# MANAGING COMPLEXITY

OTHER TITLES FROM
THE ECONOMIST BOOKS

The Economist Desk Companion
The Economist Economics
The Economist Guide to Economic Indicators
The Economist Guide to Financial Markets
The Economist Guide to the European Union
The Economist Numbers Guide
The Economist Style Guide
The Guide to Analysing Companies
The Dictionary of Economics
The International Dictionary of Finance
Going Digital
Improving Marketing Effectiveness
Management Ideas
Measuring Business Performance
Management Development

Pocket Accounting
Pocket Advertising
Pocket Director
Pocket Employer
Pocket Finance
Pocket Information Technology
Pocket International Business Terms
Pocket Investor
Pocket Law
Pocket Manager
Pocket Marketing
Pocket MBA
Pocket Negotiator
Pocket Strategy
Pocket Telecommunications

The Economist Pocket Asia
The Economist Pocket Europe in Figures
The Economist Pocket World in Figures

# MANAGING COMPLEXITY

## Robin Wood

THE ECONOMIST IN ASSOCIATION WITH
PROFILE BOOKS LTD

Published by Profile Books Ltd
58A Hatton Garden, London ECIN 8LX

The greatest care has been taken in compiling this book.
However, no responsibility can be accepted by the publishers or compilers
for the accuracy of the information presented.

Where opinion is expressed it is that of the author and does not necessarily coincide
with the editorial views of The Economist Newspaper.

Typeset in EcoType by MacGuru
macguru@pavilion.co.uk

Printed in Great Britain by
St Edmundsbury Press, Bury St Edmunds

A CIP catalogue record for this book is available
from the British Library

ISBN 1 86197 112 5

# Contents

## List of tables

# Acknowledgements

This book is the product of thousands of conversations with managers, consultants, friends and academics on five continents. Over the past 15 years I have been "making notes" while being a consultant to *Fortune 1,000* clients, building new organisations and attending many stimulating conferences. I began writing to make sense of the radical transformation going on around me in the world of organisations and business, while looking through many different windows – whether physical, such as those of a 747, the Boston Cambridge Marriott, the San Jose Hilton or the Excelsior Hotel in Hong Kong; or windows of thought, whether cognitive science, economics, strategic management, organisational behaviour, chaos or complexity.

I have been helped through being able to observe at close quarters some extraordinarily able people leading some of the most successful organisations in the world. Furthermore, I have been lucky enough to work with and learn from some extraordinarily perceptive and original thinkers across a wide range of disciplines. In all of their endeavours, they were seeking to understand and then explain the mysteries of the universe, from physics to chemistry to biology to psychology to sociology to metaphysics. They saw and interpreted the patterns emerging from their investigations in unique ways, through powerful tools.

My original inspiration was my father, Ray Wood, who, after a career as a general manager and director of fast-moving consumer goods multinationals, launched a series successful businesses in his "early retirement" from the corporate world at the age of 51.

Others I would like to thank for their help and inspiration along the way are: Henry Mintzberg, Kevin Kelly, Chris Meyer, Eric Benedict, Roger Camrass, Arie de Geus, Tony Hodgson, Bob Garratt, Peter Honey, Roger Lewin and Birute Regine, Mike Lissack, Johan Roos, Max Boisot, Jim Moore, Glenn Osaka, Stuart Kauffman, Gary Hamel, Klaus Hoffman, Robert Wood, Walter Wriston and John Reed, Ilfryn ("If") Price, Adam Brand, David Hurst, Ritchie Bent, John Halpin and Tony Page.

To my many colleagues and erstwhile "comrades" in the struggle to free South Africa (the country of my birth) from apartheid, who are now in positions of leadership, *Amandla!* We were living complexity in the 1970s and early 1980s, and the new order that is currently emerging from the chaos will be shaped by the principles we held to be true then, and for which complexity science now provides a rational explanation.

To Carolyn White, my editor, I owe a special debt of gratitude for helping me shape a book out of the mass of material I had to hand and for playing such a stalwart role in the whole editorial process.

To the many who are quoted in this book – thank you for your insights. I trust your work is done sufficient justice in what of necessity is a slim volume. If there are any errors they remain, perpetually, mine, until such time as we do another edition.

Lastly, and most importantly, this book is dedicated to my wife Suzanne, who has sacrificed more for it than anyone else – thanks for your belief in me through thick and thin. To my children, Callum and Kirstie, the most creative tutors in chaos and complexity, thanks for bringing me great joy, as well as continuously reminding me of the awesome power of the human learning and development process.

Robin Wood
*January 2000*

# 1 Introduction

WE ARE ENTERING A PERIOD IN WHICH THE WORLD IS FACING PROBLEMS
WHICH ARE NOT AS YET EVEN REALISED OR DEFINED.
Helmut Schmidt, former chancellor of Germany

AS COMPLEX AS THINGS ARE TODAY, EVERYTHING WILL BE MORE COMPLEX
TOMORROW.
Kevin Kelly, author of *Out of Control: The New Biology of Machines*[1]

## What is complexity?

Complexity is a term used to refer to a collection of scientific disciplines,
all of which are concerned with finding patterns among collections of
behaviours or phenomena. This book shows how the principles of the
new sciences (which are often referred to in shorthand as "complexity
science" or "complexity thinking") can help leaders in commercial and
public-sector organisations understand and address the challenges of
change and adaptation in today's fast-moving environment.

The central task of business leaders has often been defined as the
creation of sustainable value for stakeholders in their organisations. But
at the heart of creating value lies the leaders' ability to innovate and
implement new solutions faster than their competitors. The connecting
theme is learning from complexity: understanding it, valuing it and
managing it effectively at all levels.

Many sceptics of complexity-based approaches to management argue
that complexity is not a new phenomenon, and that leaders have always
had to be able to take decisions in turbulent environments. However, as
we move from the 20th to the 21st century we are experiencing a major
step change in the complexity of the ecosphere and sociosphere in which
we live. What is new is the sheer scale of the change that we are having
to deal with in a globalised economy. Three hundred years ago our
ancestors probably lived in a village in which they knew 20 people well,
and which they seldom, if ever, left. There were perhaps only a few
hundred different ways of making a living, and the choices about where
to live, what career to follow and with whom to mate were comparatively
simple, if heavily circumscribed by who people's parents were and the
rigidity of the social structures of the time.

1

Today, research has demonstrated that we can each be said to "know" at least 20,000 other people in our lifetime, most of them through the media, or over a telephone, Internet or videoconference link rather than face to face. In this MTV world, where billions mourned the passing of Princess Diana and experienced "personal" grief at her death, there are 80m different ways of making a living. These continue to expand as new technologies generate needs for new skills, whether they be HTML programming, genetic profiling or stress counselling for executives.

### The 500-year delta arrives

The rate of change in many parts of the world appears to be accelerating, yet few people and institutions feel able to cope with the implications this has for their future existence. Watts Wacker, a futurist, has described this situation as the "500-year delta", meaning that the end of the 500-year "age of reason" is upon us, while what he describes as "the age of possibility" is just being born.[2] During the age of reason we tried to explain the world using linear cause and effect models, which provided clear guidance on what to do in any given situation. These models were useful, up to a point; but the rising complexity of the technical infrastructure created by the industrial revolution, and the increasingly complex social arrangements that result from it, do not yield to such mechanistic thinking.

Other authors point out that we are heading into a knowledge and experience economy, where goods and services are becoming commoditised at an increasing rate, and know-how and experiences have become the new sources of value. We need new ways of thinking and understanding to survive in this age of possibility. As SRI Consulting put it in *Managing in an age of chaos: a guide for the top*:

> *The laws of causality become irrelevant in an age of chaos ... reason has effectively disappeared as a useful tool of both logic and management. Disappeared not because causality itself has ceased to exist, but because in a world driven by connectivity and universal access, the interval between cause and effect has become so infinitesimal that reason can no longer be parsed. Like oxygen or photosynthesis, we know reason is there; we know it is important. But if we spend our time searching for it, the hunt will consume our lives.*

As the durability of our assumptions decreases, so, for us to thrive and survive, does the need for learning and intelligence increase. This is manifested in several ways.

- As individuals, we sense the need to do things in less time, under more stressful conditions, than we have ever experienced before.
- As groups and teams, we find the diversity of our make-up and the potential for conflict in our functioning together increasing.
- As organisations, we struggle to create coherent and compelling working environments and corporate visions that draw on the full richness of our corporate inheritance and human potential.
- As social and national institutions, we are faced with challenges of unprecedented complexity, which require solutions that are often simply beyond the scope of our current structures and ways of doing things.

A recent article in the *The Economist*[3] emphasised that this increasing level of complexity not only causes confusion but also costs money:

> *Nobody ever thought that running a bank as huge and sprawling as Citibank was easy. But even Citi's managers were surprised two years ago, when they looked into just how complex its operations had become. Take something as ordinary as a demand deposit account. Around the world, for reasons of local regulation or history, Citi was offering not one such account but 150,000 versions of it ... To handle all this, Citi's back office needed 28 different computer systems. Citi has since launched a project to reduce its complexity by 75% and to cut the number of systems to one or two. The hope is to save more than $1 billion a year.*

### The drivers of the e-business economy

Despite the confusion caused by the scale and pace of change, it is possible to identify several driving forces behind the emerging digital economy (see Figure 1.1 on page 4).

#### Mass production and consumer choice

Mass production has created not only cars, washing machines and clothes at prices that people can afford, but also ubiquitous and cheap computing and communication devices. Now that these devices can be connected easily and cheaply via the Internet, their value and

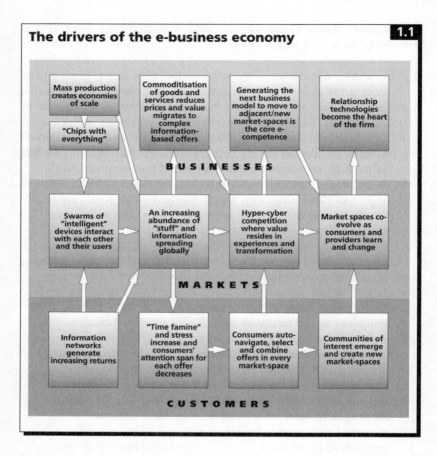

**The drivers of the e-business economy** `1.1`

Mass production creates economies of scale

"Chips with everything"

Commoditisation of goods and services reduces prices and value migrates to complex information-based offers

Generating the next business model to move to adjacent/new market-spaces is the core e-competence

Relationship technologies become the heart of the firm

**B U S I N E S S E S**

Swarms of "intelligent" devices interact with each other and their users

An increasing abundance of "stuff" and information spreading globally

Hyper-cyber competition where value resides in experiences and transformation

Market spaces co-evolve as consumers and providers learn and change

**M A R K E T S**

Information networks generate increasing returns

"Time famine" and stress increase and consumers' attention span for each offer decreases

Consumers auto-navigate, select and combine offers in every market-space

Communities of interest emerge and create new market-spaces

**C U S T O M E R S**

functionality has increased even more dramatically.[4] These Internet networks act as low-cost, highly interactive channels to supply goods and services, and the resulting commoditisation reduces prices still further and forces businesses to develop complex, information-based offers in order to compete in a crowded, often low-margin market.

In an e-business economy, consumers gain enormous power by being able to compare offers and define their own needs through communities of interest. The resulting imbalance of power creates hyper-competition among producers and retailers. Companies have to learn how to establish new sorts of relationships with their customers to reduce churn and deliver more value.

The old certainties of Fordist production methods – standardisation of product range and the reaping of cost-based economies of scale – have undergone their own process of adaptation under the strong selection pressure of customer choice. Although the effective utilisation of assets is as important as ever, producers across industry sectors have acknowledged the need to produce tailored offerings for identifiable groups of customers to create strong market positions and build brand value.

This process of increasingly finer segmentation, customer needs analysis and the bundling of products and services into offers has stretched the old production models towards mass customisation. This paradigm, drawing on flexible production technology, low labour-cost locations and information technology, has dramatically increased the amount of goods and services that the average consumer can afford, while at the same time increasing the range of offers that clamour for their attention.

### The falling cost of computing power

Over the past decade, the need to increase the functionality, quality and performance of manufactured goods has been given a boost by the rapidly falling cost of computing power. In the automotive sector, for example, chips that five years earlier would have been a core component of a computer have been relegated to minor bit players in a mini-network that encompasses engine management, braking, entertainment, climate control and maintenance monitoring.

As costs fall further and chips appear in household appliances, security systems, grocery packaging, phone cards, greetings cards and children's toys, the emerging reality of "chips with everything" raises intriguing possibilities of connectivity and distributed intelligence. For example, using a simple home network, a toaster could notify the security system that it has detected an overheat condition. This is confirmed by a smoke detector, and in response the security system rings the local fire service and the insurance company to minimise the damage. Operating and maintaining such a system could form the basis of a valuable business model.

### The changing role of information in new product development

Information has become an increasingly important input into offer creation on a number of different levels. For example:

◪ Customer preference information captured from store loyalty cards is mined to create customer need specifications for new category store-keeping units (SKUS).

- Product development combines customer needs information with technical data to create suitable product specifications. The increasing costs of R&D in many industries partly reflect increasing information intensity.
- The distribution of products is enabled by information in the chip attached to the batch packaging.
- Replenishment information is generated by wireless hand-held stock-keeping devices.

Managing the information needed to place a product in the right place at the right time is an increasingly complex task requiring significant systems investment. However, the rise of distributed intelligence has created significant additional opportunities to add value. For example, customers who order their groceries on the Internet could soon be able to connect their intelligent fridges to their grocery retailer and replenish specified items as they are used up. A simple product becomes bundled into an offer that promises the availability of a favourite snack at all hours.

The capture and use of information is also being revolutionised by the falling cost of bandwidth. Better connections between retailers, suppliers and customers mean that information can be extracted online, all the time, anywhere in the world. Open standards are playing a major role in this process.

In some cases, information is not just an important input to the offer, it is the offer. Networks such as National Transport Exchange (NTE), which link truck owners and customers with delivery requirements, now act as infomediaries, trading on the value of the information created by participants in the network. In-cab communication systems with browser capabilities are an important tool for these companies, but the economics of such businesses are fundamentally driven by the number of participants in the network: the greater the number of participants, the higher is the value of the information.

For NTE, a high number of truck owners means greater choice and competitive prices for customers. A high number of customers means a greater chance of getting a suitable load for truck owners. In this way, information networks generate increasing returns as the number of participants increases. In the same way, networks based on product standards, such as Sun's Java, offer increasing returns to participants the more dominant they become, as they lower costs and reduce entry barriers. It is no surprise that standards remain a key strategic battleground for companies wishing to dominate in the digital age.

## The increased use of IT in marketing

Conversely, using a dominant network is becoming a necessity for customers as time pressures, or "time famine", and stress increase. The need to filter offers increases as the time available for selection declines. Businesses are realising that with the increasing number of offers competing for a share of customers' wallets, being a minor player in a market is becoming an increasingly unattractive option. Being part of a network or using affinity networks as distribution channels are becoming essential to stay in front of the customer. The market value of general portals such as Yahoo reflects the importance of getting in front of the customer ahead of the competition.

The pace of change, however, is not just confined to systems of production and distribution. Even the concept of passive advertising is being stretched by new technologies that let consumers auto-navigate, select and combine offers in every market-space. MySimon™, for example, operates a website that provides advanced comparison shopping and purchasing services to online shoppers. Although this creates an extremely competitive environment for online retailers, the site also delivers merchandising, branding and promotional technology to merchants in a format that preserves an unbiased position to the shopper.

These developments mean that buyers are gaining significant power relative to sellers. While the greater availability of information is allowing greater comparison between offers, information about individual consumers is becoming increasingly valuable as the basis of future offers. Consumers are also gaining a better understanding of the value of such information to companies. At the individual level, requests for opinions on a company's products now often need to be accompanied by a tangible reward – vouchers, discounts or entry into a competition, for example – to provide an equitable exchange of value and to break into the consumer's limited attention space.

The value of information about consumers is multiplied exponentially when individuals become part of an interactive community of interest. Websites that offer individuals the chance to interact with others with the same interests create value through the generation of valuable information – discussion and widely held opinions – together with increasing retention and interest through a sense of belonging. Such communities provide valuable learning environments for businesses wishing to tailor their offers and build the elusive customer relationships. Parentalk.com, for example, set up by Procter & Gamble, provides a place where parents can interact with each other and swap information on baby products. Combined with comparison shopping engines, communities of interest swing the balance of power in favour of consumers as never before.

Businesses, to stand a chance of being first in line for the consumer's attention, must therefore enrich their offers with additional intangible benefits that transform the customer's experience of buying. This transformation can even extend to a personal transformation in the way the consumer behaves, brought about by the purchase. The Internet can provide the customer with the feeling of "I need this to be me" through interactivity and the ability to tailor the offer to the individual. At Amazon.com, for example, conducting a search for a book brings back recommendations of others that could add to the reader's understanding as well as the opportunity to review the book once purchased and share their thoughts with like-minded individuals. Such communities are being created all the time by the new generation of nimble and shrewd e-businesses, such as E-toys.com, Horse.com and Investor.com.

Online communities are one of the more common ways in which new market-spaces are being created using the Internet. However, many different business models are being developed to exploit the niches that are only just emerging on the Internet. Auctioneers such as eBay and Autobytel expand the old model of auctioneering into new territory. Integrators such as Drugstore.com allow pharmaceuticals manufacturers, warehousers, distributors and postal services to form an integrated network around the clear market signals that interactivity provides. Dell has exploited this model to offer customised PCs rapidly in response to a customer's order via the web. The supply chain has again been reorganised around a customer-facing technology that provides the clearest indication of consumer needs.

For Dell, as for other businesses across a growing spread of industries, the Internet and the systems that it drives have been placed at the heart of the organisation. The ability to reorient business processes around direct channels has become a core competency in the new digital age.

All this means that businesses will continually have to adapt their business models to engage the rapidly evolving consumer, online and physical communities. Relationship technologies are at the heart of this transformation, enabling firms to understand and anticipate their customers' needs.

## New definitions of value

In their book *Blur*,[5] Chris Meyer, director of Ernst & Young's Centre for Business Innovation, and Stan Davis, author and futurologist, describe the shape of a world in which speed, intangibles and connectivity dominate the social and economic landscape. *Blur* outlines a number of metrics that evaluate corporate performance in the connected economy: speed to market; cycle time from idea generation to new product development; and the number of electronic connections to suppliers, customers and partners. The book explores how leaders and managers can survive and thrive in the blurring world of the 21st century.

In a blurring world, the focus must be on the way in which the nature of value is changing, involving new ways to price goods, information and emotion. The implication of these new forms of exchange is a transfer of power from the producer to the customer. There are multitudes of values present in every buyer–seller exchange: economic, informational and emotional. These exchanges increasingly happen so fast that there is no time to translate them into precise monetary terms. Businesses will need to identify these hidden values and think more accurately about their worth before accepting the price proposed. The implications are profound. Companies will need to think in terms of offers, which involve merging products and services to exploit their knowledge, to give customers a value-adding experience, not just "selling them stuff".

It will be important to identify and leverage the players in an economic web. Spotting the right players and creating the right relationships is essential to developing value webs (the network of customers, suppliers and vendors on whose interaction a company depends on a daily basis). The value of economic webs generally increases with the addition of each new member.

Lastly, to create the capability to operate effectively and adaptively in this new world, it is important to learn a new set of rules for engaging with and managing human, physical and intangible resources. An understanding of the network of relationships within and around organisations, and how they produce value in conjunction with capital and other resources, is critical. The real-time organisation is fast becoming a reality. Decisions are based on performance metrics and market feedback that are generated in real time. Being simultaneously fast and agile, managing people as free agents, and investing in capital that can be leveraged or dispensed with quickly will ensure an organisation's survival in the connected economy.

The need to adapt to this tidal wave of change is felt as strongly by individuals as it is by companies. The experience of greater choice and higher service levels as consumers has led people to expect similar improvements in their roles as employees and employers.

## The business fossil record

UNLESS MANAGEMENT ACTS, THE MORE SUCCESSFUL A FIRM HAS BEEN IN THE PAST, THE MORE LIKELY IT IS TO FAIL IN THE FUTURE.

Roger Blackwell, Ohio State University

THERE IS A CHANGE IN THE RATE OF CHANGE.

Alvin Toffler[6]

What evidence is there to support the contention that evolution is accelerating, particularly in the realm of business? Figure 1.2 illustrates the growth rates of *Fortune* 1,000 companies over a five-year period. It shows that the majority of the largest companies in the world are growing at or below 10% per annum. There is a small minority of high fliers growing at 20% or more per annum and a fairly long tail of companies declining at 10–40% per annum. It is clear that a significant proportion of these companies may not be around in the next five-year period. This is a sobering thought for companies of this size, as is the statistic that only about 10% of the companies quoted on Wall Street in 1945 were still listed in 1995.

Figure 1.2 also shows that the average company only lives for around 40–50 years,[7] and that one-third of the *Fortune* 500 companies listed in 1970 had vanished by 1983. Furthermore, the share of global GDP represented by the *Fortune* 500 dropped from 30% to 28% between 1993 and 1998, despite more mega-mergers forming larger companies than ever before. The average life expectancy of all companies, regardless of size, in Japan and much of Europe is no more than 12.5 years; and some 60–70% of start-ups fail within their first five years. In the age of e-business, expect the average life span of organisations to at least halve. For at least 20% of the Jurassic Park industrial economy, particularly those in the *Fortune* 1,000, there is probably less than five years to go before they merge, are taken over or fail.

Further evidence of the acceleration in the growth and decline of firms and industries is shown in Figure 1.3, which demonstrates how, as

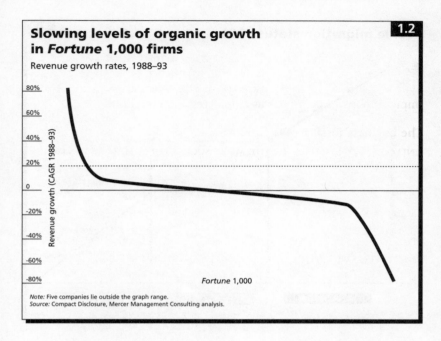

**Slowing levels of organic growth in *Fortune* 1,000 firms**

1.2

Revenue growth rates, 1988–93

Note: Five companies lie outside the graph range.
Source: Compact Disclosure, Mercer Management Consulting analysis.

industries and firms mature, they move from a value inflow to a value outflow stage. Figure 1.3 on the following page also shows, however, how some firms in the same industry can be at different stages in this process of maturation, either through the rejuvenation of a mature business (such as specialist steel company Nucor, compared with US Steel and Bethlehem Steel), or through the development of a fast-growing new market (such as Microsoft and Novell in the value inflow stage, compared with the fate of IBM and DEC in the value outflow stage).

If left to their own devices, however, it appears that firms and industries generally flow from the top left of this diagram to the bottom right as the evolutionary process unfolds. The speed at which industries and firms are moving from value inflow to value outflow has accelerated markedly in the last 50 years, according to recent research.[8]

Since the market value of the companies depicted in Figure 1.3 was calculated in 1994 some dramatic changes have taken place in their fortunes, particularly in the high-tech sectors (see Figure 1.4 on page 13). Apart from Microsoft, which has now soared to nearly 20 times its annual revenue in market value, the rest of the companies, which had demonstrated so much promise in 1994, saw their market value to

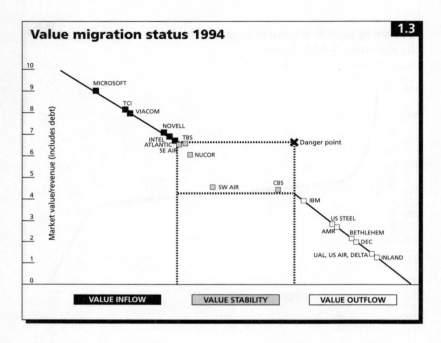

**Value migration status 1994**    1.3

Market value/revenue (includes debt)

MICROSOFT

TCI
VIACOM

NOVELL

INTEL
ATLANTIC — TBS
SE AIR
NUCOR

✕ Danger point

SW AIR    CBS

IBM

US STEEL

AMR    BETHLEHEM
DEC

UAL, US AIR, DELTA   INLAND

**VALUE INFLOW**     **VALUE STABILITY**     **VALUE OUTFLOW**

revenue ratio shrink to 6 or less, compared with their previous highs of around 8 or 9. Some of them, such as DEC, or Digital Equipment Corporation (which was acquired by Compaq), simply fell off the chart. Even Intel, one of the most admired and studied high-tech firms, has fallen slightly from a value level of 7 to 6, and cable and entertainment companies such as TCI, CBS and Viacom have fallen to values of around 2 to 3 from their previous positions of between 5 and 7.

Yet at the top left of Figure 1.4 are companies that were unknown five years ago, such as Amazon, Yahoo and other Internet and information service companies, which are operating at unheard of multiples of market valuation to revenue. What is going on?

Clearly, the markets have anticipated that global connectivity will have a huge effect on business. Some observers believe that the business world will split into two sorts of companies: "e-star" start-ups; and "Jurassic Park" global giants, which dominate their infrastructure-based industries such as energy, telecommunications and manufacturing.

Following on from this, the share of global GDP that the large industrial players, such as the current *Fortune* 500, command will drop from 27% (or $11 trillion) today to around 15% of global GDP over the next

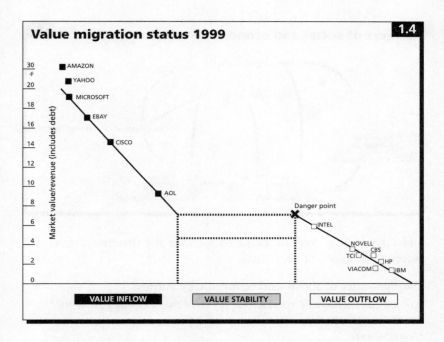

**Value migration status 1999**

1.4

decade. Most of the new value in the connected global economy will be created by small or medium-sized entrepreneurial companies, which will grow from nothing to tens of billions of dollars of revenue in the space of a couple of years from start-up. Just look at what Amazon, AOL and Lycos have achieved so far.

Future wealth will be generated from the opportunities which are emerging in the "e-tailing", telecommunications, healthcare, entertainment, travel, education and media sectors. Business models will last for no more than two to three years, and will have to evolve rapidly in Internet time. The e-stars will be solving knowledge and lifestyle problems for customers who pay highly for experiences. The speed of this evolution will be so rapid that most large global players will be left defending their patches, resulting in a continuation of the global mergers and acquisitions boom, until all large players are global in reach across most industries.

The market has already understood the potential in owning the majority of the shop-fronts in the digital main streets and malls and is valuing the number of "eyeballs" that AOL, Amazon and Yahoo have access to. In the digital economy there are valuable first-mover benefits,

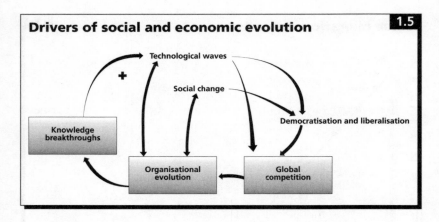

**Drivers of social and economic evolution** `1.5`

and organisations that are prepared to make the investment now will become the brands of the future.

## The dynamics of social and economic evolution

FOR AN ORGANISATION TO SURVIVE, ITS RATE OF LEARNING MUST BE EQUAL TO, OR GREATER THAN, THE RATE OF CHANGE IN ITS ENVIRONMENT.

Bob Garratt in *Creating a Learning Organisation*[9]

To survive in the growing complexity and turbulence of the current commercial environment it is essential to understand the evolutionary trajectory driving innovation and economic transformation. Figure 1.5 shows six major historical forces, which together have driven all the major waves of technological, social and organisational change that humankind has experienced.

### Knowledge breakthroughs

Over the millennia there have been several paradigm shifts in the way in which human beings make a living, each driven by a collection of knowledge breakthroughs. For example, in 1910 Albert Einstein published his *Special Theory of Relativity*. Until then the world of physics had relied on the classical laws of Newtonian physics, developed some 300 years earlier, to explain the behaviour of physical systems. Newtonian science describes a mechanical world that is linear and at equilibrium, and in which prediction and control reign supreme. In the relative world of Einstein, time and space are integral parts of the fabric of the universe, leading to unusual and unpredictable behaviour in large physical systems.

Some 50 years after Einstein, quantum mechanics revealed a world in which not even the simultaneous position and speed of an electron can be predicted with any accuracy, and in which some particles appear to be in two different positions at once, depending on the viewer's perspective. Modern physics also reveals a world in which consciousness can be causal, and in which the human brain's operation cannot be computed. This "Alice in Wonderland" view of the world would seem bizarre and illogical to a classical physicist, much as the new world of management would appear to a medieval merchant.

Such knowledge breakthroughs, even though they may appear entirely academic at the time, can transform the world around us. Everyone enjoys, for example, their own special choice of books, magazines, newspapers and suchlike, and takes for granted having them around wherever they go. Yet 500 years ago only the Catholic Church could own and publish bibles; it was illegal to own a bible, let alone any other sort of book. Then along came Johan Gutenberg, who took the idea of a printing press, first invented in China, and translated it into a working model, which he used to start printing bibles, Greek and Roman classics, Chaucer, Shakespeare and the Germanic favourites. Within a few hundred years a vast library of literature had become available to subsequent generations of scholars and students, creating rising levels of literacy and the possibility of public education and libraries.

### Democratisation and liberalisation

A breakthrough in technology generally results in greater power for those who own it or have access to it. Printed books led to the questioning of religious and secular power, and eventually universal suffrage, in combination with a variety of other powerful historical forces, which helped bring a one-person, one-vote democracy into being. In a similar way, "no one knows you are a dog on the Internet". People of all ages anywhere in the world can communicate instantly with anyone who will bother to reply, and are able to search the sum of all human knowledge on several hundred million websites through increasingly sophisticated search engines.

Of course, potentially harmful technologies such as nuclear power or weapons of any kind are so dangerous to the public good that they are generally prohibited except to those considered to be safe guardians of the technology. But these exceptions simply confirm the rule that most of the current technological breakthroughs are, in the words of Kevin Kelly, "distributive" of power to individuals.

## Global competition

The third major impact of new waves of technology is increased competition, through both the substitution of old technologies that they displace (for example, the horseless carriage replacing the horse-drawn carriage) and the emergence of new competitors applying new technologies in different ways. In the past century or two this competition has taken on an increasingly global form, as transport and communications technologies have shrunk the world. We are truly moving towards the global village predicted by Marshall McLuhan in the 1960s, and we may all soon be competing to be famous for 15 minutes in the global telecosm.

As a result of the increased effectiveness of the global economy, we have experienced a fourth decade of falling commodity prices and deflation in a number of countries. This has created a tough competitive environment for companies and countries that have traditionally based their strength on resources rather than knowledge. Even giants such as Shell and Procter & Gamble are feeling the pinch as the value of their products declines relative to the offers emerging from the knowledge and experience economy.

## Organisational evolution

As knowledge breakthroughs lead to new waves of technology, individuals and organisations co-evolve with these technologies to create new forms of knowledge. As consumers, individuals learn to identify and buy new products and services (or in this blurring world, offers), which make their lives easier, richer and longer. As workers and investors, individuals learn to use new technologies to become more productive and to earn a higher return on their time and money. The speed of learning about new technologies and ways of doing things is accelerated through the linkage between learning in the home and at work. For example, in the first wave of personal computers, most consumers had learned to use a PC at the office before buying one for the home, and the products and brands they bought at the office often appeared in their homes.

As new waves of technology and ways of doing things have evolved, so too have organisations. In simple terms, organisational forms and processes have evolved through four stages in the past few millennia.

◪ First there was the tribe, with decision-making power vested in the tribal leader and elders, which was able to cope with a low level of complexity and uncertainty in the environment. The tribal form is still in evidence in small start-up or family-run businesses where patriarchal or matriarchal authority reigns supreme.

◪ As technological and social complexity increased, bureaucracy emerged as a way of coping with the need for increasing technical and geographic specialisation. Both the Catholic Church and the Roman Empire exhibited features of this, and the late 19th-century insurance organisation written about by Franz Kafka was the apotheosis of the form. Most major governmental organisations and social institutions are still organised according to the bureaucratic model. In an extreme form, bureaucracies characterised Stalinist Russia and Maoist China, and, until recently, many emerging economies.

◪ During the mid to late 20th century the concept of business units and professional management (together with variants such as the M-form and matrix architectures) led to a variety of highly complex structures, which split responsibility by function, product, geography, site and other relevant variables. The result of these structures was a profit or cost centre, business unit or division, usually led by a professional general manager. Managerial capitalism, where there is a split between ownership and control and between shareholders and management, is characterised by this sort of structure.

◪ During the last two decades of the 20th century the idea of organising around business ecosystems, networks, architectures and processes, rather than variations on pyramidal structures, was adopted by many of the world's most progressive organisations.[10] Collaborative capitalism, where management and employees share some ownership of and control over the firm and its resources, became a feature of many modern and post-modern organisations. As we move into the seventh wave society, new technologies and social arrangements will lead to an incredible diversity of organisational forms, where it will be true to say that form fits function.

## The seventh wave society

At the beginning of the third millennium major parts of the developed and developing world economies are now living in a seventh wave

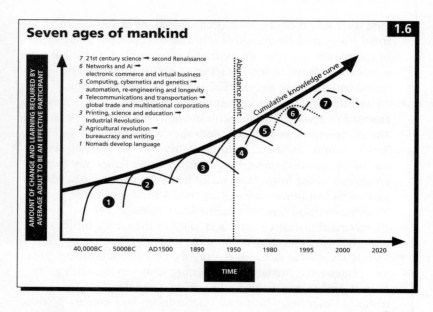

**Seven ages of mankind** `1.6`

AMOUNT OF CHANGE AND LEARNING REQUIRED BY AVERAGE ADULT TO BE AN EFFECTIVE PARTICIPANT

7 21st century science ➟ second Renaissance
6 Networks and AI ➟
  electronic commerce and virtual business
5 Computing, cybernetics and genetics ➟
  automation, re-engineering and longevity
4 Telecommunications and transportation ➟
  global trade and multinational corporations
3 Printing, science and education ➟
  Industrial Revolution
2 Agricultural revolution ➟
  bureaucracy and writing
1 Nomads develop language

Abundance point

Cumulative knowledge curve

40,000BC   5000BC   AD1500   1890   1950   1980   1995   2000   2020

TIME

society. Over three books, *Future Shock*, *The Third Wave* and *Powershift*,[11] Alvin Toffler has steadily described the major changes taking place in the world around us, leading to the "information" or "knowledge age". John Naisbitt, in his *Megatrend* books,[12] has also painted in finer detail a picture of a world that is becoming increasingly complex, turbulent and fast-moving, but also freer and richer. The author's research has led to the conclusion that there are seven waves of evolution, which can be distinguished from the time human beings left the African savannah as hunter-gatherers until they stepped into the first virtual reality machine (see Figure 1.6). Each of these waves has been driven by the six major forces outlined above.

In each wave, a particular set of knowledge breakthroughs and innovations drives the economic engine of the most advanced areas of the global economy, forming the platform on which the next wave of breakthroughs can develop. This succession of revolutions in the way in which knowledge is created and shared among people has led to fundamental changes in the way in which societies and organisations function, and has challenged the supreme power of leaders of tribes, kingdoms, countries and superstates.

Thus the common man and woman have been able to improve their standard of living and find some time to consider their own interests, needs and wants. The emergence of a middle class in any society has always led eventually to a challenge to the power of the entrenched leadership. This change in the balance of power also affects the attitudes of people to working in and for organisations, making it more difficult for employers to exploit their employees as they become enlightened about their individual and collective power and rights. This has major implications for the different organisational forms that occur at each stage. These "seven waves of mankind" form the basis of an economic "long wave".[13]

### Wave 1: the language breakthrough, 40,000BC
Human beings emerged from the mists of evolutionary time approximately 120,000 years ago somewhere in the Afar triangle in East Africa. Our tool-making ancestors soon spread across the Eurasian landmass, colonising new habitats and evolving new technologies as they went. By 40,000BC these hunter-gatherers had evolved a functional language, which facilitated their ability to develop strategies for hunting, domesticating animals and doing business.

Language provided the means for tribal power and rituals to emerge. Tribal chiefs still reign supreme over their subjects in tribal societies, much as the kings and lords of ancient kingdoms of old. Writing reinforced the power of such rulers, as the priesthood generally co-operated with the chief in restricting access to knowledge to those who could be trusted with it. The basic form of incentive and power in the tribe is physical and/or charismatic.

### Wave 2: The agricultural revolution, 5000BC–1500AD
Gradually, the nomads settled down in some places to exploit the new agricultural technologies that had emerged from innovations in animal husbandry and crop growing. Human beings relied on nature as a factory, replicating plants and animals on a scale that enabled them to accumulate surpluses and trade extensively across the known world. Writing emerged, and hierarchical structures of organisation enabled specialisation to occur. Once writing was ubiquitous, it was possible to codify the rules and regulations necessary for bureaucracies to operate. The church established the first hierarchical bureaucracies, in which an elite clerical group enforced the protocols of the church. The printing press made this much easier to do, and clerks proliferated both inside and outside the church during the Middle Ages and Renaissance.

## Wave 3: The industrial revolution, 1500–1850

The clerical elite gradually spread the ability to codify and transmit knowledge across generations. Once the concept of formal education had started, it was only a matter of time before the printing press revolutionised our ability to access new knowledge, without literally having to reinvent the wheel every time. This led to an explosion of new knowledge, culminating in the Renaissance and the Enlightenment. Once science and scientific thinking became respectable, the 500-year age of reason could begin. Now people could methodically invent new technologies that could replicate themselves and other technologies, products and services. This led to an explosion of technologies and advances in medicine, the social sciences and commerce. Some of the technologies that emerged during this period include printing, coal mining, canals, textiles and wrought iron.

The age of reason believed in itself and in progress – given the right starting point, a person could do anything. The linear thinking and technologies produced during this age, however, had some real limitations, and political and economic governance mechanisms evolved to deal with the complex problems of urbanisation and modernisation. During the industrial revolution it became necessary for more elaborate bureaucratic structures to emerge to control the increasingly sophisticated technologies being invented.

The drawbacks of hierarchy and specialisation taken to extremes became readily apparent to observers such as Engels, Marx and Kafka in the 19th century, and the human relations school in the 20th. Observation of the social effects of hierarchy and specialisation in these two centuries led to the following.

- Communism, which was meant to overcome the alienation created by the separation of workers from the means of production through collective ownership. Communism in its extreme form of state ownership of all means of production has now collapsed, but many countries have welfare systems that provide a safety net for the less fortunate.
- The establishment of trades unions and the human relations school of management. Both of these developments ameliorated some of the worst excesses of early capitalism and helped lead to the evolution of the modern organisation.

These developments enabled more workers to become more literate, educated and mobile, and (together with the development of information technology, which makes more information available to all) led to the emergence of the modern, hierarchical organisation, in which the basic forms of incentive and power are economic and informational.

The bureaucracy reached its climax in the early and mid 20th century, in the form of the functional and divisional bureaucracies described by Henri Fayol and Max Weber, and fine-tuned by the theories of Frederick Taylor on scientific management. This created a clerical elite, which, together with the dominant male oligarchies that characterised early tribes, dominated the allocation of resources.

The separation of ownership and control in such organisations led to the second wave of capitalism, known as managerial capitalism, in which managers exercised control on behalf of shareholders. In such organisations workers were considered to be merely a factor of production, on the same level as land, machinery and capital, their primary purpose being to provide physical labour in the manufacturing process. The basic form of incentive and power in the bureaucracy is economic. Many of our organisational structures are still largely designed around these principles, and are equally out of date.

### Wave 4: the transport revolution, 1850–1940

By the late 1800s it was becoming possible to move around the globe increasingly rapidly. Advances in shipping and roads led to global trading empires based on colonial patterns of dominance, and telegraphs, the wireless and the telephone enabled us to communicate across the planet. Although still only available to an elite, these technologies would transform our ability to co-ordinate trade and organise manufacture. The advances in chemistry, physics and related fields of engineering in this era simultaneously led to the emergence of the steam power, gas lighting, smelting, steel, petroleum, automobile, aircraft and chemicals industries.

New organisational forms emerged to cope with the complexity and speed of such technologies and the associated social infrastructures they enabled. Modern cities and skyscrapers evolved from these forces, and the seeds of the next wave were sown.

The modern organisation emerged during this wave. From Henry Ford's mass production lines to the divisional corporate structures of GM and AT&T, the organisational forms created during the transport revolution are still studied by MBA students. Alfred Sloan (at General Motors), Chester Barnard (at AT&T) and Alfred Chandler (at Harvard) laid the theoretical foundations for the modern organisation. Sloan developed the principle of decentralisation for big corporations, and Barnard was the first to talk about the primary role of the chief executive officer as the shaper and manager of shared values in an organisation, stressing communication, co-ordination and control as the primary functions of management. Chandler stressed the principle that structure follows strategy in an organisation, opening the way for contingency theorists in Wave 5 such as Henry Mintzberg, who described five different kinds of organisational structure which were appropriate for different purposes.

### Wave 5: the computational and electro-chemical revolution, 1940–75

The speed of industrial and transport technologies required much more sophisticated ways of managing technology, organisations and governments. Catalysed by the challenges of guiding missiles during the second world war, electronic computing was born. Some 15 years later DNA was discovered, leading us to understand that the origins of life were indeed based on chemical grammar. Organisations began to harness the new technologies, although their basic design did not change radically; traditional ways of doing things were simply speeded up. The emergence of computing and genetics laid the foundations for the late 20th-century boom in these new fields.

As part of this revolution, Peter Drucker refined the idea of management by objectives, which enabled large, divisional organisations to structure hierarchies of objectives for the purpose of control and measuring results. The most complex of these organisations became known as matrix organisations, which reached their maximum popularity in the early 1980s. Mintzberg's professional bureaucracy and adhocracy forms began to point the way to new organisational structures beyond the simple, machine and divisional forms he described as dominant in the mid-20th century.

### Wave 6: the network revolution, 1975–2010

The convergence of computing, telecommunications and media led first to corporate and government networks, and then to the Internet. An array of technology stocks is now in vogue, especially biotechnology, software, entertainment and information service providers. The network revolution has enabled electronic commerce to be born, and has given billions of people around the world the opportunity to communicate at virtually no cost with each other and with suppliers of goods and services. Breakthroughs in biotechnology and the biological sciences, together with hundred-thousand-fold increases in computing power, have led to a new wave of scientific innovation in physics, chemistry, biology and the social sciences.

The computer and the proliferation of telecommunications networks are bringing about a new form of organisation, characterised by collaborative networks and processes. The collaborative organisational form provides the flexibility, responsiveness and creativity required to enable the organisation constantly to adapt to changes in the environment through innovation. Customer focus in such organisations is achieved through the development of business and management processes. These cut across traditional functional specialisations and ensure that the focus of the organisation is on the customer.

The quality movement in the 1980s, process management, the learning organisation and knowledge management are all early manifestations of collaborative capitalism, although this is still largely an experiment to which few major organisations have committed themselves.

Collaborative enterprises recognise that intelligent, educated knowledge workers need to engage not only their bodies but also their hearts and minds in their work. Such engagement is essential to enable organisations to exhibit the intelligence, creativity, responsiveness and flexibility required in modern competitive knowledge-driven businesses. The basic form of incentive and power in the collaborative enterprise is personal mastery, linked to inspiration and persuasion.

### Wave 7: the second renaissance, 2000–

Breakthroughs in complexity science, quantum physics, chaology (the study of scientific chaos in natural and human contexts) and fractal geometry, biology and genetics, neural nets, advanced computing and networking are being applied to expand our understanding of the economic and social webs we find ourselves operating in. The new "macroscope" of connected computing now enables us to model complex systems in great detail for the first time. We have begun to see some fundamental principles emerging about the way in which life, social systems and businesses are born, co-evolve, mature and die. These principles form the foundation of the next wave of economic growth, the second renaissance. For the first time in history, the macroscope enables us to move from a technologically advanced, but warlike, argumentative species, to a socially literate global civilisation, which is becoming aware of the dynamics of its own evolution.

Rising productivity in manufacturing and services industries driven by these technologies, together with rising employment and lower inflation in most developed economies, continues to surprise politicians and economists of the old school. Global trade is now over 12% of global GDP and rising. Although war, famine and disease continue to be issues in developing countries, they become much less important in the countries moving into the second renaissance economy, where education, learning and local quality of life issues dominate the agenda. New forms of art and culture flourish just as they did in the first renaissance, particularly popular forms of self-expression and communication.

In the next few decades we will increasingly live in a blurring, connected global economy in which adaptability becomes the single most important capability an organisation can possess. The speed at which events in the global economy are unfolding is unprecedented; for example, there are now hundreds of millions of products and services traded around the globe, tens of millions of businesses, regulated by several million world, national, local government and individual groups. But the most amazing thing is that by far the largest proportion of wealth-creating interactions are self-organising, with emergent rules. In these interactions there is a high degree of recombination of existing products, services and needs driven by innovation and serendipity.

Over the past hundred years, many parts of this fluid global economy have gone "supercritical" – places such as northern Italy, south-eastern England, Silicon Valley and Hong Kong have all become dynamic nodes of global trade and innovation. The behaviour of such economic webs is increasingly unpredictable as to specific outcome. What is guaranteed, however, is the phenomenal rate of transformation in these webs, as niches beget niches. And the clock speed of these and many other parts of the global economy has increased dramatically as they evolve from industrial to knowledge economies.

The classic complexity analogy of the sensitivity of these global networks is a speculator (butterfly) flapping his wings in the Thai stockmarket in July 1997, and by August 1998 the whole of Asia is reeling from deep recession and the Russian economy is collapsing, despite the best efforts and policies of the "brightest economic minds" in the world at the IMF/World Bank/OECD. Then, for those western economies poised on the brink of what should have been a knock-on recession, a sudden, non-inflationary, full-employment miracle occurs, enabling them to land softly and recommence their growth.

A mathematical economist with the right models would be able to demonstrate that operating within this apparent "noise" are deeper patterns called strange attractors and fractals. These characterise markets and economic behaviour, giving rise to their spiky, unpredictable performance in the short term, yet yielding more consistent patterns of behaviour in the longer term; for example, economic cycles of 7–11 years.

There are signs, however, that the American and European economies are responding differently to this global recession than to previous recessions because they have become much more diverse, with many more niches. They are demonstrating the effect predicted by Schumpeter, Hayek, Kauffman and others, that combinatorial explosions take place when a supercritical economic soup has sufficient technologies, products and services to unleash major waves of innovation in an economy. This is happening right now, as the 80m traded products and services in the global economy generate niches at a faster rate than our capability to exploit them. This economic diversity is shielding the United States and the UK from the worst effects of recession in Asia and Russia, which typically have many fewer sectors to rely on for their growth and are thus vulnerable to swings in those sectors, particularly in manufacturing and commodity production.

In the new economy, even more so than in the old, the role of executives, economists and politicians becomes the creation of the conditions in which innovation and new niches can occur. At the macroeconomic or microeconomic level, this means enhancing the diversity of local communities, creating the space for innovation to flourish, enabling incentives for innovation and entrepreneurs, and rethinking the notion of value and GDP in the knowledge economy.

A long list of "new age" or "transformed organisations"[14] exists, but few have yet tackled the real issues of control that enable collaborative capitalism to flourish to the full. The world of work is also changing dramatically, with knowledge workers demanding gratification and even joy in their work. Work often spreads across a portfolio of firms, and the knowledge worker can focus his or her talents and energy on the direction that suits best.

Models of competition and co-operation both within and between organisations are currently in a state of flux. Successful collaboration requires the ability to distinguish between those that can be trusted and those with whom collaboration should be avoided. Also, in many industries, competition and co-operation coexist between firms and groups of firms, so it is necessary to know when and how to compete with a collaborator and to collaborate with a competitor.

The transition to collaborative capitalism has to be carefully monitored, measured and managed. Managing change (though usually to a more limited extent than is necessary for full collaborative capitalism) is now the primary role of leaders and managers. Although generally well-equipped with classic management approaches and tools for the existing state of affairs, most leaders and managers lack a systematic way of dealing with the waves of change rolling through their organisations. The central characteristic of successful organisations in the 21st century will be that they are capable of learning faster than their environment and their competitors, through productive collaborative working relationships within the firm and between the firm and its principal allies.

Collaborative capitalism is still in its infancy, but it is gradually gaining ground on entrepreneurial and managerial capitalism. Because knowledge work forms the heart of the 21st century organisation, it is likely that the dominant form of organisation in the 21st century will be collaborative.

Just as Darwin's "dangerous idea" of evolution revolutionised the way in which people understand the origins of life and the nature of the human species, so too is complexity theory changing the way in which many leading executives and policymakers think about, design and operate their organisations. The new sciences offer a powerful and coherent way of understanding and beneficially influencing the complex phenomena people encounter each day in the seventh wave.

## The structure of this book

This book is structured to make it an easy read for those who have little or no background knowledge of the new sciences or complexity.

This chapter provides an overview of the sources of complexity, and why businesses need to understand and master complexity to survive and thrive in the 21st century.

Chapter 2 looks at the conventional success recipes, and the role that traditional economic thinking has played in shaping how organisations are managed. Having exposed the benefits and limits of such ways of thinking and managing, the chapter then delves into the implications of thinking about organisations and economies as complex evolving systems.

Chapter 3 shows, through case studies, how companies are already applying complexity management principles in four key areas: managing and changing organisations, strategic management, information systems and operations management.

Chapter 4 takes a bird's-eye view of how the CEO and board of an organisation can consciously manage the evolution of their business. The alignment of the external forces operating on an organisation with the internal capabilities, processes and competencies of the organisation is seen to be the key to successful business evolution. Each of the forces is then explored, starting with the four externally focused elements: the business environment; business ecosystems; business design; and leadership style. The last two elements provide the bridge into the four internal elements: the organisational values, management processes, knowledge management systems and performance measures necessary for success.

In Chapter 5 the core components of a methodology known as "FutureStep" are described. FutureStep is a strategic management process designed to help companies decide how to act in an age of complexity and fast-paced change. Of the 12 FutureStep modules, five focus on diagnosis: planning the process; scanning strategic issues; developing strategic analyses; assessing organisational capabilities; and mobilising for change. The next four modules focus on strategy development: ecosystem modelling; scenario building; strategic option building; and strategic gaming and simulation. The last three FutureStep modules support the development of the strategic agenda, identification of key change initiatives and identification of strategic triggers.

Lastly, Chapter 6 draws the central themes of the book together, and looks forward to what it may be like to work in and manage businesses in a seventh wave economy.

For readers interested in pursuing some of the basic concepts lying behind the complexity sciences, the appendices provide comprehensive in-depth background briefing, as well as a list of recommended reading.

# 2 Achieving success in a complex world

THE RACE IS NOT ALWAYS TO THE SWIFT, NOR THE BATTLE TO THE STRONG,
BUT IT PAYS TO BET THAT WAY.

Damon Runyon

THE SOURCE OF REAL DISCOVERY CONSISTS NOT IN SEEKING NEW
LANDSCAPES, BUT IN HAVING NEW EYES.

Marcel Proust

In business, many lengthy tomes offer recipes for success. Whether it is the eight principles of excellence, the seven habits of highly successful people, the five disciplines of organisational learning, the four kinds of business in the BCG grid, the three disciplines of market leaders, the two by two matrix or the one minute manager, executives have flocked to find recipes that would guarantee them some kind of simple guide to being successful. Yet it is getting harder and harder to become and stay successful for any length of time.

Many success theorists believe that success is largely a matter of luck – being in the right place at the right time. Yet many individuals and organisations appear to be able to succeed more than once, in a repeatable way. This chapter explores the competencies and skills needed to manage a firm in the new, fast-paced connected economy. It compares industrial age approaches to business strategy and organisational success with the theories and practices emerging in the seventh-wave knowledge economy.

## Business evolution in the knowledge economy

The world of organisations and management is currently undergoing a rethink, as it becomes increasingly apparent that companies are unable to solve many of the complex problems they face using the current set of management tools they have been given. Complexity theory and the new sciences offer the possibility of exciting new approaches, tools and mindsets. However, great care must be taken not to misapply the concepts and theories. For example, there have been several well-intentioned but misguided applications of quantum theory to organisations. Human beings operate at a different level from atoms, and it is important to treat any inferences drawn from physics about the human world with great care.

People have always used organisations as a way to make commitments to their fellows, and to deliver on these commitments. Organisations emerge from a web of human relationships, and are then formalised through legal structures and contracts. Most organisations are formed for a specific purpose, whether business, social or pleasure. Watts Wacker states that "A brand is a promise – a product or service is the promise fulfilled". The role of organisations is to make and deliver promises.

Organisations occupy a middle ground between the chaos of markets and the order of hierarchies. All successful organisations must balance bureaucratic processes at one extreme with the fluid chaos of relationships, interests and transactions, which enable it to be innovative and alive, at the other. Of course, economic activity can and does happen without organisations. Individuals are perfectly capable of making and fulfilling promises by themselves. The days of simple promises are over, however. Networks of individuals and organisations are needed to deliver the more complex promises that are required in the knowledge economy.

In the third millennium, knowledge organisations must be capable of harnessing the different characteristics of networks, hierarchies and markets. When the costs associated with doing transactions in a socio-economic network (known as transaction costs) rise above a certain threshold, the need for an organisation to contain and manage these costs arises. However, when transaction costs fall below a certain threshold, and the conditions are right, a market will emerge.

## Networks

THE DYNAMICS OF OUR SOCIETY, AND PARTICULARLY OUR NEW ECONOMY, WILL INCREASINGLY OBEY THE LOGIC OF NETWORKS. UNDERSTANDING HOW NETWORKS WORK WILL BE THE KEY TO UNDERSTANDING HOW THE ECONOMY WORKS.

Kevin Kelly, in *New Rules for the New Economy*[1]

The knowledge economy is driven by networks. Knowledge is generated in the interactions between people, and stored in the relationships, artefacts and technologies used by those working with the knowledge. Such knowledge workers are often referred to as a community of practice, which shares specific roles, skill sets, tools and assumptions.

Most business networks extend well beyond such communities of practice, however, because as soon as someone has generated an idea, technology, product or service that may have value, then what they have produced goes to market through other networks of individuals and firms. One of the single most important success factors for any entrepreneur or intrapreneur is the size and power of their network.

The Internet has, of course, focused the eyes of the world on the economics of networks as never before. Firms such as AOL, with over 20m subscribers, have enormous power and are able to command premiums for access to their networks, well beyond anything a traditional media mogul could ever have dreamed of. Microsoft is able to command a premium of a several hundred billion dollars over its net asset value because of its installed base of hundreds of millions of users. Why are these network effects so powerful?

Robert Metcalf, the inventor of a local area network technology called Ethernet, noticed while implementing new networks that a critical mass was required to make networks succeed. He also noticed, as he put small networks together into larger networks, that the value of the combined networks multiplied rapidly. He formulated a new law, which states that the value of a network is a function of the square of its number of nodes ($v = n^2$).

This is a highly non-linear equation, which leads directly to the second fundamental law of networks: the law of increasing returns. What happens when a network explodes as its membership increases? It attracts even more members, and so a virtuous circle kicks in where the more members a network gets, the more attractive a firm/club/website/ community is to other people with similar interests, or to advertisers targeting a specific community. In turn, even more members join, making the community even more attractive, and so on, until the network runs out of potential new members, or splits itself into sub-networks, addressing more specific interests.

Network dominance is different from the dominance of a giant monopoly or oligopoly, because networks generally lower prices and increase value for their users, rather than for the owner of the network (although the owners still do pretty well, as anyone who owns Microsoft shares will know). Winners in the knowledge economy, as Brian Arthur of the Santa Fe Institute points out, are different from the classic industrial barons: "Dominance may consist not so much in cornering a single product, as in successively taking over more and more threads of the web of technology." To see this in action, see Figure 3.3 in Chapter 3 (page 81) showing the Internet network to see how many critical gateways Microsoft or Sun control in this space.

Networks, whether social, technological or biological, consist of nodes and the relationships between these nodes. The set of relationships and flows of information between the nodes in a network create the potential for value to be created. For example, people e-mailing each other or interacting in an online community over the Internet are using technological and social networks to exchange information and ideas. The value potential in these interactions will only be realised, however, if and when a contract (formal or informal) is set up and someone pays (in cash or in kind) for an exchange of value.

Although value can be created and realised through networks, markets and organisations evolved because they are often more efficient and stable ways of appropriating, realising and transferring value. What this means in the network economy is that hierarchies and markets will continue to perform most of their classic functions, although the way they do this will change dramatically.

The main difference between a pure network and an organisation is that organisations contain a hierarchy of both functions and roles, whereas a network operates on the basis of peer-to-peer relationships. The interaction between the network and the hierarchy creates some interesting dynamics and tensions, which need to be harnessed to maintain the pace of evolution in an organisation.

### Hierarchies

Hierarchies are of two kinds: formal and natural. Natural hierarchies involve the self-organisation of entities into distinct levels, so that the functionality at one level forms the basis for the operation of the next level up. For example, the hierarchy of cells in human bodies enables the major organ systems to function, but this necessarily constrains the functionality of the cells to about 256 different kinds of specialised operations, such as skin, liver, brain, and so on.

Formal hierarchies are similar to natural hierarchies in that there is a specialisation of function at each level of the hierarchy; they are different in that they involve power differences between levels in the hierarchy, and people can move up and down in terms of their roles and interactions. Formal hierarchies can thus be more flexible and simultaneously more rigid than natural hierarchies, depending on the way in which they are set up and operated.

Hierarchies perform several useful functions.

■ Simplification. Hierarchy acts as a cognitive filter[2] through a span of control of seven plus or minus two (Miller's law,[3] which states that the number of items that can be held simultaneously in the conscious mind is seven, plus or minus two). The complexity of the environment is absorbed through a hierarchy (whether four or 24 layers). Each layer acts as a filter, limiting the range and number of issues that need to be addressed at that level. This simplifies the task of the people at each level in the hierarchy, enabling the organisation as a whole to deal with complexity.

- Conservation of knowledge. Hierarchy ensures that the accumulated experience of an organisation is represented at the more senior levels, particularly where these levels have been promoted through the ranks.
- Handling the unexpected. Hierarchies enable exceptional, unanticipated circumstances to be relayed up the hierarchy for decision by more experienced, knowledgeable executives.
- Predictability. The rules implicit in hierarchies act to provide stability and predictability for the organisation's members. (As Bertrand Russell once remarked, "What people want is not knowledge but certainty.")

In natural and formal hierarchies individuals and players can specialise their roles and skills to generate specific gains:

- Productivity. As noted by Adam Smith in *The Wealth of Nations*, specialisation enables specific operations to be carried out by an individual in a production process, thereby gradually improving the speed and quality of the work carried out by each individual at each stage in a production process through the performance improvement gained through repetition of the task.
- Economy of training and knowledge. Specialisation enables workers to be trained in specific skills and disciplines, thereby reducing the amount of total knowledge they need, and the time required to acquire it.
- Control. Specialisation increases the level of control owners and management have over workers, as specialised workers require the infrastructure of an organisation and its ability to co-ordinate their efforts with other specialised workers to produce economically useful outputs.
- Rising return on investment. Specialisation increases the returns firms and individuals can earn on their knowledge through

productivity gains and economies in the acquisition and application of task-related knowledge.

Networks and markets connect the different levels in hierarchies. For example, the hierarchy represented by an organisation is connected to the next layer in the hierarchy, the economy, through the financial markets and through its own networks in its economic web. Yet at each new level in a natural hierarchy, new characteristics emerge that are not properties of the components. Thus the fluctuations in the financial markets (for example, the ups and downs of a stockmarket index) are an emergent property of all the shares of all the organisations traded in the market, rather than a property of the organisations themselves.

The drawback of hierarchies is that, precisely because they are so good at stabilising and conserving, when change is required they resist it. To make an organisation adaptive, it is necessary to go beyond the simple delayering and decentralisation initiatives that have dominated the past decade. Even flat hierarchies still seek to preserve the status quo. This is why organisations seeking to be adaptive and to evolve must balance the conservative forces of the hierarchy with the change-inducing nature of networks and markets.

## *Markets*

The explosion of new market-spaces in the digital economy owes much to the dramatic fall in transaction costs that the Internet and communications technology deliver. Online auctioneers such as eBay and QXL, aggregators such as Chemdex and exchanges such as NTE are all examples of rapidly growing market-places where everything from personal and household effects, through laboratory materials and chemicals, to transport services are exchanged online. The important functions of markets include the following.

- Redistribution. Markets redistribute surpluses, and through the laws of supply and demand ensure that a price emerges which "clears" the surplus.
- Price-setting. Markets ensure there is a price for all goods and services traded in the market.
- Benchmarks. Markets set benchmarks on value, which encourage individuals and firms to produce goods and services in the knowledge that they can earn a known amount of money for a specific unit of production or service.

Markets can only operate under conditions where a price can be determined, and where the quality of the goods or services is known or ascertainable. The alignment of interests in markets lies in both buyers and sellers finding counterparties who wish to exchange goods for goods or goods and services for money. The bargain is essentially an exchange where a buyer pays in money (or in kind) for something the seller no longer wishes to own. In the case of a service, the seller is selling time that they no longer wish to own, as well as their skill and knowledge. This symmetry must be present for markets to work. Where such symmetry does not exist or cannot be arranged, hierarchies are more effective in meeting people's needs and getting things done.

Markets exhibit both complex and chaotic dynamics, depending on their state. When markets are driven by large doses of optimism and energy (for example, in a bull market where prices rise as demand exceeds supply), or are settling down and consolidating after profit taking, or when pessimism and lethargy prevail (for example, in a bear market where prices are falling and supply exceeds demand), they generally exhibit complex behaviours. At critical turning points in a market, however, the dynamics can become chaotic, as anyone who has been involved in a stockmarket crash can testify.

Market structures were used effectively during the 1980s and 1990s to break up large nationalised corporations through privatisation, and internal markets were created within decentralised organisations to improve efficiency and make businesses more competitive. Markets are now fusing with networks, so that communities, commerce and content join together into what many believe is a virtuous circle of increasing returns for all involved. Complex adaptive systems, methods and tools are particularly well suited to dealing with this rich, interactive world of multiple feedback loops, emergent value propositions and market phase transitions.

### Organisations as complex evolving systems

Complex evolving systems share several common characteristics.

- Self-organisation. All living systems are self-organising, and this extends with equal force to the social and economic worlds. In organisations, self-organisation occurs in many different ways. Think, for example, of what happens around the coffee machine or water dispenser. There is a grapevine of informal gossip and information sharing, which enables different possible combinations of relationships to emerge from the "co-incidences" that happen during informal interactions. Think of the way new ideas emerge in a group of managers, in laboratories, or even in the boardroom; they self-organise out of the rich soup of existing knowledge and relationships, and cannot be programmed in any formal way.

◪ Creativity. Surprising characteristics can emerge from the interaction of the components of a network, which are not properties of the components themselves. At the human level, for example, the collaboration of a group produces outcomes that are not possible to predict by simply summing the behaviour of the individuals involved, just as the outcome of the interaction of billions of neurons in our brains produces consciousness, which is not a property of the neurons themselves.

◪ Non-linearity. Small causes can produce large effects in human systems. The "butterfly effect" (where the movement of the wings of a butterfly in Brazil can alter the state of the weather in Texas) is a well-known chaos theory example, but the effects of non-linearity can clearly be seen in human affairs. For example, as mentioned in Chapter 1, the collapse of the tiny stockmarket in Thailand in late 1997 led to the Asian economic crisis a few months later and the collapse of the Russian economy several months later. In a personal relationship, the wrong word used at the wrong time can lead to the disruption or ending of the relationship – small causes, but large effects.

◪ Memory. Complex systems have memory, not located at a specific place but distributed throughout the system. Any complex system has a history, which is crucial to the behaviour of the whole system.

◪ Adaptability. Complex adaptive systems can reorganise their internal structure without the intervention of, or in response to, the intervention of an external agent. Such a pre-adaptation or adaptation may enable the system to have a higher probability of survival under changing conditions in its ecosystem and environment, and is the result of unconscious learning.

The unique feature of organisations, compared with technologies, processes and infrastructures, is that they consist of networks of relationships among human beings. That is, they are an emergent property of these networks of relationships and the commitments made between the people in these relationships. As well as the five characteristics outlined above, there are four more features that characterise human relationships and organisations.

- ◪ Being. Humans have authentic presence and needs, and cannot simply be treated as a resource. The way in which people experience themselves in an organisation enables or constrains the potential of what an organisation can become. The experience of individuals enables them to form an interpretation of themselves and their world. The relationship between these different interpretations is what people are dealing with in the interactions of individuals in organisations.
- ◪ Identity. A person's identity is a function of the interaction of their being and their relationships. The quality of these relationships is a strong driver of the kinds of outcomes that are possible in an organisation. Innovation, for example, is possible only in a collaborative environment that creates the conditions in which creativity is possible.
- ◪ Conscious learning. Networks of relationships are capable of conscious learning, just as the individuals that comprise the nodes in the networks are. Whether knowledge is created and shared in an organisation will depend on the quality, number and types of relationships within an organisation, and between the organisation and its economic web.
- ◪ Coherence. Individuals and organisations are both sense-making entities. The extent to which the organisation operates as a network of relationships enables individuals to make sense of their work and their world, and will strongly influence the coherence of the organisation and its sense of purpose. Such purpose can only be grounded in the coherence and meaningfulness of people's work to themselves, their colleagues and their customers. At its heart, coherence requires an alignment of context, viewpoint, purpose and action that enables further action.[4]

In these respects, organisations are different from any other entity grounded in the operation of a network, and it is through these differences that their unique characteristics arise. So what does all this mean for managing complexity? The principles of complex adaptive systems and of organisational evolution described above are reflected in the real world of organisations in many ways.

There are two main types of organisations operating as complex adaptive systems. The first is organisations that have been applying such principles unconsciously, but successfully, and have often discovered in retrospect that they have been doing so. These are known as the "implicit complexity" group. The second type, less numerous but growing rapidly, comprises firms that have been consciously applying the principles of complexity. These are known as the "explicit complexity" group.

Whether the application is explicit or implicit, both groups of firms have adopted the following management styles.

- Instead of micro-managing, managers spend time setting general direction and minimum specifications. They focus on the desirable outcomes and leave the process of getting to these outcomes to those responsible. This rule frees members of the system to self-organise and to adapt to meet the unique challenges of the situations they encounter in their own creative way.
- They have a limited set of simple rules, which provide a general framework within which employees/members can interact freely, limited only by the general sense of direction and minimum specifications already agreed.
- They create spaces for creativity by relinquishing control and generating trust. It is difficult for creativity and innovation to emerge in an organisation without self-organisation. In turn, self-organisation cannot happen unless there is an informal network in place, suffused with sufficient trust in its own capabilities to allow it to begin to generate experiments "outside the box". The informal network will not support such experiments until managers relinquish some control, and support learning and the mistakes that learning requires.
- They encourage diversity and recombination. The most robust systems in nature are the most diverse; and diversity comes about through the endless recombination of elements already within a system to create new entities that have not previously existed. This can be easily kick-started in most organisations by encouraging many small-scale experiments, where the cost of failure is sufficiently low to allow innovative learning and breakthroughs to happen.
- They support initiative and personal responsibility. If individuals in an organisation do not take responsibility for their own work

and develop their own plans to add value, then little value will be added by practising the principles of complexity in that organisation. The approach is characterised by "paradoxical" leadership, which gives direction without being directive, is authoritative without being controlling, is strong while being open to influence and is clear in situations of uncertainty.

Chapter 3 and Appendix 2 provide several case studies of these principles being applied in organisations.

## What does business success really mean?

The desire to be successful appears to be as common as breathing in the human race. Of course, what each individual means by success varies enormously, but each of us, in our own way, has some kind of picture of what we are and what we would like to become. In a real sense, who we are will determine what success means for us and how we might go about striving to achieve it (or not, as the case may be).

Organisational success has been defined in many different ways, but a predictive model of business success has so far proved as elusive as the Holy Grail. A large number of variables might be selected as potential determinants of organisational behaviour and performance. Much of the research done to date has categorised these variables into groups with headings such as "environment", "market", "organisation", "management", "culture", and so on. The relationships between these variables and the performance and behaviour of firms are not well understood. Some commonly accepted measures of business success in the modern, economic model of the firm include:

- profitability;
- satisfied stakeholders such as customers, shareholders, employees;
- revenue and profit growth;
- growth in market share;
- growth in market value (stockmarket capitalisation).

If some or all of these (mainly financial) measures constitute success, then what are the prerequisites for achieving them? Grinyer, Mayes and McKiernan[5] investigated the causes of decline or improvement in performance in 25 British companies between 1984 and 1985, as measured against a control group of 25 firms. They found the same mix of economic and organisational variables as Peters and Waterman did in the *In Search* of *Excellence* sample of ten American corporations in 1981/82[6]. Goldsmith and Clutterbuck's 1984 survey of 23 British firms found a similar mix of variables[7], as did Peters's 1987 list in *Thriving on Chaos*[8]. The four lists of variables are shown in Table 2.1 on the following page.

The assumption in these popular recipes for success is that the organisations that "get it right" in each attribute will prevail, irrespective of the environmental challenges or opportunities facing them. Subsequent evidence, however, suggests that, on the contrary, such recipes for success do not predict superior long-term performance, as is illustrated by the fact that over two-thirds of Peters and Waterman's 1982 excellent companies were no longer excellent five years after publication of their book.

Other authors have developed models of organisational performance that include both economic and organisational variables. In an introduction to a paper[9] on the subject, Hansen and Wernerfelt comment:

> *In the business policy literature there are two major streams of research on the determinants of firm performance. One is based primarily upon an economic tradition, emphasizing the importance of external market factors in determining firm success. The other line of research builds on the behavioral and sociological paradigm and sees organizational factors and their fit with the environment as the major determinants of success. Within this school of thought, little direct attention is given to the firm's competitive position. Similarly, economics has disregarded factors internal to the firm. Theoretical or empirical evidence of linkages to performance abound within each paradigm, but surprisingly little has been done to integrate the two and evaluate the relative effect of each on firm profitability.*

Hansen and Wernerfelt decomposed the inter-firm variance in profit rates into economic and organisational components, and found that both sets of factors are significant determinants of firm performance. Their further findings are that the two effects are roughly independent, and that organisational factors explain about twice as much variance in profit rates as economic factors.

Table 2.1 **Traditional variables used to explain company success**

Peters and Waterman, *In Search of Excellence*
1. A bias for action
2. Closeness to the customer
3. Autonomy and entrepreneurship
4. Productivity through people
5. Hands-on, value-driven
6. Sticking to the knitting
7. Simple form, lean staff
8. Simultaneous loose-tight properties

Goldsmith and Clutterbuck, *The Winning Streak*
1. Leadership
2. Autonomy
3. Control
4. Involvement
5. Market orientation
6. Zero-basing (or stick to the knitting – keeping in close touch with the fundamentals of the business)
7. Innovation
8. Integrity

Grinyer, Mayes and McKiernan, *Sharpbenders*
1. Good management
2. Appropriate organisational structure
3. Effective financial and other controls
4. Sound product/market posture
5. Good marketing management
6. High quality maintained
7. Tightly controlled costs

Peters, *Thriving on Chaos*
1. Higher value-added
2. Responsiveness
3. Making products that work
4. Service
5. Flatness of organisation
6. Innovation
7. People-centred
8. Leadership

## Success depends on interconnections

The difficulty with success recipes is that they ignore the fact that much of what determines an outcome in a situation is a function of the complex array of factors in the situation and their interconnection. John Kotter, professor of leadership at Harvard Business School,[10] puts it like this:

> *Imagine walking into an office and not liking the way in which it is arranged. So, you move one chair to the left. You put a few books on the credenza. You get a hammer and re-hang a painting. All of this may take an hour at most, since the task is relatively straightforward. Indeed, creating change in any system of independent parts is usually not difficult.*
>
> *Now imagine going into another office where a series of ropes, big rubber bands, and steel cables connect the objects to one another. First, you would have difficulty walking into the room without getting tangled up. After making your way slowly over to the chair, you try to move it, but find that this lightweight piece of furniture won't budge. Straining harder, you move the chair a few inches, but then you notice that a dozen books have been pulled off the bookshelf and that the sofa has moved slightly in a direction you don't like. You slowly work your way over to the sofa and try to push it back into the right spot, which turns out to be incredibly difficult. After 30 minutes, you succeed, but now a lamp has been pulled off the edge of the desk and is precariously hanging in mid-air, supported by a cable going in one direction and a rope going in another.*

The difference between the office of independent parts that we are used to, and the office in which everything is interconnected, is the difference between managing simple mechanical systems and machine-like organisations in the industrial age, and managing complex adaptive systems and organisations in the knowledge age. These tasks are completely different, and the tools and approaches developed for the one will not work well for the other. Thus although there may be simple formulae to describe the recipe for success for the office of independent parts, the use of such recipes in the complex, interconnected room may prove to be not only an exercise in pure frustration, but also disastrous.

So success means many different things, depending on where you are in a particular system. If you have insight into the model that informs the operation of the highest level system, then success is a function of the effective operation of that system. For example, a group of companies may judge its success by the return the group as a whole makes on its capital. If, however, your awareness is restricted to the level of one of the smaller systems which contributes to the group, then success will to be seen in the context of that "smaller level". It is also possible that success at this level may be in conflict with success at the higher level. For example, the managers of a subsidiary may want to make a substantial investment in, say, new technologies in order to retain or build a competitive advantage, only to find they are overruled at a higher level by those focusing on the group's overall figures for the following year.

In an earlier age, tragedy occurred when individual herdsmen allowed too many animals to graze on common land. In the short run this did no harm; indeed, initially it may have stimulated growth. In the longer run, however, the overgrazing destroyed the grass on the common land, causing the animals to starve and leaving the community in difficulty. A similar situation can be seen today in destructive market share wars based on price cuts alone, where too many competitors are chasing too few customers with commodity products.

The notion of success is thus a direct function of the level of system being observed. The interactions between a successful individual such as "Chainsaw" Al Dunlap, a corporate raider who bought companies and stripped them of their assets, and the surrounding system are often antagonistic. One of the last companies Al bought, Sunbeam, never recovered from his chainsaw and went bust. Even Al eventually lost his money. Corporate anorexia brought about by continual downsizing may make a fast buck for a while for a few people, but in the longer term it saps the strength and competencies of an organisation. This is not to say that downsizing or rightsizing is always a bad thing; sometimes, if done intelligently, so that the value drivers in a business are not destroyed, shedding some weight can be highly beneficial in the longer term.

Organisational complexity arises largely because organisations themselves comprise many people and multiple components, each with different aims, needs and wants. Depending on your perspective, the approach you choose to interact with or lead them will vary.

### Three schools of thought

Take three managers, each of whom has recently returned to work from a particular training programme at three leading business schools. Each business school takes a very different approach to describing how organisations succeed.

The first manager, who went to a summer programme in competitive strategy at Harvard Business School, may explain how his organisation works in a rational way, describing how particular individuals and stakeholders have set objectives and strategies, and how specific programmes are being implemented to make these things happen. He would also describe the competitive forces acting on the organisation, its relationship with its principal allies, suppliers and customers, and how the organisation's structure, systems, staff and skills are aligned to the organisation's strategy. He would draw on many case studies to illustrate how a step-by-step rational process was used to analyse critical success factors, industry structure and shareholder value added (the rational economic approach).

The second manager, who attended a two-week organisational change workshop at McGill University, may describe her organisation as being subject to the whims of outrageous fortune, where many of the key variables critical to the success of the organisation are subject to external influences. The story in this case would revolve around serendipitous events, in which key players in the organisation and its environment were thrust together, out of which emerged exciting new products or services, and in which new markets were accessed or created. She would describe the behaviour of specific individuals and organisations as key to the outcomes in her firm, and how their interpersonal chemistry and management styles were critical to what happened at each of the organisation's stages of growth. Models of visionary leaders would be cited to show how her firm could become more entrepreneurial in its performance. The context of her story would be that her firm was in a Darwinian kind of environment, where natural selection operates on populations of firms, and that shared vision together with the right purpose, processes and people are the keys to enable growing firms to survive in this tough evolutionary process (the behavioural approach).

The third manager, who has just returned from a high-powered summer programme at a leading European business school, may explain that his organisation is essentially a socially constructed reality, in which different coalitions of stakeholders are interacting using a variety of paradigms and processes to generate stories of the past, present and future. Such stories are helping the organisation understand itself and its business ecology, enabling a process of accelerated learning to occur

Table 2.2 **The driving forces in the industrial and knowledge economies**

| Industrial economies | Knowledge economies |
|---|---|
| Scale and physical assets | Connectivity and intangibles |
| Oligopolies | Ecologies |
| Market share | Value share |
| Product/market selection | Relationship and value web selection |
| Experience curve | Economic web |
| Equilibrium | Phase transitions |

Source: Chris Meyer, 1998.

among the various key stakeholders in and around the business. This organisation is using methods and approaches such as business ecosystem mapping, strategic options, scenarios, and strategic gaming and simulation to navigate the complexity and uncertainty in and around it. These generate a coherent and compelling strategic agenda, which enables the organisation to be more nimble than and out-manoeuvre its competitors, changing the rules of the game in their industry (the strategic learning approach).

These three examples show the different roles executives play in improving organisational performance. However, the learning approach to strategy and organisations may be the most appropriate in the complex, fast-moving knowledge economy of the early 21st century. Table 2.2 summarises the major differences between the driving forces of the industrial and knowledge economies.

Predictors of firm performance in the last decade have become more organic than their counterparts in the previous three decades, as the reality of human, complex, adaptive systems becomes apparent. Culture, particularly, is a variable, though difficult to measure, which recognises the importance of meaning, symbols and communication in an organisation.

### Success in the traditional economy
Traditional microeconomic and macroeconomic models rely on two principal assumptions: the rational behaviour of the seller and buyer (to maximise their economic gain or profit); and perfect information about the state of demand and supply in a market. The classic tools of economics, such as production functions, cost curves and price setting

demand and supply curves, cannot operate without these assumptions.[11] It is true that certain markets (such as the foreign exchange markets in free currencies) are virtually perfect examples of this sort of economic theory.

The economic paradigm explains behaviour and performance using models that measure explicit variables, such as accounting information and market and industry statistics. The organisational behaviour model relies on the measurement of some external variables, such as size, history and environment, together with more implicit variables, such as management quality, culture and style. The payoff in an economic game is likely to be fairly hard, in the form of assets, cash, or promotion, whereas the payoff in a sociopolitical game is often intangible, such as a change in behaviour, a motivated employee or a shared perspective.

Transaction cost theory has been applied with some success to explain the exchange of information and goods between firms, but it is limited to situations where there is a market between organisations or between large departments in organisations where costs are readily calculable. Of course, a great deal is made of the reduction in transaction costs brought about by the Internet and the communications revolution. Although this is true, it does not shed much light on what makes for success in the network economy.

The other major drawback of classic economic models and transaction cost theory is their reliance on one or more stable equilibrium points to determine costs and income. This results in static models that do not reflect the dynamic nature of organisations and their environments. Transaction cost theory takes no account of the transition costs involved in the almost continuous changes organisations need to make in their affairs if they are to adapt and survive.

Economic approaches have limited predictive ability except at high levels of aggregation. Such levels of aggregation explain little about how high performance is to be achieved under conditions of uncertainty. The economic approach does not quantify (nor can it, since they are intangible) variables such as culture, decision-processes, or cognition and irrational factors such as personality.

The traditional economic approaches work best where:

- a degree of certainty prevails in markets, and large volumes of reasonably accurate data are available about macroeconomic and microeconomic variables;
- returns on assets and capital are being judged, or where

continuous or batch production makes capital intensity and large-scale infrastructure important, and people are comparatively unimportant in the overall equation.

## The evolution of traditional business strategies

In a traditional economy, high market shares and experience curves become extremely important as they enable firms to achieve economies of scale, which are essential for profitability in a world of physical assets where the law of diminishing returns holds true. The law of diminishing returns states that for every unit of capital invested in an asset, the return on that asset will reach an optimum level through the experience curve effect, then start diminishing, as no further productivity gains can be made from the asset.

This is because physical laws limit what assets can be made to do, and how much they can be made to "sweat". Although total quality management (TQM) demonstrated that incremental improvements in productivity can be achieved in assets that are already well utilised, these returns begin to run out unless more dramatic changes are made to the way things are done. In any event, it could be argued that the major contribution of TQM was the way it motivated workers operating in mass production environments to do a better job and work more effectively in teams.

### From the 1950s and 1960s ...

In the late 1950s and early 1960s strategic planning became popular. From the work of Selznick and Andrews, in the tradition of Harvard Business School case studies, came the design approach to corporate planning. The message here was strategic fit, and the method was to figure out from case studies and previous experience which strategy was the best fit for where the organisation was at the time. The useful SWOT (strengths, weaknesses, opportunities and threats) analysis emerged, as well as the distinction between the formulation and implementation of strategy.

Along with the design approach to strategy, the planning school developed out of the work of Igor Ansoff, based on systems theory, cybernetics and engineering. Professional managers championed this way of thinking, which led to the formalisation of planning, programming, scheduling and budgeting. The central actors in this approach were planners, who controlled immense staffs of analysts and programme managers. The environment this required was one in which procedures dominated, and checklists of factors that needed to be "controlled" drove the management agenda.

This worked well, particularly in the domestic American market, where demand exceeded supply for most consumer and business products and services in the 1950s and 1960s. This led to a simple, stable business environment, where forecasting and programming worked. Following the changes unleashed by the start of the sixth wave economy, and the decline of the industries in which strategic planning had succeeded, the planning school began to decline.

This led to the rise of what Henry Mintzberg, professor of management at McGill University, summarised as the "positioning school".[12] The work of Dan Schendel in the 1970s and then Michael Porter in the 1980s, derived from military history and economics, was championed by major consulting firms and military writers. The positioning school focuses on analysis, calculation and facts. Its central actors are analysts, which is why it is beloved by the classic strategy boutiques and executives who have learned these techniques. The positioning school thinks of the organisation as a large machine, where deliberate strategy rules the roost. This approach is most useful when assessing industrial age markets and mature industries.

### ... to the 1980s and 1990s

In the 1980s and early 1990s, business strategy continued to rest on the works of these "old masters". Michael Porter, professor of strategy at Harvard Business School, wrote two best-selling business strategy books, *Competitive Strategy* (1980) and *Competitive Advantage* (1983). Porter's work assumes that economic considerations are primary in determining the performance of organisations, particularly market share. The analytical framework of the competitive positioning approach is based on extensive empirical research into the dynamics of competition in various industries during the 1970s and 1980s, relying heavily on data from the Profit Impact of Market Strategy programme (PIMS).

The facts about market share are well known.[13] The PIMS database generated surprisingly consistent results between 1965 and 1990: market share is the primary determinant of profit. The PIMS programme emerged from General Electric corporation in the 1960s and developed into the Strategic Planning Institute, established in conjunction with Harvard Business School. Since then over 30,000 businesses from most industries, in many countries, have contributed information about their business over a period of five or more years.

Porter's key framework is the five competitive forces, which explain profitability within an industry and firm. Industry structure is held to be the main determinant of industry profitability, and the position of a firm within an industry the main determinant of its profitability. Thus an industry with a monopolistic or oligopolistic structure, with few or no new entrants, small customers with little or no power, no substitutes and little competitive rivalry, is likely to be highly profitable for the few firms that dominate it. Where there is a great deal of competitive rivalry, customers are large and powerful, new entrants abound and the number of new substitutes for the products or services produced by the industry are rising, profits will be lower. So in large, mature industrial firms, the key is to establish a dominant market position relative to competitors, and to reduce the number of new entrants or substitutes through regulation, lobbying or (in less developed countries) cronyism.

### Adding value

The value chain model developed by Porter and his colleagues provides a useful framework to describe the way firms add value through their activities. Value-adding activities can be analysed in different firms, leading to an understanding of the relative competitive advantage that different combinations of activities can yield in different firms. Every firm is a collection of the activities it uses to transact its business (that is, design, produce, market, deliver and support its product). Such activities are remarkably consistent whether the product flow is physical, such as a cement production line, or abstract, such as the compilation of items of information for a newspaper. Porter refers to the set of activities causing the product to flow from the input to the output ends of a firm as primary activities. He refers to other activities conducted by the firm as support activities. These activities consist of flows of materials, services and information required to ensure the continuity and integrity of the product or service flow. A simplified version of value chain theory is represented in Figure 2.1.

The value chain works from left to right: organisations take in a variety of inputs from suppliers, and together with their own resources transform these inputs into outputs that add value to customers. These inputs and outputs can be goods and/or services. In manufacturing businesses the inputs and outputs are generally physical things; in service businesses they are usually human labour and/or information. Design, procurement, production and operations, distribution, and service and support are typical stages in the primary processes of a value chain. Personnel, finance and administration are typical functions in the secondary or support processes in a value chain. Information technology

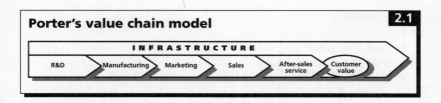

**Porter's value chain model** `2.1`

INFRASTRUCTURE

R&D — Manufacturing — Marketing — Sales — After-sales service — Customer value

can be used to enable people to add more value in their organisation's value chain by automating and re-engineering business processes.

Porter's competitive analysis framework is often used to identify the areas in the value chain that will provide the greatest competitive advantage, which has led to the popularity of benchmarking processes and systems to determine their value-adding characteristics. The principal tenet of the positioning approach to competitive strategy, led by Porter, was that research revealed that market share was a major driver of profitability.

### Performance variables

The PIMS database measures nearly 500 variables, of which a core of 15 account for about 80% of performance over a three- to five-year period in most of the 3,000 firms in the database. Variables such as market growth, market share, capital intensity, rate of innovation, productivity and relative quality are captured in this core group of variables. Although such information is useful in focusing the mind of management on major issues, the PIMS variables measure macro-phenomena over long periods of time.

The PIMS programme found that predicting how well a firm would do in the future depends largely on its market environment, its current competitive position (its market share, quality, price, and so on) and the nature of its production structure. According to the findings of research using the PIMS database, high values in the following areas are strong predictors of business success:

- absolute and relative market share
- relative quality
- real market growth
- industry concentration
- operating effectiveness
- capacity utilisation
- value-added per employee

but low-moderate values in these areas are desirable to avoid failure:

- ◪ investment intensity
- ◪ fixed/working capital mix
- ◪ customer power
- ◪ distribution complexity
- ◪ moderate levels of innovation.

The PIMS research demonstrates that incremental return on investment is not related at all to historic return on investment. In other words, how well the firm did in the past bears no relation to how well it will do in the future. The major criticism of PIMS is that its findings are based on 30,000 or so industrial firms, predominantly large manufacturers, and that service companies, financial institutions and knowledge businesses are largely absent.

The pure economic approach to organisational performance is essentially an external control model of the business. Outside forces such as market attractiveness and competitive position influence decisions about internal variables such as production and organisational structure. Of course, not all organisations are founded for economic reasons or judged by economic criteria. Other evidence also suggests that strategy follows structure, rather than vice versa. What is value-added is a value judgment itself, on the part of both the producer and the consumer. The economic approach assumes rational decision-making, based on facts – the relevant facts dictated by the economic model being used.

Much of the way in which organisations operate, however, depends on a great deal of uncertainty, and theories of leadership and management have developed to explain how leaders navigate such uncertainty. The inherent problem is that although today's decisions have a great effect on tomorrow, no one can ever have perfect knowledge about today's, let alone tomorrow's environment. It is possible to go so far as to say that some firms create order out of chaos, in situations where little or no information is available before the event.

Fritjof Capra, a well-known quantum physicist and ecologist, has criticised traditional economics for being based on highly aggregated data, inappropriately derived from microanalyses, resulting in elaborate quantitative models describing fragmented segments of economic activity – all based on tacitly assumed neo-classical concepts. Although economic approaches to understanding organisational success can yield some insights, they have failed to provide any systematic evidence of improved performance as a result of such insights.

## The knowledge approach to future business success

In a knowledge economy, the principles of biological evolution can be a useful guide to what organisations must do to survive and prosper. Biological evolution has always had as its primary feature the perpetuation of a wide diversity of species, capable of adapting to the widest set of environmental niches. The limited resource base for which all organisms have to compete in physical ecosystems, however, results in the survival of only those species which have a competitive advantage, that is, which are able to secure more than their proportionate share of the resource base and utilise it efficiently.

Biological evolution goes through a number of stages. First it generates variety, which is then selected by interaction with the environment. The variations that succeed through many successive generations then become fixed. For biological evolution to work, diversity is generated through processes of self-organisation, in which the recombination of the components of an organism into different kinds of forms is enabled through spontaneous mechanisms such as mutation, sexual reproduction and more complex processes operating at a social level.

No species of any kind has ever become so successful that it has dominated the landscape of an ecology: whether the ecology is a planet, a rain forest or a small pond. The same phenomenon holds true in economies: organisations are subject to the forces of natural selection, together with the business ecosystems of which they form a part. Organisations that are well-positioned, aligned, ready and adaptive prosper because they are able to continue functioning over long periods of time in a wide variety of circumstances.

To continue functioning over long periods of time in a wide variety of circumstances is easy to say but hard to do. In evolutionary terms, failure is the norm: more than 99.9% of all species, companies, languages, cultures and technologies that have ever existed are now extinct. The entities that did not survive either became too complex to adapt to the changes in their environment, or failed to manage the complexity around them in a way conducive to their survival.

Humans have been particularly successful at technological evolution. They have extracted and utilised matter, energy and information from the environment with a minimum of effort, thereby supporting and proliferating their descendants and genes.

The evolution of technological knowledge and new technologies is perpetuated principally by the communication of benefits, and reinforced by tradition and sanctions. In the personal computer industry, for example, the benefits of the graphical user interface (GUI) incorporated in products such as the Macintosh or Windows has meant that the GUI has become the standard way of interacting with a PC. At the other extreme, the spread of nuclear technologies has been limited by the enforcement of a variety of nuclear non-proliferation treaties, backed up by severe sanctions.

To apply some of the insights and metaphors of biology to organisations and industries, it is helpful to think of individuals and organisations as adaptive agents. Each adaptive agent seeks to maximise the welfare of itself and those near and dear to it. This involves competing for resources and opportunities, as well as collaborating with other players when this makes sense.

Societies and organisations are composed of many adaptive agents interacting with each other. These adaptive agents can be of three kinds: people, computer programs and machines. Of course, people are by far the most intelligent and adaptive kind of agent, and most of the richness of organisational behaviour comes from human interactions. Adaptive agents operate in complex feedback networks, which often generate surprising and counter-intuitive behaviour.

The primary feature of evolution in a social and organisational context is that entities co-evolve with each other in a rich tapestry of interactions. Co-evolution happens at many levels, such as between companies, government departments, charities, local authorities and communities.

### Business strategy in the knowledge economy

In the knowledge economy, the principles of business strategy are being transformed. Instead of a focus on physical assets and economies of scale, the drivers of success reside in connectivity and intangibles. For example, Microsoft has a market value five times that of General Motors, with only one-fifth of its turnover. This value is created by a network of incredibly complex connectivity, in which Microsoft manages thousands of relationships with its partners to produce the 20m lines of software code used to write this sentence in Word and Windows 98.

Businesses increasingly need to develop and manage complex ecologies of organisations around themselves so as to succeed. Take the case of AOL. Although initially its founder, Steve Case, had only to manage a moderate web of other players to create value for its customers, as soon as the Internet browser arrived AOL had to create a new ecosystem of players around itself to survive. This complex web now includes Sun, Netscape and Bertelsmann in Europe, where AOL is now the largest Internet service provider, and more alliances are becoming necessary daily as Steve Case and his team seek to defend AOL's position against the inroads of Microsoft. The selection of partners with whom to collaborate is now becoming a life or death issue for most firms.

However, there is no substitute for original strategic thinking, even in a digital economy, or especially in a digital economy. Strategic thinking is a means of introducing revolution into the evolutionary process. Strategy accelerates or guides evolution by taking evolution to another level. Competition and co-evolution between ideas, beliefs and paradigms can be managed and designed to test new business models and ensure that they are robust before and during implementation.

At the core of complexity-based strategy lie economic webs. An economic web is a set of firms acting as nodes in a network, interconnected by a web of relationships, contracts and transactions across which flow resources and information. Such webs are often referred to as a business ecosystem. Economic webs lie at the heart of business evolution, for it is the co-evolution of the players, relationships and resources in an economic web that drive innovation and thereby evolution. So how can executives start to think differently, and learn to co-create desirable futures for themselves and their organisations under these conditions?

Shared strategic maps and models are the most effective ways of exploring new business ideas and options, as they provide a rapid means of simulating and testing the models through experiments. In a broader context, new kinds of mind-tools enable adaptive agents to operate on themselves and their internal models, making it possible for them to recognise and change these models before the threat of extinction (planning as learning, for example). Such maps and models are known in complexity science as internal models.

Every adaptive agent in a complex adaptive system has an internal model, which anticipates certain features of its environment. In the case of people, such models are socially constructed realities, which arise from the structure and dynamics of the individuals and their interactions with their environment. The accuracy of the shared internal models held by a management team of their firm and the nature of its business environment is usually one of the factors determining the ability of an organisation to adapt to its environment and co-evolve with the business ecosystem in which it operates. Internal models vary from the simplistic and rigid to the rich and highly adaptive.

This is where the cognitive and cultural schools of strategy have much to say. The principal message in the cognitive school is that how people frame reality shapes the way they can imagine and conceive of business opportunities. Such an approach places the mind in the role of the central actor, where change is mentally constructed and the strategy development process is emergent. The cultural school sets limits on what is possible in an individual mind and establishes that much of strategy emerges in, and is shaped by, a cultural context.

Where the cognitive and cultural approaches to strategy end, the entrepreneurial and learning approaches begin. Joseph Schumpeter, a well-known Austrian economist (and coiner of the phrase "gales of creative destruction", which he used to describe how economies evolve), is the father of the entrepreneurial school. Championed by small business people, the popular business press and progressive leaders such as Percy Barnevik, a former head of ABB, the entrepreneurial approach to strategy emphasises the bold stroke of leadership and the vision of the leader in securing new business opportunities. In an environment full of dynamic niches, the leader's intuition and vision enables the organisation to access adjacent possible spaces in the market-place.

The learning approach to strategy originated in the work of organisational theorists Richard Cyert, James March and Karl Weick in the 1960s. Following the popularity of the learning organisation movement and chaos theory in the early 1990s, the learning approach has been revitalised. Through teamwork and collective learning processes, the outcomes of organisational learning became apparent. For example, Arie de Geus, head of planning at Shell until 1992, stated in his famous *Harvard Business Review* article "Planning as Learning" that: "The ability to learn faster than your competitors may be the only sustainable competitive advantage."[14]

So, in layman's terms, by "playing" with their internal models institutions are capable of learning to adapt more quickly by influencing natural evolutionary forces to their benefit. The competition and collaboration between components of internal models (called "memes" by some, after Richard Dawkins's term) takes place in the minds of strategy-makers against the backdrop of the strategic landscapes in which they operate.

Most people are familiar with the natural and constructed landscapes around them. They instantly recognise the difference between the Himalayas and the English Lake District, or New York City and Moscow. What is confusing in the fog of commercial and political battle is that mental landscapes are not so immediately obvious. Not only is the nature of the terrain unclear, but it is often difficult to identify which players are on the terrain with us, and whether they are friend or foe.

At its simplest, a strategic landscape is a representation of those parts of the natural and constructed landscapes around them that people need to be able to navigate to survive and prosper. As in nature, different kinds of social and business ecosystems establish themselves on different landscapes – the savannah, the Mediterranean and rain forest ecosystems all have their equivalents in the world of business. Strategic learning involves building accurate and useful models of such landscapes and ecosystems to enable executives and their organisations to navigate them more effectively and to develop robust strategies and moves.

From a complexity perspective, the formation of emergent patterns in a messy process of innovation seems more like the real world than the idea of executives sitting in smoke-filled boardrooms making elaborate plans which are to be carried out to the letter. The environment in which the learning model operates is complex and dynamic, working best in adhocracies and professional, knowledge-based firms. The approach also works well in evolving situations in which unprecedented changes are happening, and appears to be the most suitable approach for adaptive organisations in the seventh wave economy.

### The role of strategic learning

The way to build future success in the age of e-business is to design an organisation which can not only adapt to current circumstances, but is also able to influence the circumstances in which it finds itself. Learning enables individuals, organisations and ecosystems to:

- change conditioned behavioural routines to be more adaptive;
- generate and evaluate a wider range of hypotheses about the future;
- select appropriate mind-tools and environments to enhance their learning, thinking and implementation capability.

The learning process should be as conscious as possible, and scenarios are a helpful technique for working through new ideas and strategic options. This process is known as strategic dialogue, and is illustrated in Figure 2.2 on the following page.

De Geus provides an excellent description of how Shell developed its scenario process in the *Harvard Business Review* article referred to

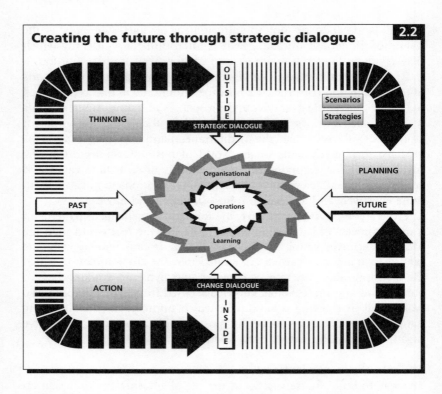

**Creating the future through strategic dialogue** `2.2`

earlier. He describes Shell's successful response to Standard Oil's market tactics earlier this century, and then says:

> *Outcomes like these don't happen automatically. On the contrary, they depend on the ability of a company's senior managers to absorb what is going on in the business environment and to act on that information with appropriate business moves. In other words, they depend upon learning, or, more precisely, institutional learning, which is the process whereby management teams change their shared mental models of their company, their markets, and their competitors.*

Learning is the key competency required by any organisation that wants to survive and thrive in the knowledge economy. Strategic learning focuses on the helicopter view of how organisations adapt to a changing

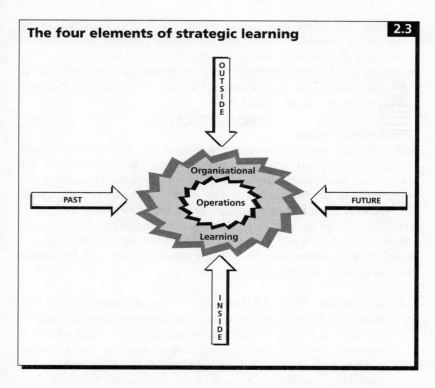

**The four elements of strategic learning**　　2.3

OUTSIDE

PAST　　Organisational　　FUTURE
Operations
Learning

INSIDE

world and create their own futures. The four elements that need to be balanced to achieve strategic learning are shown in Figure 2.3:

- the past, which needs to be interpreted and understood in the context of today;
- the future, which needs to be created from desirable elements of the past together with new elements;
- the external environment, which needs to be viewed as a source of possibilities (both good and bad); and
- the internal environment of the organisation, which must change to accommodate and seize possibilities of varying kinds.

In many organisations the pressure of events crowds out the opportunity to learn and develop. Rapid change of any sort (rocketing growth, serious shocks or sudden decline, for example) will make it difficult for the organisation to get ahead of its own operational necessities and think strategically about the future. Then, when the environment changes, it is unprepared for such change and begins to show signs of stress and potential failure to cope. This is why it is so important for all organisations to keep organisational learning alive, as this competency is the key to sustainable success in a rapidly changing and increasingly complex world.

### Consciousness counts

Both conscious and subconscious processes drive individual behaviour. Consciousness is an emergent phenomenon, an outcome of the interaction between biochemical, neurological and electromagnetic phenomena in the human brain. The extent to which an organisation can be said to learn is thus a function of the extent to which networks of relationships can be said to be gaining new knowledge, framing and reframing shared mental models, and applying such knowledge and models to make better strategic and operational moves. Such learning is likely to be both of the following.

- Subconscious. Below the threshold of conscious awareness, in which case the organisational learning process is operating as a form of imprinting or conditioning. Such organisational reflexes are largely built into the corporate culture, and into its day-to-day routines. As a result, such learning accumulates unexamined assumptions, which often result in the organisation failing to adapt or innovate.
- Conscious. Here the team, group or organisation becomes self-aware, and aware of the relationship between the team, group or organisation and its environment. Where there is awareness of the learning process (metalearning) and what is being learned, it is then possible to direct the organisation's attention to those trends and possibilities in itself and its environment that require consideration and, in some cases, a response.

Unfortunately, far too many organisations operate at the level of subconscious learning or instinct. They are thus incapable of directing their collective attention to strategic possibilities and vital turning points in themselves and their environment, and therefore fail to develop an appropriate strategic intent to pull them forwards into the future before their competitors.

*Making it happen*

As an organisation continually learns how to satisfy the changing demands of its stakeholders and its environment, it will itself be making many choices, wittingly or unwittingly, among a diverse array of possibilities in a number of key areas.

- Scenarios and strategies: diverse sets of assumptions about the future, which drive a variety of strategic directions, options and tactics.
- Products, services and offers: a range of products, services and technologies, which it does and can offer.
- Markets: a variety of market segments, value propositions and opportunities.
- Stakeholders: different coalitions of stakeholders with contrasting interests and ambitions.
- Partners: current and potential partners in joint ventures, alliances and other players in the ecosystem.
- People: groups and teams of people who can carry out the organisation's purpose.
- Cultures: different value systems and ways of seeing the world.

The strategy of an organisation will reflect a mix of these choices, and the degree to which they can be intelligently implemented will make or break the future of the organisation. The making and implementation of strategy, although an organisation-wide process, is developed by groups and individuals, each of whom will have a different perspective on the world. Such perspective and management styles often differ radically.

In embarking on a process of strategic dialogue, it is essential to develop a shared vocabulary and set of concepts for strategic thinking. For example, executives need to agree about the following.

- A business is a set of processes that deliver superior value to a large enough customer group, and at a low enough cost relative to price, to generate value (wealth) for the stakeholders. This is the major goal of a successful strategy, and it is achieved through developing competitive advantage.
- Competitive advantage is developed through applying a firm's distinctive capabilities to relevant markets.
- Distinctive capabilities are developed by exploiting key resources using business processes that harness the firm's core competencies.

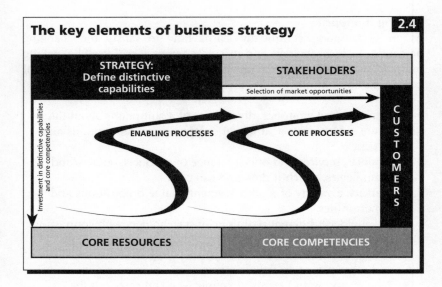

**The key elements of business strategy** 2.4

This process is accelerated through learning at all levels in an organisation.

The fundamental strategic questions are therefore as follows.

- Which core competencies, resources and processes should the firm invest in to develop the its distinctive capabilities, and to realise its vision and strategic intent?
- In which markets are these distinctive capabilities relevant, such that customers will pay for the value generated by them?
- What does the firm need to invest in these relevant markets to realise its vision and strategic intent?

As shown in Figures 2.4 and 2.5, a good strategy describes how, over time, an organisation will develop the core competencies it needs for the future. To do this it needs a vision of its future business ecosystem to provide a foundation for organisational foresight. Such a vision is replete with a variety of possible, relevant business ideas for the future, which may require different arrangements of the business ecosystem components and the organisation's value chain. Such potential business designs provide multiple options for the organisation, enabling it to succeed in whichever future it finds itself.

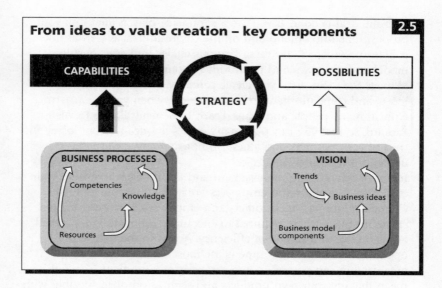

**From ideas to value creation – key components** `2.5`

*Fifteen survival tips for businesses*

In the knowledge economy, the windows of opportunity are opening and closing so fast that few firms that are not already on Internet time will survive. What does this mean for the rules of thumb that executives need to guide them in this turbulent, but exciting world?

1  Embed intelligent technology into everything you sell and operate in your business. It is cheap, and customers will love you for it. Just make sure it offers really valuable features, as opposed to gratuitous functionality, otherwise you will annoy them with irritating appliances, gadgets and buttons.
2  Make everything you offer interactive. Ensure customers and prospects can interact with you across many different kinds of media. Cross-thread the media offers so that they come back to you and your partners.
3  Distribute knowledge to everyone in your organisation. As they will have to make the key decisions in this fast-paced world, ensure that they have the information they need.
4  Exploit increasing returns. If you already operate in a market or service a community, ensure that you offer them fresh commerce deals, as well as fresh content. Make sure the deals you do with your commerce providers brings those "eyeballs" back to your community

after the deal is done. If you are a commerce player, then link your propositions into onland and online communities, as well as hot content providers. Build these virtuous circles into your business model and processes and the minds of your people.

5 Manage the value webs you create carefully. There are many feedback loops, and some unintended consequences, when you are a partner with so many people and firms. Learn to be neutral, like Hewlett-Packard, so that you can play many games at once without losing the trust of your partners and allies. Do not sign any exclusive deal unless it is absolutely strategic.

6 Invest in relationship management and technologies to ensure your customers, suppliers and employees are all co-investing with you. Connect customers to customers and employees to employees, and create intimacy where required to encourage innovation and speed.

7 Focus on opportunities, not efficiency. Access to the right opportunities at the right time is the most valuable thing an organisation can possess in a fast-moving environment. This will mean making your own products and services obsolete, together with your partners, before your competitors do, so you can create the room for new things to emerge in your business.

8 Develop your portfolio so that you get enough hits. In the complex adaptive economy of the 21st century, all industries will become like the movie, toy and pharmaceuticals industries of today – blockbusters there will be, and also many flops. Demand will be volatile in markets where fickle online consumers can change suppliers at the click of a mouse.

9 The world is a giant photocopying machine. Outsource anything that is not absolutely core to your business and focus on what you do best, otherwise you will find other players outpacing you in their innovation and learning curves in the areas where you are not so good. But do not outsource your core competencies – that way lies suicide.

10 Stick to open systems of all kinds. These systems, whether in software, hardware or trade, learn faster and enable you to gain access to more information and better partners. Remember that you need to be part of a fast-moving, rapid-learning value web to survive in the third-millennium economy of 100m or more niches. These webs can only grow and survive as a part of open systems.

11 Give away version 1.0, or the first ten, 100 or 1,000 copies of your product, service or offer. If it is any good you will be able to sell the

upgrades or the next batch. Whether it is business cards, software or machine tools, free samples, demonstrators and beta versions are the way to get offers into the market-place rapidly and to develop a following.

12 Make it easy to join in. Consumers and businesses will navigate themselves to the place where they feel comfortable to buy. Make it easy to become a member of your value web, club or community. In the network economy the trick is to get people and firms in the door first, then let them decide what they might like to buy from you. Hard selling is out; network selling is in.

13 Nothing fails like success. As windows of opportunity get shorter and shorter, you will need to re-evaluate your business model every six or even three months. You will also need to be part of an innovative network of firms and customers to ensure that your offers and organisation are evolving rapidly in Internet time.

14 Become an explorer, and hire and partner with hunter-gatherers and free agents. They will be pre-eminent in an economy where market-spaces come and go as rapidly as do the game on the Serengeti plains or in the Kalahari desert. Speed and anticipation are crucial, especially when flash crowds storm into new market-spaces and make billionaires of 27 year-olds almost overnight.

15 Balance between the edge of chaos and order. Grow requisite complexity in and around your organisation, so that it can move to the edge of chaos when required and also maintain the stability of your operating core and values in the centre. Ensure you have some still and sacred places left when you come in from surfing the waves of the e-business age.

## Summary

Complexity science provides an explanation of why the strategic management practices of major corporations will need to change radically to cope with the pace of change in the 21st century. Anticipation, flexibility and intelligence are the principal characteristics required in organisations able to master their destiny in such a complex, fast-moving world.

As a result the nature of organisations is changing dramatically, from the modern vertical structure to the post-modern collaborative, network-based structure, providing a healthy balance between control and learning, hierarchies and networks. Such a design facilitates the emergence of intelligence in an organisation.

Anticipation is the key to generating the lead time required to create a desirable future for an organisation. A business strategy for a specific future is not required or possible, as this would imply the ability to predict the future. What is needed is a requisite variety of options centred on a core theme for the business, which can then be played out as appropriate under the different possible future realities.

Strategic learning and dialogue have thus become the driving forces of strategic management. They are the key enablers of real-time, online learning in an organisation, which enables executives to adapt their mental models to the changes in the world around them. Such adaptation assists executives in making more appropriate and timely business moves faster than their competitors.

Strategic dialogue also provides the process through which innovation can be generated, thereby providing the platform on which a desirable future for the organisation can be created. Such a future inevitably draws its robustness and resilience from the competitive advantage provided by the unique value proposition and business design of an organisation.

Where the strategic dialogue generates possibilities, the business change process provides the capabilities required to deliver on those possibilities that become part of an organisation's strategic direction. The strategic and change dialogues should be aligned to stimulate and guide transformation in the most effective manner possible.

All of this implies that a radically different management process is needed to take organisations forward into the 21st century. The core of such a process is the use of evolutionary and network thinking to sensitise executives to the implications of multiple possible futures for their business, and to stimulate the strategic thinking required to provide the organisation with the options it needs to become flexible and more intelligent.

# 3 Complexity management in action

TO NAVIGATE UNCERTAINTY, EMBRACE COMPLEXITY.

Complexity-based approaches to management have begun to spread rapidly throughout business and government over the past decade. Many organisations are beginning to use concepts, frameworks and tools derived from complexity theory. They include: AT&T, BT, Hewlett-Packard and Sun in computing and telecommunications; General Motors, Deere, Unilever and United Distillers in manufacturing; Citicorp, Barclays and NASDAQ in financial services; as well as others in such sectors as retailing and defence.

This chapter outlines various complexity approaches in practice. The criteria for selecting the examples were as follows.

- The application had to have been published or mentioned at a public conference.
- The organisation had to be gaining or had gained some advantage from the complexity-based application compared with other methods it had previously used.
- New insights were generated in the development and use of the application that would be useful to other managers in similar situations.

To gain a fuller picture of current complexity applications being applied in practice, it is useful to think of the applications of complexity arranged across a field defined by two axes as shown in Figure 3.1 on the following page. The x-axis represents the physical to virtual spectrum of applications spread out across space, from the concrete, physical world on the left-hand side, to the virtual world of brains and cyberspace on the right.

On the left-hand side of the x-axis are applications implemented in the physical world; for example, the General Motors paint shop scheduling application developed by Dick Morley, which enables paint booths to bid for trucks to paint, by representing the booths as adaptive agents in an internal market. This application outperformed all previous scheduling technologies used by GM.

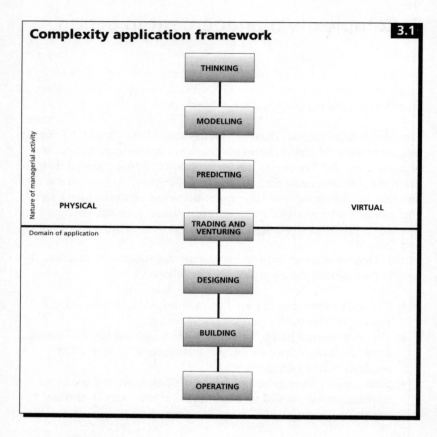

**Complexity application framework** 3.1

THINKING

MODELLING

PREDICTING

*Nature of managerial activity*

PHYSICAL

TRADING AND VENTURING

VIRTUAL

Domain of application

DESIGNING

BUILDING

OPERATING

On the right-hand side of the x-axis are applications of complexity implemented in the natural world. For example, Karl Sims of Genetic Arts produces both surreal and natural film sequences using cas (complex adaptive system) algorithms. Sims's sequences are used by many of the major film companies to produce special effects and artificial worlds in their productions.

The y-axis represents a spectrum of human activities from thinking to action, with a number of stages in between. At the top of the y-axis lie the applications of complexity employed by thinkers, strategists, modellers and forecasters. Thinking about businesses as nodes in economic webs and business ecosystems, for example, makes a fundamental difference to the way in which strategy is developed.

At the bottom of the y-axis are applications, which involve running a particular function within an organisation. For example, British Telecom (BT) uses adaptive agent software to help manage its telecommunications network more effectively.

Figure 3.1 has four major quadrants, which are shown in more detail in Figure 3.2 on the following page. The four quadrants are as follows.

- Strategic management. The top right quadrant of Figure 3.2 shows thinking or virtual activities, such as scenario thinking, which are typically strategic in nature.
- Managing and changing organisations. In the top left quadrant are the thinking/physical applications of complexity. For example, the design of organisations around organic, adaptive models and the development of decision-making processes using fractal, cybernetic principles.
- Information systems management. The bottom right quadrant represents the operating/virtual applications, typically involving the development and running of complex information systems that are both adaptive and intelligent. For example, an application that uses intelligent agents to search the Internet for keywords relating to an enquiry from a questioner and then provides an intelligible answer processed by neural networks using complex adaptive systems techniques.
- Operations management. In the bottom left-hand quadrant are examples of the operating/physical applications – the hard physical world of making and moving products and services. For example, the scheduling of cement trucks so that they are able to respond rapidly to changes in demand for ready-mixed cement, by being adaptively routed to the nearest location with the highest need, was one of the early business applications of complexity.

In Figure 3.2 the boxed company names indicate companies discussed in more detail later in this chapter.

## Two cases of how organisations adapt

The stories described in this section relate to the top left-hand quadrant of Figure 3.2. The first is about a chief executive who faced some difficult challenges on assuming the helm of the exploration division of a major oil company.

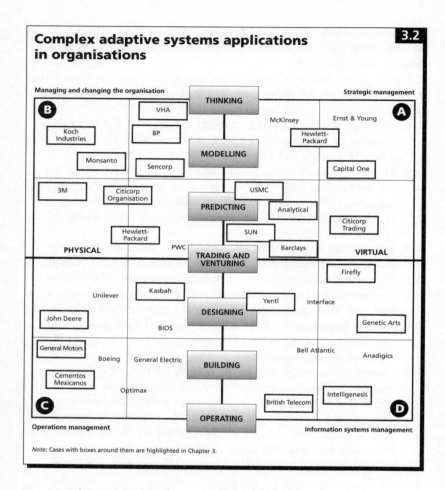

## Complex adaptive systems applications in organisations

**3.2**

Managing and changing the organisation / Strategic management

**THINKING**

**B** / **A**

VHA

Koch Industries · BP · McKinsey · Ernst & Young

Hewlett-Packard

Monsanto · **MODELLING**

Sencorp · Capital One

3M · Citicorp Organisation · USMC · **PREDICTING** · Analytical

Citicorp Trading

Hewlett-Packard · SUN

**PHYSICAL** · PWC · Barclays · **VIRTUAL**

**TRADING AND VENTURING**

Firefly

Unilever · Kasbah · Yentl · Interface

**DESIGNING**

John Deere · Genetic Arts

BIOS

General Motors · Bell Atlantic · Anadigics

Boeing · General Electric · **BUILDING**

Cementos Mexicanos

Optimax · Intelligenesis

**C** · British Telecom · **D**

**OPERATING**

Operations management / Information systems management

*Note:* Cases with boxes around them are highlighted in Chapter 3.

*From underperforming bureaucracy to global leader: the case of BP*
When John Browne became head of BP Exploration in 1989 he was determined to create more value for both customers and shareholders. Although BP was successful, Browne knew that the world was changing and that in the face of an uncertain future, the business had to become more adaptive.

So what did he do? He did not call in the strategic planners or continue to restructure and rationalise assets. Instead, he took a more courageous step and decided to raise the creative tension. Moving with, rather than against, the increasingly heightened turbulence of the early

1990s, Browne established the preconditions necessary for creating such tension and deliberately moved the organisation to a situation that was at the edge of chaos. That is, the point at which a natural equilibrium is found between chaos and order, comparable to the conditions in the evolving natural world. Browne and his team were consciously evolving BP into an adaptive organisation, one that would be better able to survive and prosper in today's uncertain and turbulent times.

Opening up an organisation and sharing information is the start of creating value, both internally and externally. As the dividing line between customers and suppliers becomes fuzzy, the organisation's external environment, or ecosystem, becomes impossible to predict. The success of the organisation then becomes as dependent on the other organisations in the web within which it operates as on its own strategy.

One of the questions Browne asked was: how do I get value out of this system? He grasped that one of the keys to creating value today is to understand that a business cannot evolve in isolation; it has to co-evolve and create value through collaboration with others. The business ecosystem replaces traditional concepts of industry and market with economic communities of interacting organisations that together deliver and consume goods and services. These ecosystems are complex networks of players that go far beyond traditional competitors, customers and suppliers. They comprise communities of organisations that collaborate and compete in economic webs of relationships.

Browne's strategy for BP included process improvements, major outsourcing, asset sales and, more importantly, total changes to its corporate culture. The company adopted new business thinking and a new relationship to its business web. It forged new approaches to developments, new working relationships with contractors and new alliances.

Browne introduced a portfolio of assets, which he called his federation of assets, and allied this with an entrepreneurial business design driven by consistent decentralisation and united by a single common strategy. In 1989 there were 13 levels of management; by 1994 there were just five. It was up to each company to understand how it related to other players in this business ecosystem so that they could co-evolve to create unique contributions to emerging customer groups and markets. The task for management was to create and sustain an organisation that was able to do this spontaneously.

Browne freed the energy in BP, creating room for different thinking. Employees were initially sceptical about achieving their set targets on time, yet the targets were reached one year early. The stockmarkets recognised the achievement, but the process of maintaining the creative tension in BP continues. Part of strategic dialogue is to maintain the creative tension and keep the organisation moving.

At BP organisational capability was changed. Central functions were reduced or removed and business operating centres and assets chose their own routes to implement changes. Internally, the organisation co-evolved with each department and function, and externally, it co-evolved with its suppliers and customers. In a global market, companies should learn how to work in a world of business ecosystems where they can get other players to co-evolve with their visions of the future.

One key to successful business evolution is to let go of centralised control. In these complex times no one at the centre of an organisation can know what questions to ask, let alone what the answers are. Good management today, like evolution, is a way of collaborating with each independent part of the whole organisation and surviving in the face of incipient chaos.

BP increased the value of its share price by a factor greater than ten in a period when other companies were seeing marginal improvement in their share prices. The overall benefit of company-wide transformation was measured in billions of dollars. In 1998 BP announced that it was merging with Amoco to create the second largest oil company in the world.

### Engineering evolution through adaptive cultures: the cases of 3M and Hewlett-Packard

3M was founded in 1902 as the Minnesota Mining and Manufacturing Company when two railway executives, a doctor, a lawyer and a meat market manager bought a mountain to mine corundum for the manufacture of sandpaper. By mistake the founders bought a mountain containing worthless mineral, so they reinvented the company and imported garnet grit from Spain. The knowledge of adhesives they gained from manufacturing sandpaper enabled the company to go on to invent Scotch tape and Post-it notes. Without knowing it, the company has selectively pursued an edge-of-chaos strategy, combining innovation with stability. How has it achieved this? The 3M culture, values and method of organising lie at the heart of its achievements. The secrets of much of the company's success lie in its unconscious application of the complexity principles and rules outlined above.

It is useful to compare 3M's experience with that of Hewlett-Packard (HP). The author and his colleagues since 1994 have carried out 13 different projects across most parts of HP's organisation in the United States and Europe. HP was founded in 1939 as a manufacturer of electronic equipment, became a defence contractor in the second world war, and then developed a powerful position as a producer of electronic test and measurement equipment. By the 1970s HP had begun to produce calculators and computers, and by the 1980s it was helping to pioneer the Unix movement in software. The laser and inkjet printer businesses grew out of breakthroughs in HP's laboratories in the 1980s and became world leaders in the 1990s, by which time HP had also become a leading player in enterprise and personal computing.

3M and HP have continued to grow and renew themselves since their founding, and have both remained successful members of the *Fortune* 500 for over 30 years. Together, they are good illustrations of a number of rules and principles of applying complexity theory in business.

THE THREE RULES OF ORGANISATIONAL EVOLUTION: CO-EVOLUTION, ADAPTIVE
AGENTS AND INTERNAL MODELS

To co-evolve in complex, rapidly moving environments, 3M and HP have structured their businesses in such a way that their business units maintain strong links with their local geographic and technical environments. Now a $15 billion organisation, 3M at one time had over 60,000 products. It has always organised its business units into small groups of around 150–200 people, in a similar fashion to HP. In both organisations, when a business unit gets close to or exceeds this magic number it is usually split up or has parts hived off to new units.

At 3M there is an unwritten rule that scientists can spend up to 15% of their time on "skunkworks", pet projects that may result in new products for the company. At HP billions of dollars a year are spent on HP Labs, where scientists are encouraged to think far ahead into the future. Each HP division has its own laboratories looking into productive applications of the new technologies that are continually popping up within and around the company. In both organisations, research is usually carried out in a collaborative fashion with external or internal partners, often including customers. In this way, co-evolution within market-places that are crucial to accessing future opportunities is encouraged.

Importantly, both organisations ensure that the internal models they use to run their businesses and develop their strategies are coherent and in touch with reality. To achieve this they regularly bring external perspectives into their organisations to accelerate the strategic learning they need to stay ahead of competitors and in touch with potential new sources of value creation. Both organisations regularly deploy techniques such as ecosystem modelling, scenario thinking and strategic gaming (see Chapters 4 and 5 for further details), particularly at strategic breakpoints in the history of a business or an ecosystem.

THE NINE ORGANISATIONAL COMPLEXITY PRINCIPLES: SELF-ORGANISATION, EMERGENCE, NON-LINEARITY, MEMORY, ADAPTABILITY, BEING, IDENTITY, CONSCIOUS LEARNING AND COHERENCE

Both 3M and HP have organisational cultures and structures that encourage self-organisation and emergence. Yet such self-organisation is contained within clear commercial frameworks and entrepreneurial cultures, so that each business unit is expected to reach specific quarterly profit, growth and productivity targets. Both businesses have strong organisational memories, which are carried in their values and culture.

The "HP Way" and 3M's values are remarkably similar: both cultures place a premium on trust and respect for individuals. As the bedrock value, the freedom this gives to members of the organisation is balanced by the second value of achievement and contribution. This ensures that both cultures are meritocracies, where progress in the organisation is achieved through measurable contributions to the success of the organisation rather than cronyism. The third value, integrity, ensures that the identity of members of the organisation is authentically expressed, and that slickness and hype are virtually non-existent in both cultures.

Integrity also ensures that tensions between individual and corporate purposes and values are acknowledged and worked through (rather than simmering destructively under the surface as they do in so many organisations), thus underpinning coherence. Another core value is support for individuals through training and counselling, which helps safeguard the other three values.

These four values form the basis of any culture that seeks to create the conditions for self-organisation, emergence and coherence, working from the bottom up. Although they can be successful at the level of the individual, they will not necessarily ensure that the values permeate the whole organisation. All kinds of corporate or group attitudes can stifle individual intitiative unless the organisation consciously adapts. Such conscious learning and non-linearity need to be cultivated in groups and teams.

This is where the values of flexibility and innovation, a chance to learn by mistakes, informality and open communications, are essential. They encourage conscious learning and a state in which a group or team can achieve results out of proportion to their effort. Such non-linear results require certain preconditions, and are certainly not simply the product of chaotic conditions or messy situations. They require groups of individuals who have deep insights into their craft, and who are able to create the conditions for outstanding results with nudge-like interventions.

William McKnight, a former CEO at 3M, helped the company to become a leading supplier to the automotive industry by simply building on insights that 3M people were getting through their close contact with the bodyshops that bought their sandpaper. Once the bodyshop has fixed the bodywork on a damaged vehicle, it must be spray-painted to look as good as new. Given the rough finish that welding and panel-beating often leave on the metal surface of the car, painting turned out to be one of the most expensive operations in a bodyshop, as many coats were required to achieve the required finish. One of the biggest causes of this roughness was the coarse sandpaper being used at the time, which always clogged up with grit.

A smart 3M salesman noticed this problem and talked extensively to his customers to find a solution. Eventually, 3M invented "wet and dry" sandpaper (trademark Wetordry Waterproof Abrasives), which enabled sanding belts to be used with water spray so that a fine finish was achieved before spraying, resulting in an outstanding quality of finish on every car. At the same time, special tapes were developed that enabled various parts of a car to be sprayed without affecting other parts and could be easily removed without pulling the paint off. McKnight fully supported the efforts and risks his people took to develop superior products. 3M is now one of the leading suppliers to the world automotive industry, selling thousands of outstanding products and services as a result of this co-evolution with its customers, driven by learning by mistakes, open communications and conscious learning.

THE FIVE RULES OF COMPLEXITY MANAGEMENT: GOOD ENOUGH VISION, MINIMUM SPECIFICATIONS, SPACES FOR CREATIVITY, ENCOURAGEMENT OF DIVERSITY AND RE-COMBINATION, PARADOXICAL LEADERSHIP

HP is an example of an organisation unconsciously applying some of the five rules of complexity management at the highest level. However, it is important to understand when reading this analysis that HP is in the process of making some hard decisions about its future direction. Growth has stalled and something different needs to be done to get it going again. What is interesting about HP is that, having faltered several times in its history, the principles by which it has operated have remained consistent, even as it has adapted to new ways of creating value.

First, as mentioned above, the HP unit size remains between 150 and 200 people, the upper limit of who can be known and trusted in a face-to-face network by the members of the network. This means that the 100,000 or so people in HP are split into roughly 500 business units of fewer than 200 people each, with the balance taken up by head office and support functions. Each of these units, or "boxes", has operational autonomy and is expected to make a profit, as well as to take charge of the development of its own product portfolio, supported by HP Labs.

The general managers of each of the 500 autonomous boxes are responsible for managing their box and for managing innovations around it. For example, the LaserJet division continually searches for new spaces around its box, and comes up with a continuous stream of improvements to make laser printers better, faster and cheaper. Occasionally, a discontinuity comes along like colour laser printing, which HP then uses as an opportunity to cannibalise its existing product line before its competitors do. This discontinuity is known as being in the grey space around the LaserJet box.

Where HP has had real difficulty in innovating is in the white spaces between the boxes and the grey spaces. For example, although HP has known about and used the Internet for years, and was one of the first companies to have an intranet, the Internet business opportunity fell between the many HP boxes, straight into white space. This meant that HP was slow to develop a coherent e-business solution set for its customers. Only in 1999 was HP able to focus with sufficient critical mass in this space through the launch of its e-services business, despite the fact that work was already under way in 1995 to define and capitalise on this emerging opportunity. The time and the difficulty of co-ordinating the HP boxes required to exploit the enterprise Internet opportunity meant that IBM, with its e-business offering, was able to leap ahead in becoming viewed as the business Internet company to deal with.

Thus, despite the company unconsciously observing the basic principles of complexity management, HP's difficulties stemmed from having to build a new business for the Internet age from the bottom up, rather than using a combination of top-down and bottom-up approaches. Microsoft is a good example of a company that used the top-down impact of Bill Gates's U-turn on the Internet in 1995, combined with the bottom-up creativity and experience of its various software divisions, to reinvent its offerings and its business model.

A further reason for IBM and Microsoft getting the Internet right before HP, apart from the constraints embedded in the company and its culture, is that HP was being pulled in two different directions in the marketplace. It needed to maintain its strong position in the Unix computing world while trying to build an even stronger position in the Wintel world. Its neutral positioning in the market combined with fears of alienating some of its key customers and business partners slowed down attempts to reinvent the business for the Internet age.

## Strategic management

Moving to the top right-hand quadrant of Figure 3.2, the following examples are of firms that have applied complexity principles to their strategic management processes.

### Economic modelling: the case of Citicorp and the global banks

John Reed was just 47 when he headed towards Santa Fe in Citicorp's Gulfstream jet late in 1986. As the CEO appointed to follow Walter Wriston, he wanted to understand why traditional economists had been unable to foresee the early 1980s debt crisis. Citicorp had lost $1 billion and had $13 billion in doubtful loans.

The scientists and economists Reed met in Santa Fe heard him describe how existing neo-classical economic theory and computer models did not give him or his executives the kind of information they needed to make real-time decisions in the chaotic world of the financial markets. Elaborate models with 4,500 equations and 6,000 variables failed to account for the social and political factors that drove the real behaviour of the markets. Such models assumed that the markets would settle back into equilibrium despite the economic and political shocks that had kept coming since the first OPEC crisis in 1973.

The scientists described how advanced computer graphics could help visualise mountains of data as intelligible patterns; how artificial intelligence techniques using adaptive agents could evolve and learn from experience; and how chaos theory could be used to predict stockmarket prices and other seemingly random phenomena. Towards the end of 1988, Brian Arthur and his colleagues at the Santa Fe Institute Economics programme were beginning to make headway in their computer modelling, with adaptive agents in a primitive stockmarket who could make bubbles and crashes happen just like they do in the real economy.

At Santa Fe they had begun to develop increasingly complex models of the markets, as had a number of exiles from the Los Alamos laboratories down the road. Citicorp started funding the Centre for Adaptive Systems Applications (CASA) in the early 1990s. It now has 50–60 scientists and programmers developing and testing models used by the bank and its clients. This has helped Citicorp to achieve some of its best results, despite the increasing levels of turbulence in the market-places in which it operates. Although the bank and its officials will not divulge details of exactly what they are doing, insiders have revealed that in crises such as the devaluation of the Mexican peso in 1997, the models enabled the bank to outmanoeuvre its competitors and the market, significantly reducing the losses it might otherwise have made.

Since the mid-1990s, many other banks have got in on the act. Morgan Stanley, an American investment bank, has employed theoretical physicists to help fund managers allocate money between different asset classes. The $5 billion Legg Mason Value Trust mutual fund has beaten the Standard and Poor's (S&P) 500 index for several years in a row, and William Miller, the fund's manager, has attributed much of this exceptional performance to his analysis using models and insights from complexity theory.

Barclays Global Investors, the world's largest institutional investment company, has been highly successful with its strategy that incorporates non-linear modelling. Called NeuAlpha, this long-short portfolio strategy has significantly outperformed the S&P 500 index since its launch in 1996. Barclays collects data on several companies from a variety of sources, and then puts this information into a model that predicts stock price changes. Neural nets are used to sample company data for attributes, and provide insights to investors as to how to distinguish good stocks from bad stocks. The bank's portfolios are then generated and managed based on the availability of the securities within target price ranges and how the stocks' risks hedge against each other. So far the rate of return has been some four percentage points (or around 13%) better than the S&P index.

More recently, a new model of the economy, called Aspen, has emerged from the Sandia National Laboratories. Most economists consider Aspen to be a major step forward. As a Nobel prize-winning economist, Lawrence Klein, says: "This is probably the best thing that's come along in a long time." A new research community is emerging around this model, focusing on modelling economic actors as agents using genetic algorithms. Still in the prototype stage, Aspen has already surprised its authors. While simulating the effects of a downturn, the synthetic companies did something totally original for which they had not been programmed: they learned to co-operate, just as real companies do to help their suppliers over a rough time.

Aspen's make-believe world can have 10,000 households, 1,500 factories, stores, banks and government agencies, and potentially 100,000 agents or more. Aspen is currently being used to model unusual things such as underground economies in Eastern Europe and trade breakthroughs such as the North American Free Trade Agreement (NAFTA). Such simulations are helping economists find new insights, which put the real world in a new light.

There is still much more to do in understanding economies. Some of the puzzles are just beginning to yield their secrets, such as why stock prices are so volatile and where economic growth comes from. Researchers such as Brian Arthur and Stuart Kauffman of the BIOS Group, an offshoot of the Santa Fe Institute, continue to speculate and model how economic niches emerge, and to explore how economic diversity makes it easier and easier to create new goods and services once the innovation rollercoaster gets going. In Kauffman's view, the economy follows the same kinds of self-organising paths as life and matter. Hyper-growth economies, such as Silicon Valley, parts of northern Italy and some of the Asian tiger economies, provide rich models of how such economic lift-off can occur through interlocking webs of technologies, organisations and cultures.

### A *revolution in military affairs: the case of the US military*

Following the end of the cold war and the fall of the Berlin Wall, there was a revolution in military affairs. After two conventional world wars in the 20th century, the role of the military was to plan for a third world war on the plains of Central and Eastern Europe. "Red" versus "blue" war games and simulations were the order of the day. Then the Warsaw Pact fell apart, and Saddam Hussein invaded Kuwait. A review of military affairs in the early 1990s in American and NATO forces suggested that factors such as "strategic lift",[1] peacekeeping and the ability to contain local wars would be more important than the ability to defeat a crumbling Soviet bloc. Fighting on a digital battlefield, and keeping the peace among warring clans in distant corners of the world, would literally be a different ballgame from aiming conventional and nuclear forces at a "red threat".

The result of this review was a change in military policy and practice on both sides of the Atlantic. During the early 1990s in Washington, DC, Andy Illachinski at the Centre for Naval Analysis and Josh Epstein at the

Brookings Institute had developed very different approaches to modelling battlefields and social systems, both drawing on their experience of advising the military using advanced computer simulations. Across the Atlantic, modellers in the UK and NATO Centres for Defence Analysis were developing similar modelling and simulation techniques. At the same time, the US Marine Corps (USMC) was developing new approaches to its own operations and doctrines of warfare under General Paul van Riper, and General Gordon Sullivan was creating the vision and capability for "Force XXI" in the US army.

Illachinski's ISAAC simulation pitted red against blue forces using adaptive agents to represent the individual soldiers on an imaginary battlefield. Although more useful for conventional war gaming than some of the new roles facing the military, ISAAC was nonetheless a breakthrough. Watching an ISAAC "battle" on the screen, it is possible to see tactics and strategies emerging from the simple rules programmed into each adaptive agent. Pincer movements, concentration of force, tactical dispersions: all the classic military manoeuvres are replicated by these silicon soldiers with only simple rules, such as how far they can see and fire, how aggressive or cautious they are and how much they stick together or disperse as a force.

Epstein and his colleague, Rob Axelrod, went in another direction entirely. They wanted to see if they could model a social system from simple agents upwards. In Sugarscape, the model starts with a several hundred agents who have a metabolism (slow to fast), vision (short to long) and the ability to move randomly around a digital landscape on which there are two sugar mountains. Long-sighted agents with slow metabolisms accumulate more sugar than the short-sighted folk with fast metabolisms and survive longer. Add some spice mountains to the sugar mountains and trade emerges among agents long on sugar and short on spice (and vice versa). As the model increases in complexity with the addition of sexual reproduction and other characteristics common to homo sapiens, so more and more of the dynamics and features of social systems we take for granted emerge spontaneously on the screen. Warfare breaks out, castes form, capitalism emerges – all the dynamics of competition and co-operation we have come to expect from our own species.

J Mitchell Howell and his colleagues have been applying complexity techniques to tackle the difficulties of adaptive planning in missile defence systems; specifically, the timely allocation of interceptors to incoming missiles. Military officers have to make decisions within minutes about how to respond to multiple threats with independent and random arrival times and different targets. Given limited resources, how can these decision-makers deploy them to best effect? Mitchell used different kinds of autonomous agents to track threats and launch missiles with a bidding system, whereby each agent can bid to perform a service to defend a target. Which agent gets to perform the service depends on the value functions programmed into the system, so that the contention between the different goals of the system is traded off in a market-place, which selects the optimal combination of services for any given moment in time. The system is constantly searching for better solutions in real time, rather than trying to anticipate every possible scenario it may have to deal with.

Bruce Hubanks of Texas Instruments has been working on a logistics approach that allows agents to self-organise, and thus adapt more easily to changing situations in delivering the "right stuff at the right time in the right place" for the military. Current military logistics is labour-intensive, prone to error and slow to respond, given the need to create detailed schedules weeks or months in advance and trying to abide by them. For example, how does someone co-ordinate 300 aircraft with 900 crew members flying 500 missions a day among 280 different airports? The answer lies in developing a self-organising system, which is characterised by a large number of distributed processing elements, communicating using a shared protocol, continuously planning and executing operations, and learning through multiple data inputs. Each element of military logistics is treated as a cluster and networked like the Internet, so that if one node of the network is taken out alternative routes are available to carry out the function. When further developed, this system is likely to transform military logistics.

General Paul van Riper of the usmc has taken a different angle in applying complexity theory in military affairs: the human perspective. According to van Riper, warfare and international relations are both arenas characterised by their complex, evolving nature, and are thus prone to chaotic and unpredictable outcomes. The usmc is bringing the ideas of complexity and dynamic systems together to create a description of the complexity of combat. This is being used to find the attractors for different states the marines may find themselves in, and to provide valuable tools for developing tactics. For example, genetic algorithms are being used to breed architectures for usmc command-and-control systems, and the Swarm software from the Santa Fe Institute is being used to create more realistic synthetic combat environments in which to train Marines.

In the chaos and confusion of war, the USMC believes that the only way to succeed is to push decision-making down to the marines who are on the spot. By doing this while retaining a simple hierarchy designed to keep everyone's job manageable, you should create high-speed, chaos-proof leadership, which enables the marines to respond to any number of scenarios equally effectively, and to take better decisions faster than other players in a situation. This is why van Riper and his team have been instilling the new sciences into all ranks of the military to create a new, more adaptive understanding of their role in the 21st century.

### Developing foresight in hi-tech ecosystems

One of the methods Hewlett-Packard has found exceptionally useful in developing effective strategies to "create the future" (a phrase used in many parts of the organisation) is business ecosystem modelling. As described elsewhere in this book, a business ecosystem is a web of organisations working together in both competitive and collaborative relationships, which is visible as a coherent community to both those within the ecosystem and those outside it. For example, Microsoft, Intel and a host of other players (including HP) form the Wintel ecosystem, so named for the high profile of its major offering, the Windows operating system using the Intel chip set. The Wintel ecosystem is orchestrated by Microsoft and Intel through a network of key gateway relationships with software, hardware and telecommunications firms. To illustrate the power of such a way of working, Microsoft and Intel's combined current revenue makes up only about 3% of the trillion dollar revenue of the ecosystem.

The classic value chain approach is worse than useless in the development and implementation of business strategy in such a complex and rapidly evolving system. It is almost impossible to define at a high level who is a customer, a competitor, a collaborator or a supplier in a system evolving so quickly, unless you are talking about a local region of the system at a specific point in time. To develop effective strategies, HP models business ecosystems in which it is involved, and plans and mounts campaigns around new offerings with its ecosystem partners. To illustrate how difficult (but vital) this activity is, consider Figure 3.3.

Some of the crucial relationships between the players in both the Wintel and Unix ecosystems are illustrated in Figure 3.3.[2] There about six key players in the central cluster that act as gateways between the Wintel and Unix ecosystems; HP is one of them. This is potentially a great advantage, if used wisely, but it also puts HP in a difficult position. How can it enter into a joint venture with an important player in the Unix

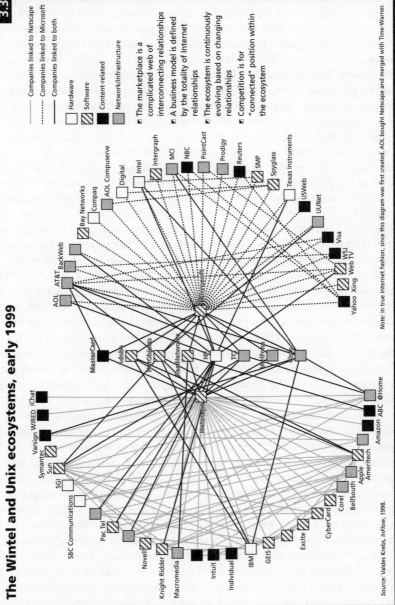

# The Wintel and Unix ecosystems, early 1999

**3.3**

Companies linked to Netscape
Companies linked to Microsoft
Companies linked to both

☐ Hardware
▨ Software
■ Content-related
▦ Network/infrastructure

■ The marketplace is a complicated web of interconnecting relationships
■ A business model is defined by the totality of Internet relationships
■ The ecosystem is continuously evolving based on changing relationships
■ Competition is for "connected" position within the ecosystem

*Source:* Valdes Krebs, *InFlow*, 1998.

*Note:* In true Internet fashion, since this diagram was first created, AOL bought Netscape and merged with Time-Warner.

81

ecosystem without upsetting Microsoft or Intel? How can it improve its bargaining position in the Wintel ecosystem by leveraging its position in the Unix ecosystem, and vice versa? The answer is with great sensitivity and care, as it is public knowledge that the scions of Sun and Oracle are on public record as "Bill baiters", and Bill Gates is equally antagonistic about Scott McNeely, Larry Ellison and their products. Yet HP's chairman has to sit down in meetings with all these people, on many different occasions (though usually in different rooms), to hammer out a deal about a particular product or area in HP's $47 billion business.

In such high-stake, complex games, HP has to develop many different scenarios of the future possible states of the business ecosystems it is involved in if it is to make good decisions about its next moves. These scenarios are used to both develop and destruction test a variety of game plans and strategic options that HP may have in a particular business area. They rely on detailed modelling of the specific zone of an ecosystem, which is relevant to a particular business decision, to understand how that ecosystem interacts with other adjacent ecosystems, and what this means today and in the future for HP and its partners.

The techniques HP uses to do this include some of the modules outlined in the description of the FutureStep process in Chapter 5. The use of ecosystem modelling is most powerful when it is applied as a collaborative decision-making process together with business partners and customers. Although this is not always possible or advisable, the time taken to make good decisions is compressed dramatically. The process also enables players who may not know each other well to develop a common vision of the future for a specific offering or area they are involved in (and alternative ways of getting there) together.

Increasing returns – a characteristic of information-sector organisations operating in the knowledge economy – describes the law operating when a product's value increases in proportion to the number of other products like it in the market-place (especially if, like telephones, faxes, Internet browsers or PCs, they are able to communicate with each other). Complexity-based swarm strategies are now being deployed successfully by many organisations in launching new products. For example, when in 1994 Netscape offered an early version of its browser software free over the Internet, more than 4m copies were downloaded within a few weeks.

Other firms have also exploited this phenomenon. While working at General Electric, Paul Graziani developed a $3m product to process vast amounts of data into a two-dimensional view of orbiting satellites. When GE discontinued the product, Graziani set up Analytical Graphics, christened his product the Satellite Tool Kit and priced it at $10,000. But in early 1997 after Graziani started giving the software away free, orders for it started pouring in. Through add-ons and upgrades, the company's revenue exceeded $7m in 1997 and doubled in 1998.

Other examples of business ecosystems in the high-tech arena include the economic communities centred on Microsoft and its allies, Mitsui and its allies, General Motors and its allies, and Motorola and its allies. A classic example is the ecosystem that grew up around mainframe computers before the advent of the personal computer. In the 1970s the ecosystem leader in this industry was IBM, which in its day produced excellent mainframe and mid-range information processing systems.

Many companies existed in the IBM biosphere, where many exotic species could survive. IBM provided the pricing and quality benchmark for other mainframe manufacturers (including the BUNCH – Burroughs, Univac, NCR, Control Data and Honeywell – ICL, Fujitsu, Bull and others), as well as the makers of supercomputers (Cray and Cyber) and minicomputers (DEC, Prime, Wang and several others). Everything was evaluated in terms of its price and performance relative to the IBM System 360 and 370 mainframes, and later the 308x and 309x range of mainframes and System 3x midrange.

The mainframe industry sheltered thousands of microchip, component, software and service providers, which had to adapt to a rapidly diminishing market-place during the late 1980s and early 1990s when IBM wrote off several billion dollars in an attempt to turn itself around. The reason for this sudden and permanent decline in the mainframe ecosystem was, as almost everyone now knows, the rise of two new ecosystems. These centred on Motorola (maker of the 68000 chip series for Apple PCs) and Intel (maker of the 808x and 80x86 range of microchips that form the basis for Microsoft DOS and Windows PCs).

The Intel ecosystem includes hundreds of computer hardware vendors such as Compaq, operating software vendors such as Microsoft (DOS, Windows, Windows NT) and IBM (OS2), and software developers and other microchip vendors such as HP and clones (such as AMD). It also increasingly includes telecommunications, cable TV and government organisations. The Intel ecosystem has now convincingly eclipsed the Motorola ecosystem as a result of:

◪ the increasing influence and success of Microsoft, now the world's dominant maker of PC operating systems (90% market share) and applications running on Intel chip designs;

- the deliberate campaign waged by Intel to stimulate processor-intensive customer applications in areas such as voice, video, data collaboration and high-bandwidth networking;
- work with suppliers to fix PC architecture problems including plug-and-play hardware components, processor to video-card communication and ATM (asynchronous transfer mode) standards for local and wide area networks.

So 20 years ago IBM dominated the global market for computers with a market share of over 40%; now the Intel ecosystem and Microsoft between them dominate this market with a share of about 60% for Intel and 90% for Microsoft in PC chips and operating systems respectively.

Whether a business operates in an industry subject to rapid product innovation such as the high-tech sector, which demands increasingly large investments in high-risk new products, or is in a more stable industry where commoditisation, removal of government protection or trade barriers and narrower margins are squeezing profits, the effects of changes in industry structures and business evolution are far-reaching. Competitive advantage in business ecosystems requires the ability to:

- identify opportunities to build business process architectures that provide superior value-propositions for the end customers and drive customer-valued innovation across the ecosystem;
- provide leadership or create the alliances necessary to form and nurture an ecosystem through its different stages of development;
- build a competitive position in the ecosystem and industry that is inimitable and non-substitutable, durable and superior.

## Managing information systems

Turning to the bottom right-hand quadrant of Figure 3.2, this section looks at how companies are using complexity theory to manage information systems.

As the network economy spreads, it is being driven and enabled by a number of new technologies: the Internet, fixed and satellite digital networks, PCs and personal digital assistants, and hundreds of billions of smart chips embedded in every conceivable appliance. At its heart are a burgeoning number of intelligent agents and smart-bots, operating as complex evolving cyber-systems.

At Microsoft Research, real-world agents that grapple with uncertainty in the context-sensitive goals of people and organisations are being developed. Two projects in particular, Lumiere and LookOut, deserve mention. Lumiere focuses on methods and architectures for inferring a user's goals and informational needs by considering an ongoing stream of user and system activity. LookOut explores the concept of mixed-initiative user interfaces, centring on designs for agents and interaction that assume people and automated reasoning systems will collaborate with one another to achieve goals.

At the other end of the corporate scale, Intelligenesis, a start-up founded by a software wizard, Ben Goertzel, has designed an intelligent agent-based program capable of searching the 250m web pages on the Internet to answer any question anyone might care to ask. Goertzel has deployed every known complexity technique, including smart neural network technologies, to develop his program, and has now found venture capital backers for his enterprise. The Intelligenesis programs are currently being used by financial professionals on a test basis, and trading activities carried out using the programs have already beaten the stock exchange indices by a handsome margin. Information and news selected over the Internet by Intelligenesis software are fed into trading programs, and these programs are already outperforming trading experts. Goertzel's programming is based on complexity-derived, agent-based software principles, and he regularly attends complexity science conferences looking for new techniques and ways of doing things.

Managers at BT have several reasons to be impressed with the work being done in their organisation using multiple agent systems. For example, a program called Adept has been used to develop a system to produce quotes for designing networks and providing services. The system receives a customer service request and generates quotes for building and operating the network. Half a dozen agents can be involved, representing sales, customer service, legal, designers and credit checking. This has led to a new way of managing at BT called agent-based workflow, where managers are able to delegate mundane aspects of their work to software agents while they focus on more important areas such as customer service, team management and strategic planning.

In other parts of BT researchers have developed programs modelled on ant colonies, which send out intelligent agent "ants" to explore alternate routes through the network. Thousands of ants return with information about the fastest routes through the network, enabling the network to reconfigure itself in microseconds to avoid bottlenecks. The goal of this program is to make the network self-managing. A tougher problem now being tackled is how to enable BT to overhaul its network to be fully digital in an adaptive way. The cost of doing this using traditional methods is currently estimated at $46 billion, and it would take ten years at BT's current annual spend of $4 billion. Researchers are studying complex adaptive systems in nature to give them clues as to how they might do this faster and at less cost.

On a slightly different front, Karl Sims has been exploring the opportunities for designing complex evolving digital creatures in his work in the world of movie-making. Using genetic algorithms and other complexity-inspired techniques, Sims literally evolves artificial life-forms out of silicon on to the screen. As movies become more digital, work like that of Sims is likely to become a key part of movie-making, and the evolutionary tree of cyber-creatures is sure to become as complex and fascinating as the real evolutionary tree of the 30m organisms currently inhabiting the earth.

Patti Maes, while a researcher at the Massachusetts Institute of Technology's Media Labs, came up with the idea of a program that uses intelligent agents to make recommendations to buyers of products on the Internet, based on its ability to match a buyer's preferences with those of other buyers, and then to make recommendations on other products of interest. For example, My-Launch, Firefly's music vendor, asks customers for their ten favourite music albums. It then takes the ten recommendations and compares them with the other 500,000 Firefly members interested in music. Firefly then works out where in "taste-space" customers belong, places them near the group of people who like the same sort of music, and then tells them what other albums they might like based on their suggestions. Online booksellers such as Amazon.com and bn.com (Barnes & Noble) are using similar technologies to sell more books and make customers smarter shoppers.

Maes has since sold Firefly to Microsoft, and is developing Yentl and Kasbah, two other applications developed using intelligent agents. Kasbah focuses on finding the best bargain on the Internet for any product or service imaginable, and then facilitating a deal including payment for the purchase. It will also enable bartering to occur. Yentl is an online dating agency with a difference. It will use intelligent agents to sift through all the other lonely hearts on the Web and find a sample of ideal mates, as well as help screen partners, and arrange meetings and contacts.

Throughout the world researchers and programmers from organisations as diverse as NASA, Daimler-Benz, Boeing, IBM, NTT, General Motors, Telecom Italia, Siemens and Sony are exploring and exploiting the opportunities for complexity-based programming in a wide range of areas. These areas include: personal agents for e-mail, scheduling and travelling; business agents for workflow and network management, negotiation, price discovery and information arbitrage; and tools and techniques for process control, traffic control, knowledge management and monetary instrument standards.

## Operations management

Turning lastly to the bottom left-hand quadrant of Figure 3.2, this section reviews companies applying complexity principles to operations management.

### Concrete success

One of the first business applications of complexity theory in the world of operations management occurred in Guadalajara, Mexico, a few years ago. At Cementos Mexicanos (Cemex), staff used to be reluctant to answer the phone for fear of angry customers shouting at them and wanting to know the whereabouts of their delivery of ready-mix cement. Now this has all changed. Lorenzo Zambrano, a 53-year-old Stanford MBA graduate whose grandfather consolidated Cemex into a modern company in the 1920s, decided to enable employees to keep commitments by investing heavily in state-of-the-art systems, which included a high-powered application of complexity theory.

It began when Cemex IT executives were visiting Fedex, observing how the massive delivery company handled high-volume operations while maintaining impeccable customer service. They saw how empowering employees with advanced technology, enabling them to make good decisions on the spot, turned an endless stream of minor crises into a way of dealing quickly with problems and satisfying customers. But how could they implement this in the chaotic environment of Guadalajara, where unpredictable weather, unreliable builders and crazy traffic made the life of a cement-truck driver miserable? The answer was to reinvent the way cement was delivered from the ground up.

Cemex created the DSO (dynamic synchronisation of operations) system and scrapped its traditional dispatching approach. When a cement order arrives the centralised dispatch centre allocates a truck based on the probability of demand for the day, against the background of a complex forecast of all the factors that could influence demand such as weather, traffic, project delays, and so on. Orders are relayed to trucks using global positioning system (GPS) relays and onboard computers, so that the position of every truck is known all the time by the dispatch department, and last-minute problems can be ironed out over the radio.

Dynamic scheduling of Cemex's trucks relies heavily on IT, but the use of complexity principles extends to the conversations and commitments of the company's managers and workers. The theory (and practice) is that successful systems are driven by loops of people working to fulfil commitments. Operators on the spot are given authority and the information to make instant commitments, backed up by the flexibility of the dynamic scheduling system. The traditionally adversarial relationship between management bureaucrats and Mexican workers has been broken down and replaced by trust and the opportunity for workers to move up from the shop floor to dispatch and to management. Cemex has achieved a small miracle with its radical approach: $30m in annual savings, a high degree of customer satisfaction and a 3–5 year advantage over its competitors.

## Painting by numbers

North of the border, at General Motors, a different kind of problem was being solved: how to paint trucks, sweeping away old assembly-line schedules and forging a better system. In Fort Wayne, Indiana, Dick Morley, holder of more than 20 American patents including the programmable logic controller, saved GM $1m and cut the code required to schedule its truck-painting operations from several hundred lines to four. Morley and his colleagues invented a system that turned the traditional top-down scheduling approach upside down. As the type of truck arriving at a spray-painting booth, and the colour it needs to be sprayed, are inherently unpredictable, Morley decided to apply a complexity-based solution to the problem.

Each paint booth was given a "chicken-brain", which enabled the booth to bid for a truck coming down the line. The bid would be shaped by whether the truck required the same colour paint already in the booth, or whether the job was marked urgent. Each paint booth interacted with the scheduling program based on a few simple rules of behaviour. Each is programmed to keep busy and bids on each job are based on its ability to do it. The key to this operation is what Morley describes as programming behaviour, not states; in other words, programming not what is going to happen, but how to make it happen. The bottom line is that GM made savings of $1m in nine months, and is achieving high-quality throughput with the minimum of problems. By embracing complexity, GM found efficiency.

## Reaping benefits

Meanwhile, in Moline, Illinois, Bill Fulkerson was helping the world's largest farm equipment manufacturer implement a genetic algorithm based approach to scheduling that both pumped up production and enhanced efficiency. Fulkerson explains that the sheer variety of farm equipment products Deere & Co sells makes production scheduling one of the company's biggest challenges. For example, Deere's seed planter production facility is required to produce seed planters to suit dramatically different sowing conditions. Deere planters can be configured into as many as 1.6m distinct products. In 1992, at a new site, Fulkerson had the opportunity to prove that genetic algorithms could outclass teams of analysts doing schedules on spreadsheets.

Since then Deere has put in five genetic algorithm based systems. The benefits of having the system include substantial improvements in throughput, resource utilisation and schedule reliability, along with better supply chain management and increased rescheduling flexibility. Under the old system Deere would have to cancel tons of orders in the master schedule every six months, whereas under the new system, 1–5 individual orders are cancelled every six months, not because of production bottlenecks but because of marketing conflicts or other external causes.

The technology on which this breakthrough is based, genetic algorithms, is based on population genetics. Just as in real-life evolution, "GA optimisation" evolves a good solution through repeated recombination of a population of candidate solutions. Genetic algorithms are effective at searching large, complex problem spaces, such as deciding how to schedule the manufacture of the 30–100 units a day in a typical Deere assembly plant. Multiplying out the number of possible combinations, it is not long before you have a number larger than the number of atoms in the universe. Deere & Co has succeeded in solving these complex problems, thanks to Bill Fulkerson and the inspired teams who originally came up with the idea in Moline.

## And the list goes on

As complexity-based approaches continue to evolve, the range of industrial problems being solved is increasing dramatically. For example, the CASA scientists mentioned earlier in this chapter have worked on a variety of problems involving automatic learning by computers in complex environments. They have developed car braking systems that learn about the road surface, together with vehicle control systems that stop a vehicle in the best way during a panic stop. In manufacturing, CASA has developed process control systems that learn the behaviour of processes as they evolve; for example, drift-plasma processing of semiconductors, distillation columns and stirred tank reactors. Other advances have been in areas such as the extraction of patterns and tracking from satellite images, and the modelling of businesses and manufacturing enterprises.

# 4 The wheel of business evolution

Leaders and managers have always had to make choices, often between complex alternatives and in compressed timeframes. Given the increasingly short windows of opportunity in which a capability or a business can be launched and made a success, there needs to be a way of compressing this complexity into manageable chunks. The wheel of business evolution is a framework and set of tools which enables managers to:

- prioritise the various programmes and initiatives for strategic and operational change in their business;
- co-ordinate the various change initiatives in the organisation;
- benchmark progress made in those change initiatives;
- balance the efforts made and resources devoted to change initiatives in accordance with their relative priorities and inter-relationships;
- link change initiatives tightly to the strategic innovation process known as FutureStep, which is described in Chapter 5.

The wheel of business evolution contains eight sections, as shown in Figure 4.1 on the following page. This chapter explains the origins of the wheel in research carried out at London Business School (LBS) and how the wheel can be used to achieve strategic, organisational and managerial alignment. At the end of the chapter, each of the eight sections of the wheel is illustrated with typical profiles of companies that have used the wheel to analyse strategic issues within their organisations.

## Origins of the wheel

The wheel of business evolution was developed through research carried out by the author at LBS between 1989 and 1995, in conjunction with 24 major organisations, including ICI, BUPA, Lloyds, Prudential, Rover, Sainsbury's, TSB, Wedgwood, W H Smith and Xerox. The research also set out to investigate how major organisations went about the complex processes of organisational change and transformation, in an attempt to understand whether the change management process could be managed more effectively.

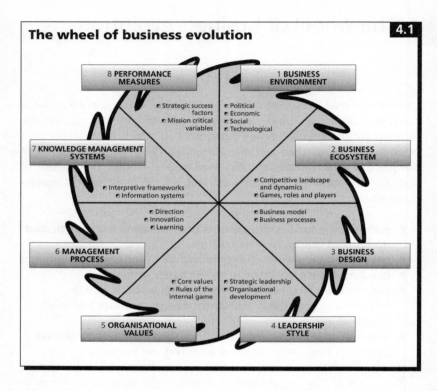

The focal question in the research was: what role do management systems (and by implication management) play in the success or failure of their organisations? This question was designed to challenge some of the most cherished assumptions of classic management theory, such as whether:

- ◪ major investment in management, planning and IT systems leads to better organisational performance;
- ◪ control is always central to superior organisational performance; and
- ◪ hierarchically organised divisional forms using classic management systems are capable of adapting quickly in rapidly changing environments.

The principles underlying the design of the wheel derive from cognitive and complexity science, strategic management and organisational behaviour. The sequence of the eight segments reflects the learning cycle that occurs when outside-in or bottom-up learning takes place. The leadership style, values and nature of the management processes in the firm will shape the way in which such knowledge is generated, codified and diffused.

The main conclusions of the LBS research were as follows.

- There is a strong correlation between long-term strategic performance in a business and the level of alignment between the eight wheel variables. In particular, the alignment between the business environment, business ecosystem and the other six variables is critical.
- There are several different ways in which organisations can successfully manage change, depending on their specific situations and environments.
- There is tremendous scope for improvement in an organisation in the process of alignment between the leadership style, organisational values, management processes, knowledge and information management and performance measures, and management tools and systems. The alignment process is messy, inefficient and often ineffective, as it is not consciously managed according to a coherent agenda by the management team.
- There is a need for more effective ways of managing the process of business evolution, and for tools that can support the change management process in the often unique circumstances in which organisations find themselves.

It was clear from the evidence that although the culture and climate for adaptive, collaborative knowledge work was being championed by a number of the organisations surveyed, they were experiencing great difficulty in changing the mindset and behaviour of the management team and the people in the organisation.

There were several other barriers to achieving their goals of becoming customer-focused, quality-driven, process-managed learning organisations.

- The current organisational structure often hindered collaboration or made it impossible.
- Short-term performance pressures made the creation of a learning environment difficult and resulted in risk averse behaviour, which was not conducive to innovation and entrepreneurship.

- There was a lack of vision and leadership at the top, or too much vision at the top without other visions being shared or communicated.
- Information and management systems were barriers to sharing knowledge and information.
- Functional silos focused too narrowly on specialised roles and tasks rather than broader competencies and capabilities.
- Management processes and workflow were fragmented, with islands of automation.
- Budgeting and planning processes resulted in territoriality.

Most of the 72 directors who participated in the research felt that there was a great need for a more coherent management framework, which would enable them to recognise the main issues in managing the complexity of adaptation and transition in their organisations. Since the research was completed, several major multinational corporations have used the wheel of business evolution as an integral part of their change management process to great effect.

### Managing the interactions between the inside and the outside
To understand how to use the wheel, it is useful to think of two broad domains of activity occurring within and around a firm.

- The external domain. This describes the world of possibilities external to a firm, over which it has little or no control. Within this world there are stable elements (some of which may be predetermined), trends and uncertainties.
- The internal domain. This describes the world of capabilities within a firm, which are a function of decisions and commitments by the firm, over which it has total, or at least some degree of, control or influence.

These two broad domains each have a number of sub-domains (see Figure 4.2).

### The external domain: landscapes of possibility
The external domain can be usefully divided into four levels of sub-domain, in which the lower levels are contained within the higher levels.

- At the highest level is the business environment. This is a set of

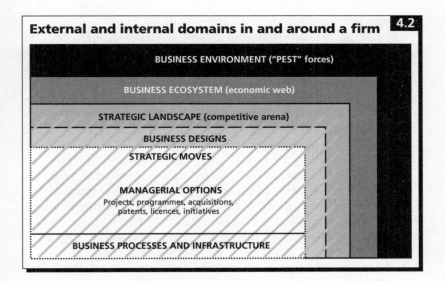

**External and internal domains in and around a firm** 4.2

BUSINESS ENVIRONMENT ("PEST" forces)

BUSINESS ECOSYSTEM (economic web)

STRATEGIC LANDSCAPE (competitive arena)

BUSINESS DESIGNS

STRATEGIC MOVES

MANAGERIAL OPTIONS
Projects, programmes, acquisitions,
patents, licences, initiatives

BUSINESS PROCESSES AND INFRASTRUCTURE

political, economic, social and technological actors and forces,
which are largely outside the control and influence of a business and
can potentially have a positive or a negative impact on the business.

◪ At the second level is the business ecosystem. This is a community
of organisations and stakeholders (players) operating within a
particular business environment, which collaborate and compete
in an economic web of relationships. This web of relationships co-
evolves through time subject to the general forces in the business
environment and the specific moves made by the web of players.

◪ At the third level are strategic landscapes. These are the locations
in a business ecosystem in which competition and collaboration
take place between players according to the rules of the game they
are playing. The players and the landscapes co-evolve depending
on the nature of their interactions and outcomes.

Both business ecosystems and strategic landscapes can evolve in very
different directions. To anticipate some of these possible directions and
the strategic moves that would be appropriate, it is helpful to build
scenarios. These are different possible future configurations of the
business ecosystem, each of which has different implications for the
design, operation and management of a business. Scenarios can also
describe how the specific strategic landscapes for a product, process or

infrastructure play out under different rules of the game.

The external domain comprises a land of possibilities for the firm. Such possibilities can be both positive (new business opportunities, for example) and negative (competitor entry into a firm's most profitable market, for example). In the language of complexity, this land of possibilities can sometimes become "supra-critical", where small changes in initial conditions at the micro-scale lead to large effects at the macro-scales in the business environment. This kind of chain reaction can be the result of the following.

◪ Microeconomic events, such as product and standard lock-ins, which lead to increasing returns and high barriers to entry, as in the case of VHS in video players and Microsoft Windows in the case of operating systems for personal computers.
◪ Macroeconomic events, such as the economic crisis that hit East Asia during 1997.
◪ Political events, such as a change of government, which result in markedly different economic and social policy.

### The internal domain: capability space

The domain internal to a firm can also be usefully divided into four levels of sub-domain, in which the lower levels are again contained within the higher levels.

◪ At the highest level are business designs. These describe different possible configurations of a business idea, how this idea adds value, and how it is embodied in distinctive capabilities to create sustainable competitive advantage. Like species in natural ecosystems, business designs have fitness and sustainability functions. These can be improved in a number of ways, either through more appropriate strategic moves being made on the strategic landscape, or by thinking of a broader range of robust and complementary options from which to make strategic moves.
◪ At the second level are strategic moves. These are groups of activities and assets (such as projects, programmes, acquisitions, licences, patents, and so on) that are intended to improve the strategic position of a business, product, offer or technology on a specific landscape. Such moves can improve the fitness and sustainability of a firm if they are selected from a broad range of options, and co-ordinated through an adapative strategy process.

- At the third level are options. These are alternative strategic moves which can be made depending on which scenario (pure or hybrid) the firm believes it is operating in. Options link to real, financial, economic and shareholder value-added measures, as each option can be compared with other options or to what will happen if the option is not followed.
- At the last level are human activities and business processes. These are the primary building blocks of the capability of a firm. Without such activities and processes business designs, strategic moves and options would be hollow blueprints or recipes, rather than embodied value-adding systems.

The internal domain contains the worlds of management and organisations, where the familiar events and rituals of work are played out against the backdrop of the external domain (or outside world, as it is more usually known).

## Managing business evolution using the wheel

The wheel of business evolution is split into four quadrants representing the outside or external environment and four quadrants representing the inside or internal environment. Change can be generated in at least two ways.

- Through events or interactions in the external environment (or exogenous change); for example, the threat posed by Japanese motor manufacturers to the American Big 3 in the 1980s, which created the need for a response from the American organisations.
- Through events or interactions within the firm and its internal environment (or endogenous change); for example, when Apple Computer launched the first few waves of personal computers into the world, generating changes within the environment of the firm.

Most real-world change that organisations have to deal with is a complex combination of these two kinds of change. The wheel enables an organisation to map the trajectory of change it is experiencing and to establish the nature of the change it is going through or generating.

Over time, without any major internal or external perturbations to their environment, most organisations will settle towards the ordered end of the scale between chaos and order. For example, Sencorp appears to have been able to select its operating environment well enough to avoid any major disruptions to its operations over the past 40 years. It is at times like these that near-perfect alignment between an organisation and its environment is possible, although such cases appear to be less and less frequent.

In the turbulent business world such conditions of equilibrium are for most managers and organisations an unattainable paradise, but the wheel is a framework that can help them manage complex change.

## 1. *The business environment*
The classic PEST framework (political, economic, social, technological) identifies four of the many possible categories of external factors that affect the ability of an organisation to survive and prosper.

Although it may sometimes seem difficult to influence some of these categories, over time many firms have shown that they can change their environment; for example, by negotiating with governments to change the rules of the game. Webs of relationships among countries, corporations, markets, economies and technologies are continually co-evolving. At one level, individual actors or firms might only be able to influence events in a small way, but the industrial and information revolutions described in Chapter 1 have both been driven by an ever-increasing avalanche of small actions, leading to radical change in the business environment for all firms.

The supra-critical soup of interconnecting economic webs and technologies delivering increasing returns in the information and knowledge sectors of the global economy is now a very real factor in the global business environment, generating chaos for some, order for others and complexity for most.

It is crucial for an organisation to understand what sort of business environment it is encountering, as this will determine the rate of change the organisation has to deal with. The broadest classification of environments is that of Fred Emery, who defines four environmental types (see Figure 4.3).[1]

- ⬛ Random/placid. No predictable pattern to this non-competitive environment exists. Strategic planning adds little value owing to the unpredictable nature of the environment. Firms would be isolated and have only infrequent contact with each other. In this case a strategy is often as good as the best tactic. A resource-rich, isolated environment such as a start-up firm in a high-growth market or a large monopoly are examples.

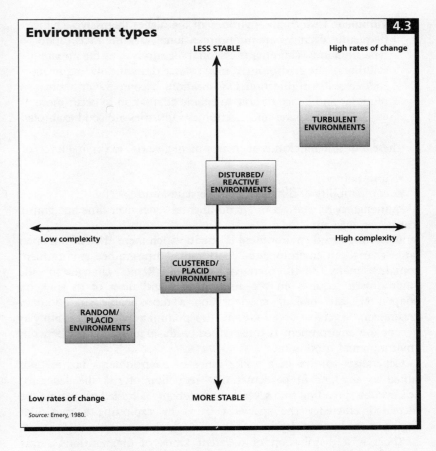

**Environment types** `4.3`

LESS STABLE — High rates of change

TURBULENT ENVIRONMENTS

DISTURBED/ REACTIVE ENVIRONMENTS

Low complexity — High complexity

CLUSTERED/ PLACID ENVIRONMENTS

RANDOM/ PLACID ENVIRONMENTS

Low rates of change — MORE STABLE

Source: Emery, 1980.

- Clustered/placid. Such an environment is non-competitive, but sufficient causal consistency allows learning and planning to take place on a limited scale, enabling a niche to be discerned and protected. A monopoly industry or government bureaucracy are examples.
- Disturbed/reactive. Sufficient population density allows competition for the optimum niches to occur, creating some instability at a higher level. The niches themselves change only slowly, however. Planning now becomes essential for competitive purposes and survival. Organisations become larger and more complex. Oligopolies and particular professional industries are examples.

▣ Turbulent. In such an environment the niches themselves change frequently. Changes are multidimensional, creating catastrophe-type situations. Planning is essential for survival, as the apparent stability of the environment may change dramatically, requiring sudden shifts in direction. Organisations become flatter, more modular and hence flexible to enable adaptation to occur more easily. The computer and electronics industries are good examples.

These four different kinds of environment give rise to varying levels of:

▣ uncertainty;
▣ compatibility of different resource states; and
▣ frequency of changes in environmental states over time (the grain).

A coarse-grained environment is one in which there are few (but often large) changes in environmental conditions. A fine-grained environment contains many small, frequent changes. Rapid change in the environment requires an organisation to spend most of its time on adaptation, thus making specialisation a more viable strategy than generalism. Specialist organisations also dominate when uncertainty is low or the environment is fine-grained, with large differences between environmental conditions.

Generalists survive in a wider range of environments but are not suited to any one in particular. The reduction of risk the generalist achieves by spreading into several environments is traded off against the increased efficiency the specialist gains by exploiting a particular environment in great depth.

There is a distribution of different kinds of organisations across environmental conditions, and there are also limitations on organisational structures in different environments. Organisational form (a specific configuration of goals, boundaries and activities inferred from an organisation's structure, patterns of activity within the organisation or the normative order that characterises a particular organisation) is related to the particular type of environment in which the organisation operates.

A population of organisations that can survive and reproduce itself better than other local populations within certain constraints (at a number of different resource levels, for example) constitutes a niche. (The implications of niches are explored further in the next section on business ecosystems.) Constraints are both external and internal. Examples of internal constraints are:

- sunk costs;
- internal political constraints that make the redistribution of resources difficult;
- constraints emanating from history and tradition; and
- reduced or limited information received by decision-makers as a result of present activities and structures.

External constraints include:

- legal and financial barriers to market entry and exit;
- legitimacy considerations, which delimit the organisation's flexibility in changing form or activities;
- the problem of collective rationality (where the conflict between optimal rational strategies for individual buyers and sellers leads to disequilibrium at a collective level when enacted); and
- external constraints on the availability of information.

The process of variation, selection and retention by which successful organisational forms survive and proliferate in particular environments is illustrated in Figure 4.4 on the following page. The resource dependence perspective links environmental effects with internal political processes in organisations. Different environmental states affect the distribution of power in an organisation, which in turn affects who succeeds to administrative positions and what point of view comes to characterise the organisation's decision-making. This in turn affects the actions and structure of the organisation.

Provided this process works comparatively quickly and smoothly, such actions and structures should provide an appropriate response to the environmental challenges and constraints in that particular situation. This view of the organisation implies a looser coupling between organisations and their environments than would be implied by economics or population ecology, as power is seen to be an important intervening variable between environments and organisations.

There appear to be close links between the performance of an organisation and the degree to which it is capable of satisfying the demands of its environment. The linkages between the environment, strategy, structure and performance of an organisation have been well demonstrated by a number of researchers. Further linkages between the environment, senior management style, the distribution of power and decision processes have also been adequately demonstrated.

**Process of adaptation to environments by organisation**

4.4

ENVIRONMENT
(uncertainty, resources, constraints, contingencies)

SELECTION OF ORGANISATIONAL FORMS

ORGANISATIONAL FORM DETERMINES DISTRIBUTION
OF POWER WITHIN ORGANISATION

SELECTION/REMOVAL OF MANAGERS

ORGANISATIONAL ACTIONS/STRUCTURE

DECISION CONTENT

CULTURE AND VALUES

Source: Pfeffer, J., *Organizations and Organization Theory*, John Wiley, 1978.

Attractive environments, in which performance is expected to be superior, are simple, stable and munificent (growing). Unattractive environments, in which performance appears to suffer, are complex and unstable and exhibit low or no growth. There are always exceptions to the typical performance in different environmental conditions; these over- or under-achievers may be better at adapting to their particular environment.

## 2. Business ecosystems

In the simpler times of the late industrial age, it is possible to identify approximately 15,000 discrete industries that were more or less vertically integrated and interconnected with other parts of the economy through markets, suppliers and customers. Any business ecosystems that existed were generally local clusters of firms and industries that interconnected to provide some form of national or local competitive advantage. In the past 50 years of economic history this pattern has changed radically. Information technologies have enabled the demassification of industries and the emergence of horizontal value webs between hundreds or thousands of firms, resulting in specialisation, a focus on core competencies and outsourcing on a global scale. The information technology and communications industries have been at the forefront of these developments.

Within the socio-economic webs operating at the macro-level in the global business environment are tens of thousands of value webs, or business ecosystems, which interconnect to make up the global economy. A business ecosystem is defined as a co-evolving economic community supported by a foundation of interacting organisations and business processes, producing goods and services of value to customers. These organisations and processes are shaped by customers, suppliers, lead producers and other stakeholders. The organisations in the ecosystem co-evolve their capabilities and roles over time, and generally align themselves with future directions orchestrated by one or more central organisations. The particular organisations holding leadership roles may change over time, but the function of ecosystem leader is valued by the community because it enables members to move towards shared visions and to find mutually supportive roles when they so desire.[2]

Business ecosystems reside in strategic landscapes created by different kinds of environmental conditions. For example, in the natural world, ecosystems operate in landscapes as diverse as deserts, volcanic islands, high mountain regions, fertile river plains, foothills and swamps. Specific kinds of ecosystems thrive in specific landscapes. For example, savannah grasslands thrive on wide open plains with cool winters, and Mediterranean ecosystems thrive in mountainous landscapes near oceans and seas in only three climatic belts capable of providing wet winters and hot dry summers.

Just like biological ecosystems, business ecosystems come and go at a surprisingly rapid rate. Whether it is Amazon rain forest or Arctic wilderness, technological and social change can have major and often devastating impacts on biological ecosystems. As the rate of change in the business environment increases, so too do business ecosystems become more fragile and transitory than they ever were. Business ecosystems go through four basic stages in their existence.

STAGE 1: PIONEERING

In this stage the ecosystem is getting started, much as the elements in the primordial soup began to mix with each other and form new compounds and forms of life. In business terms, however, this is a much more conscious process, where the pioneers are exploring and innovating in the new territories opened up by the emergence of new ideas, knowledge, processes, fields, technologies and/or resources. Some explorers are merely good innovators, lacking the competencies to integrate or systematise. They are generally absorbed into organisations or alliances that have the capability to replicate most rapidly and cost-effectively.

Effective replicators (such as Ford, Coca-Cola, McDonald's, Apple, Microsoft, Body Shop, Virgin and Direct Line) create a basin of attraction into which resources, technologies and customers flock once the basic value proposition is established and proven. At this stage the business ecosystem is still young and impressionable, so major shocks to it can wipe out the emerging forms of life. This is why the concepts of portfolios, nurseries and other forms of protection for fledgling business ideas are required. There is a high extinction rate at this stage in the ecosystem, hence the expression among venture capitalists: "pioneer and disappear".

STAGE 2: EXPANSION

Once the pioneers who have not disappeared have established their niches, they begin to expand them at a rapid rate. How they do this depends very much on the nature of the business model they are using. Business models are often intuitive, implicit in the way in which the founder sets about doing business. (It is only recently that business economists and strategists have begun to talk about business models as explicit approaches to setting up and running a business.) Ford's approach was based on vertical integration, mass production using assembly lines and product simplicity (leading to the "any colour so long as it is black" approach to design). This scalable architecture led to a 48% market share in the United States by 1914 from a cold start in 1905.

Microsoft took a different route. Bill Gates embedded MS-DOS into the IBM personal computer for the lowest price of any of the seven competing operating systems at the time (1981). A copy of MS-DOS was then carried into the world with every IBM PC shipped. Between 1981 and 1987 IBM managed to dominate the desktop for PCs (until more powerful clones such as Compaq and Japanese competitors emerged), and Microsoft expanded from a tiny software company into a giant, eclipsing General Motors in its stockmarket valuation by the early 1990s.

McDonald's was a classic case of a failure in franchising by the McDonald brothers in San Bernardino, California, until Ray Kroc worked out a more robust way to expand the McDonald's concept throughout the United States. By limiting franchises to local areas rather than states, and by exercising ruthless quality controls on the raw materials and production methods in each McDonald's restaurant, Kroc was able to expand McDonald's faster than any of its fast-food competitors in the 1950s and 1960s. The McDonald's business design also had one secret ingredient: the entrepreneurial energy of the "mom-and-pop" teams that Kroc was so good at finding. Good franchisees had to be hungry and prepared to work the long hours required in setting up a franchise.

In the expansion phase, organisations expand as rapidly as they can until they hit an environmental buffer of some kind: shortages of customers, people, resources, suppliers, and so on. When this happens the maturity phase of the ecosystem begins. During the expansion of the auto industry many kinds of dependent species also managed to gain a foothold in the ecosystem. For example, motor insurers, oil companies, road builders and component suppliers all expanded greatly as the motor manufacturers expanded. In this phase such interacting players in the ecosystem begin to have strong mutual effects on each other and end up in a co-evolutionary set of relationships.

STAGE 3: MATURITY

In this stage the players in the ecosystem begin to struggle over the rewards and profits generated by the ecosystem. Labour unions, insurance companies, foreign competitors, governments and regulators, suppliers and customers all compete for the wealth being created by the ecosystem. Alternative ecosystems begin to arise, which compete for customers and resources with existing ecosystems.

This is the ecosystem stage that is most familiar within economics and management theory. Porter's work on competitive advantage, and the PIMS database on which that research was based, both owe much of their power to the fact that they explained the workings of the mature stage in most of the industrial ecosystems in the developed world.

In the case of Ford, this stage of the ecosystem was reached between 1930 and 1970, when the company battled with General Motors and Chrysler for dominance in the United States and Europe. During this long period of maturity, innovation continued in product and technology terms, but the way in which the major players in the ecosystem carried out their business (that is, the business model) remained largely unchanged. It did not change until Japanese motor manufacturers such as Toyota evolved their own distinctive ecosystem through parallel evolution after the second world war.

The focus of the Japanese ecosystem was to build limited numbers of cars with minimal capital, few resources and highly dedicated employees. The production system thus emphasised careful, continuous co-ordination of efforts and optimisation of resources, together with the ideas of W. Edwards Deming, who launched the quality revolution. The ecosystem had evolved by the 1970s into one that focused on customer-led design, concurrent engineering, flexible manufacturing, networks of just-in-time suppliers and learning-oriented workers. All this was held in place by a set of statistically refined management practices, which led to a highly innovative ecosystem developing vehicles in half the time, with half the labour and at half the cost, compared with the American auto manufacturing ecosystem.

Microsoft and McDonald's are both still in the expansion phases of their ecosystems, as they struggle to meet the new territories that have opened up to them through globalisation. Yet each has undergone a mini-maturity phase, which, although not as dramatic as the motor industry, was still important. Microsoft went through a phase when it was not clear whether Windows would ever equal the power of the Apple Macintosh. IBM set about developing OS2, which posed a threat from another front. It was not really until the issue of Windows 95, NT4 and Office 97 that it became clear that Microsoft had successfully made it through a period of renewal.

The take-off of the World Wide Web and web browsers such as Netscape in 1995 almost left Microsoft as "roadkill on the information superhighway", until Gates made a decisive U-turn on Internet strategy and set the company on the road to becoming the most dominant provider of web technology. Life cycles in the IT industry are much shorter than those in other industries, which explains why pioneering, expansion, maturity and renewal can all take place in 18 months with some products.

Before its globalisation McDonald's went through a maturity phase in its business in the United States in the late 1970s. Burger King and other fast-food retailers made significant inroads into McDonald's market share, particularly where franchisees had got fat after having made their millions. McDonald's had to buy up many of these franchises to revitalise them, and to reinvest in new store and food concepts to reverse the decline. This is another example of the way in which the length of the different stages can vary enormously between businesses, as well as the fact that a company can have different parts of its business in different stages at the same time.

STAGE 4: RENEWAL

Ecosystems can die (much as horseless carriage makers did when automobiles came along), to be replaced by others that take root in the debris left over from their demise. Equally, some players can adapt – and thereby renew themselves – to survive. Ford's response to the Japanese manufacturers was to renegotiate its labour contracts in the early 1980s, gaining flexibility in its job structures and enabling it to institute total quality programmes across all its plants. It then transformed its supplier network and established a just-in-time network of long-term relationships. This dramatically improved Ford's performance and cost position, enabling it to at least stem the loss of business to the Japanese.

Other companies in the same ecosystem, such as General Motors and Chrysler, failed to make the transition as quickly. Chrysler had to be rescued by the American government, and General Motors is only now becoming competitive with the Japanese through learning from the success of its NUMI and Saturn new-concept plants. Rover is the only British mass motor manufacturer left in the UK, and it is owned by BMW. Japanese manufacturers and Ford dominate the rest of the industry – the British auto ecosystem failed to survive global competition.

Within business ecosystems different kinds of games are being played. Some are win-win (akin to infinite-sum games), some are win-lose (similar to zero-sum games) and some are lose-lose (negative-sum games). The best way for an organisation to make strategy in an ecosystem, however, is to change the rules to play to its strengths, if it can. Many ecosystems are win-win for those players who are capable of creating enduring relationships within robust value propositions. For example, the Wintel ecosystem has managed to create a (so far) unbeatable value proposition, dominating the desktop for PCs with its operating systems, software and chips.

Sometimes the principal focus is on competition between ecosystems (such as between the IBM/Motorola and Wintel ecosystems, or the Japanese and American motor manufacturer ecosystems). The key to survival is the speed at which the ecosystem can evolve to meet the challenges of a changing strategic landscape and the innovations in competitive ecosystems.

Using scenario planning techniques it is possible to model different possible states of the ecosystem, to understand what kinds of games are or might be played, who the players are or might be and what roles each of them takes or could take in the ecosystem. This enables the organisation collectively to get its mind around the different possible competitive strategies it and its competitors might adopt. Another important insight is to understand the health of the ecosystem as a whole, and which other ecosystems it might need to challenge or work with in the future.

Such scenarios, representing different states of the ecosystem or different moves between different ecosystems, can then be used to test a variety of different business models or strategies for robustness and flexibility. The collective learning of the group undertaking this process then results in a vision statement (which ecosystem it would like to play in and what the ecosystem would be like in its most desirable form), together with a statement of strategic intent (how it might move into such an ecosystem, or bring such a state about, that is, its strategy).

Given that the vision and strategic intent provide the guidance system for the organisation from this point onwards, the implications of the nature of the business environments and business ecosystems for that vision and intent need to be embodied in the nature of the organisation that is designed through the change process initiated by the wheel. This is the key to ensuring that all organisational units within the global framework can make local intelligent responses.

As business ecosystems evolve, the value in the ecosystem migrates from zone to zone in the value web, depending on the dynamics of co-evolution taking place between the different players in the web. As business ecosystems mature, so do the pioneers in the ecosystem undergo value migration from their part of the ecosystem to new players, as has happened with IBM giving way to Microsoft, or GM giving way to Toyota and other Japanese players. This is known as moving from value inflow to value outflow, as shown in Figures 4.5 and 4.6.

The migration of value in the computer industry can be seen clearly in Figure 4.7 on page 111, which tracks the stockmarket value of various firms over several years. The four charts in Figure 4.7 demonstrate how important it is to track the migration of value for any business that desires to sustain its existence in a business ecosystem. Chapter 5 describes the strategic process that enables value to be tracked, and then enables a business to be redesigned to track the profit in the business ecosystem.

## Value migration in computing

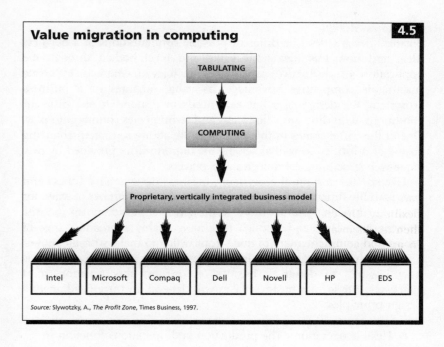

Source: Slywotzky, A., *The Profit Zone*, Times Business, 1997.

## Value migration

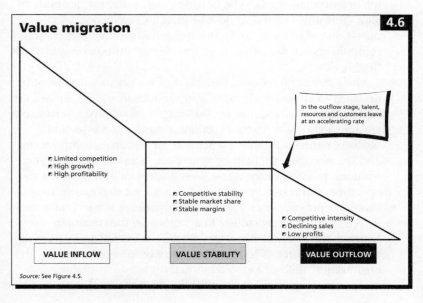

Source: See Figure 4.5.

## 3. Business design

Business designs describe different possible configurations of a business idea, and how this idea adds value and is embodied through the application of distinctive capabilities to relevant markets to create sustainable competitive advantage. As value migrates in a business ecosystem, the design of a business needs to respond to the different conditions, with different value webs and technologies coming into play. One of the cornerstones in this process is the ability to discern changing customer priorities, as well as seizing the opportunities provided by new value web structures, technologies and players.

Like species in natural ecosystems, business designs have fitness and sustainability functions. These can be improved in a number of ways; for example, through making more appropriate strategic moves on the strategic landscape, and through making available a broader range of robust and complementary options from which to make strategic moves.

Given a particular strategic intent (the function of the business), it is now possible to design a business to express this function most effectively. The form a business takes will depend on three fundamental design principles.

- Flexible operations. The production and operations function in the organisation needs to be designed with sufficient flexibility to allow learning and change to take place in production and operations. Modularity and interchangeability of business process components are two of the principal design attributes required for flexible design.
- Creative structural tension. The fabric of the organisation must be designed to allow for creativity and innovation in and around the organisation. This requires the building in of creative, constructive tensions between different functions, business processes and business partners. Healthy contention for resources, competencies and infrastructure overlaid by synergistic business processes and common interfaces help create a productive balance between co-operation and competition in and around the organisation.
- Customer pre-eminence. Flexibility and creative tension must be driven by a corporate culture that focuses on the customer. External and internal customers must be respected and valued as the primary source of legitimacy for any process or activity in an organisation. Both process and virtual organisation design components are useful in establishing the horizontal, customer-

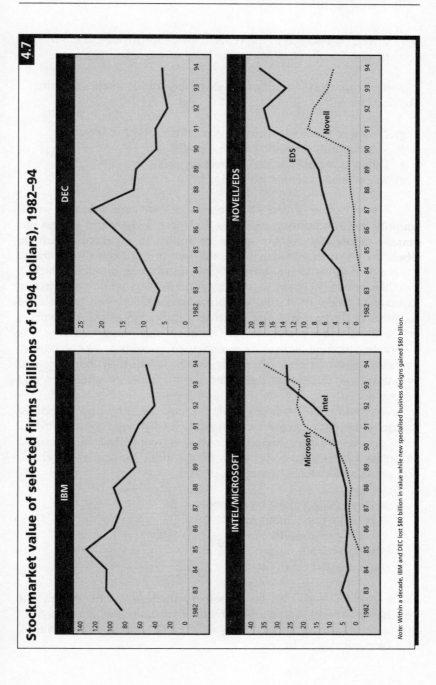

**4.7**

## Stockmarket value of selected firms (billions of 1994 dollars), 1982–94

*Note:* Within a decade, IBM and DEC lost $80 billion in value while new specialised business designs gained $80 billion.

driven (as opposed to the vertical, hierarchy-driven) culture needed to enshrine the customer at the heart of the organisation.

Some important questions need to be asked when designing a business.[3]

- Customer selection: Which customers do I want to serve?
- Value capture: How do I make a profit?
- Differentiation: How do I protect my profit stream?
- Scope: What activities do I perform?

The world of work consists primarily of tasks and activities, which combine to form business processes. Each task, activity and process has specific inputs and outputs, and is controlled in a particular fashion. Workflow processes and activities range from programmatic to emergent. An example of the former is Sainsbury's distribution business, which is run like an army. Power is at the centre and the store workforce is expected to follow fixed rules and procedures. Examples of the latter are scientists in the R&D area of a pharmaceuticals company, or playwrights and authors, where power over the workflow and power to change it is highly decentralised and can be reconfigured instantly to take account of changing circumstances. There are many off-the-shelf business and organisational designs available for specific types of situations and functions.

Some 22 different kinds of generic business designs (or profit models, as named by their categoriser, Adrian Slywotzky) have been identified. Four or five of them are well known to economists and business strategists, as they embody some of the basic principles of classic economics and business strategy research:

- Relative market share profit model
- Experience curve profit model
- Cyclical profit model
- After-sales profit model
- Specialisation profit model

Other models, such as the customer solutions profit model, the switchboard model and the blockbuster model, are less familiar. Most businesses rely on a combination of these profit models to retain control of their particular profit zone.

## 4. Leadership style

Leadership style is a property possessed by both individuals leading an organisation and the firm itself in its business ecosystem. To make a unique contribution within a business ecosystem and to find a special niche for a firm, a specific kind of leadership style is required within the business ecosystem for the role the firm wishes to play. This style also underlies the way in which campaigns need to be orchestrated to create and maintain success.

New styles of business leadership are required to deliver a particular strategic intent and vision. New strategic styles of leadership are also necessary to transform hierarchical management structures so as to liberate the leadership potential within them.

Leadership must concern itself with three interacting elements if it is to comply with the principles set out above in relation to successful value web orchestration and business design.

- Strategy development towards a vision. The ability to articulate a clear vision and develop a strategy leading towards that vision must be evident in the leadership group. This group is usually not restricted to senior management. It includes people in all walks of life around the organisation who are able to share in or contribute to the strategic dialogue.
- Strategic influence in and around the organisation. Those involved in corporate change or transformation around new strategy must have strategic influence inside and outside the organisation. The ability to swing hearts and minds behind a vision so that a number of shared and aligned visions emerge in and around the organisation is crucial. This includes the ability to work within the current confines of a corporate culture, yet to redefine such a culture from within, and the necessary credibility and standing in the organisation to be taken seriously and to be allocated the necessary resources to make change happen.
- Organisation and culture building. Change leaders must be skilful in building the corporate processes, systems and mindsets to support a new business design and strategic intent. Making change stick in a sustainable way is crucial to successful implementation of new strategy. Without such lock-in, organisations usually regress towards their old ways of doing things once the stress of change is over.

The kind of leadership and management style of an organisation and a particular management team can vary from top-down, centralised and formal at one extreme to bottom-up, decentralised and informal at the other. Leadership and management styles are a function of several aspects of the way in which:

- the direction of the organisation and its strategy are determined;
- the energy and commitment of the people in the organisation and other stakeholders are harnessed in a common direction; and
- results are measured and monitored.

Senior managers in an organisation will exhibit their specific leadership and management style through characteristic power relationships, choice of communications media and communication styles. Particular individuals, such as Lord Hanson (Hanson plc), Richard Branson (Virgin), Anita Roddick (the Body Shop), Lee Iaccoca (ex-Chrysler), the late Akio Morita (Sony), Percy Barnevik (ABB) and Lew Platt (ex-Hewlett-Packard), exhibit very different management styles, which often characterise their organisation. Other organisations may have a collective leadership and management style, in which case no particular individual will be uniquely identifiable as the primary source of the style. In this case it is helpful to think of individuals or groups who exemplify of the style.

### 5. Organisational values
Organisational values describe the network of expectations about what is desirable behaviour in a firm; they describe "the way things get done around here". This network of expectations is generally dynamic, and evolves together with the network of relationships and business activities of a firm. In this sense, values describe the "how and why" of what happens in an organisation, rather than the "what, where, who and when". The motivation for behaviour and the behavioural style form part of the value set in an organisation.

The core values of the organisation and the rules of the internal game must support the strategic intent and business design. Part of the role of leaders in any organisation undergoing change is to discern which of the current values and rules are helpful to the new direction and which are not. Important change levers, such as organisational structures and organigrams, the physical layout of operations and offices, remuneration policies and incentives, promotions and dispatches, should be used wisely to change the rules of the game in favour of the new strategic direction and the new change leaders.

Organisations are made up of networks of relationships between the members of the organisation, and the networks of others outside the organisation. These networks operate according to the cultural rules in and around an organisation. They can range from mechanistic closed (for example, United Parcel Services, which structures its networks of relationships using hierarchical, mechanistic principles) to organic open (for example, Hewlett-Packard, which operates as an adhocracy, with a strong internal market and open networks).

The organisational type also describes how the network of relationships codifies and diffuses knowledge, which forms the basis for the wealth-creation process. The culture and value system that underlies and operates this value-creating knowledge system is a function of the mindset and culture of the particular organisational type. Does the culture encourage the playful reconfiguration or recombination of its components and network of relationships, or does it prohibit such creativity? Is the organisation driven by fear and survival needs only, or does it also recognise the need for development and self-actualisation in its members?

In turn, the mindset and culture of an organisation result in characteristic ways of thinking about and dealing with the world. Conservative organisations would, for example, exhibit a focus on the past, a low level of internal diversity, an internal focus and a hierarchical approach. Radical organisations would be future driven, with an external focus and a high degree of internal diversity, and would be more individualist in nature.

Organisational values also exist at a minimum of two levels: the legitimate (or formal) system, and the shadow (or informal) system. The legitimate, formal system contains the codified and articulated commandments, which everyone knows ought to be obeyed. However, as such commandments may not be as adaptive as the informal system in the organisation, there is often a great deal of divergence between "do what I say" and "do as I do". The latter become the unwritten rules of the game, and usually become more important in driving actual behaviour than the ideals and rituals of the formal system. This is particularly true in times of rapid change, as at present.

In an organisation where people have purely economic goals, the culture is likely to become competitive, with even a "dog eat dog" attitude. The glue of relationships and shared infrastructure may not be sufficient to prevent such an organisation disintegrating through the short-sighted self-interest of its constituents. Other organisations have been described as living organisations, which are based more on a sense of community and sustainability, as well as the need to attain economic goals.

Either of these types of culture may be autocratic (command-and-control) or democratic, but whether guidance is exercised top-down or bottom-up, co-operation generally emerges if a long-term game can be discerned, in which there are consequences for breaking the rules or cheating. Organisational cultures are vehicles by which these tensions are held and resolved, and organisational values are the components from which cultures are formed.

## 6. Management processes

Just as real change leaders need an appropriate leadership style and supportive values to drive a new strategic intent and vision, so too must management processes provide support for change. Management processes are those clusters of activities required to enable, support and control the key operational business processes. They include core enabling processes, such as selecting and managing people, managing operations, managing money, building and maintaining infrastructure, managing reputation and brands, and developing and managing information systems.

The strategic management process, stakeholder management, and business and organisational development processes must also operate in the appropriate manner to lead and reinforce change. The design of these processes and their interfaces with the enabling and operational processes is therefore an important responsibility of management in implementing a new strategic intent and vision.

The technologies for management and management systems in an organisation range from classic financial systems and budgets to elaborate strategic and quality management methodologies, underpinned by anything from a mainframe with 5,000 dumb terminals to an elaborate network of client-server PCs. Management systems exist in functional dimensions, including finance, marketing and sales, production and operations, research and development, and human resources, as well as in cross-functional areas such as the following.

◪ Strategic management: directing and facilitating the strategic process, managing the co-evolution of the organisation and its market-place. This includes reviewing and evaluating the strengths and weaknesses of the business and the opportunities and threats in its environment, both present and future, and ensuring that strategic and management processes enable the organisation to respond to and influence changes in the environment to the organisation's advantage.

- Innovation management: ensuring that the concept of the business and its products and services are different from and better than those of competitors or substitutes. Managing the innovation process and developing the core competencies of the organisation required to compete in the future.
- Stakeholder management: identifying direct stakeholders in the business, developing good relationships with them, and recognising and caring for their legitimate interests.
- Direction setting: determining organisational vision and mission, and guiding the pace of operations and development. Ensuring alignment to the mission in the organisation and exercising strategic control to this end.
- Development: developing, coaching and supervising management and staff to build the distinctive capabilities of the organisation and delight present and future customers. Transforming the organisation and its capability to learn and adapt to ensure its continued high performance.
- Organisational design: designing organisational form to fit function, and setting and monitoring the design process and standards. Re-engineering the design to ensure that the form of the organisation continues to anticipate its function.
- Performance management: determining the performance measures and systems to enable strategies, policies and other important dimensions of the business and its environment to be monitored. Monitoring the performance of managers and making timely and appropriate interventions to improve performance.

These processes comprise the "what" of management, but it is also important to explore the "how" aspect of the management process. In some organisations, management processes are extremely tight, regulating most of the key variables through a command-and-control approach; the military is a perfect example of this tight structure and approach. Other organisations, such as HP and 3M, manage mainly through shared values, and initiatives and programmes are encouraged to emerge and replicate within the values of the organisation.

Tight management processes rely on formal organisation structures and processes to align individuals and groups. This management approach promotes a rational decision-making style. Loose, self-organising management processes encourage individuals and groups to operate as semi-autonomous, self-organising agents, relying on values and care and connection to provide alignment. This approach requires a far more intuitive style of management and decision-making.

### 7. Knowledge management systems

One of the cornerstones of any modern organisation is the way in which knowledge is created, shared, stored, harnessed then recycled or renewed. Interpretive frameworks and information systems lie at the heart of knowledge management. They are the key to the way in which value is created by all organisations. Knowledge management grew from four primary drivers.

- Re-engineering. Re-engineered organisations realise that knowledge is one of the kinds of glue that enables organisations to do what they do. Business and management processes rely on the quality of knowledge being applied within them, and are only as good as that knowledge.
- Intellectual capital. This is increasingly being regarded as an asset and a primary factor in corporate success.
- Core competency competition. Core competencies (integrated bundles of skills deployed within the strategic architecture of a firm) are now regarded as the only sustainable basis for competing in hyper-competitive markets, where products and services become obsolete much faster than the knowledge that produced them. Core competencies are difficult to emulate because they are based on profound kinds of knowledge, which are secret, protected or simply difficult to acquire. Such competencies prevent emigration of customers as they build loyalty into an organisation, brand, product and/or service, and are maintained through enabling processes.
- Information management. Apart from a few much-hyped cases, such as the Merrill Lynch Cash Management Account and the American Airlines Sabre reservation system, information technology investments appear simply to have enabled firms to keep abreast of their competitors, rather than leapfrog them.

Many books were written about knowledge management during the 1990s, but for the purposes of the wheel of business evolution, the following aspects are of crucial importance.

DIVERSITY: STYLE OF KNOWLEDGE EMERGENCE

Is new knowledge generated and applied in a firm predominantly through top-down processes, or does it emerge from the bottom and work upwards? For knowledge to be useful in feeding corporate intelligence and instinct, it must be captured, catalogued and transferred, without stifling the creativity of those generating and using knowledge. Top-down processes generate uniform styles of knowledge, which may have general applicability in a fairly homogeneous environment and be easier to transfer. Bottom-up processes generate great diversity of knowledge, but this will be harder to transfer.

FLEXIBILITY: TRAINING AND DEVELOPMENT

How are training and development driven in a firm? Is it mainly by task- and role-defined skills needs, or is the focus on more general competencies and personality? The more complex, dynamic and frag- mented the environment a firm is operating in, the more training and development is needed to focus on general competencies rather than role-defined skills, as it is difficult to define specifically what knowledge will be required where and when in advance.

INNOVATION AND ENTREPRENEURSHIP

How good at coming up with innovative new ideas and applying them in the business are people in an organisation? Are people generally bureaucratic or entrepreneurial? Bureaucratic organisations usually have lots of data and little knowledge. The key knowledge in a bureaucracy is in the systems and procedures used to process data and generate information. There is typically little innovation in bureaucracies. Entre- preneurial organisations, however, reward the spontaneous generation of new knowledge that adds value, and allow their members considerable freedom to innovate.

PERVASIVENESS OF INFORMATION

How centralised and rigid information systems in a firm are will determine the extent to which information can be made pervasive. Centralised, rigid information systems (for example, mainframes with dumb terminals) lock up information and knowledge and make it difficult to play with. Decentralised, flexible information systems (for example, networks of PCS and information appliances) enable individuals, teams and groups to take ownership of information and shape it to their own ends. Information is thus much more likely to become pervasive in such an environment.

LOGICAL DEPTH OF INFORMATION

Whether a firm's management information systems deliver mainly operationally focused information or strategic information will determine how much logical depth there is to the information. The more logical depth there is, the more strategic the information can be. Operational information is generally closer to data, but strategic information becomes transferable, actionable knowledge with a high impact once it is deployed.

## 8. Performance measures

Different performance measures are required to provide feedback to executives on the results of their actions. This is a vital part of the learning loop, which enables an organisation to develop its intelligence and succeed. Such intelligence is not only represented through the core competencies and distinctive capabilities, but it is also evident in the structure and behaviour of the organisation.

Performance measures vary from high-level, strategic measures, such as market share or customer satisfaction, to low-level, operational measures, such as cost per unit. It is crucial in an organisation wishing to succeed that there is a balance between strategic, operational, functional and financial performance measures, and that these measures are driven appropriately by balanced customer, internal, stakeholder and learning and innovation measures.

Some questions to ask when developing and applying effective performance measures are as follows.

- Are the measures appropriate to the vision and strategic intent?
- Do they measure the strategic dimensions of the business design?
- How well are performance measures integrated with the value and cost drivers in the business model?
- Do the management processes make extensive use of current performance measures?
- How good is the organisation at using performance measures for the purposes of improving control and accelerating learning?

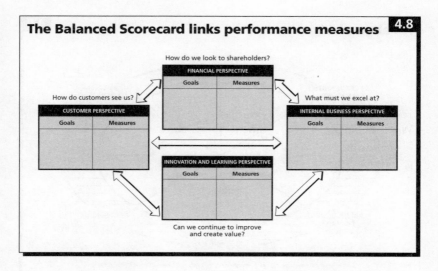

**The Balanced Scorecard links performance measures** 4.8

- How extensive is the use of the major performance measures at different levels in the business?

The measures used to manage the performance of a business comprise a range of strategic and operational measures (summarised in frameworks such as Norton and Kaplan's Balanced Scorecard, for example – see Figure 4.8). They include the following.

- Strategic measures: market attractiveness (industry structure, growth, concentration, innovation, customer power, logistical complexity) and competitive strength (relative market share, relative quality, intellectual property, customer coverage).
- Organisational measures: leanness, culture, incentives, training and development, structure, purpose, process.
- Operational measures: customer satisfaction, product or service excellence, capacity utilisation, capital intensity, productivity, outsourcing.

Depending on the emphasis placed on different measures in an organisation, its information and performance measures can vary between operational fixed (for example, the 99% replenishment rate on the shelves of a Sainsbury's store) and strategic flexible (for example, Microsoft's goal of standards ownership on the information superhighway).

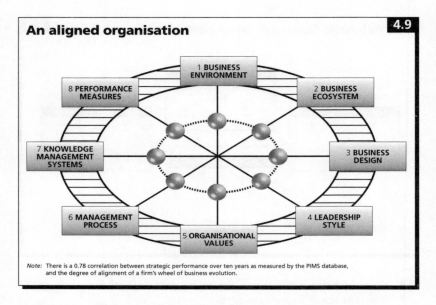

**An aligned organisation** `4.9`

Note: There is a 0.78 correlation between strategic performance over ten years as measured by the PIMS database, and the degree of alignment of a firm's wheel of business evolution.

## Interpreting profiles on the wheel of business evolution

### The meaning of alignment

A wheel was chosen deliberately as a useful way of representing the personality of an organisation as revealed by the responses to a questionnaire (see Appendix 3). The circular design enables differences in wheel profiles to be picked up quickly, and also gives rise to some characteristic shapes.

The most important aspect of a wheel diagnosis is the degree to which a firm is aligned with its environment and business ecosystem, as the degree of alignment has a strong correlation with the strategic performance of an organisation. Figure 4.9 shows a perfectly aligned wheel.

An organisation is aligned if its strategic intent and management and business processes are appropriate to the challenges of its environment and the nature of its business. The research evidence shows that over a five-year period the strategic and financial performance of the 24 organisations studied was significantly correlated with their degree of alignment. In other words, superior alignment results in superior performance.

Alignment profiles are essentially a snapshot of the main factors

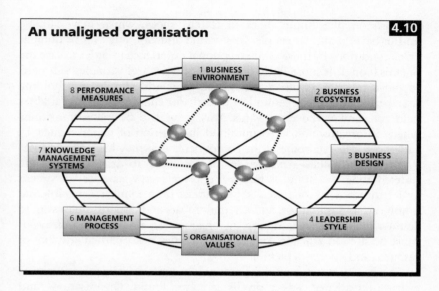

**An unaligned organisation**　　　4.10

*(diagram labels:)*
1 BUSINESS ENVIRONMENT
2 BUSINESS ECOSYSTEM
3 BUSINESS DESIGN
4 LEADERSHIP STYLE
5 ORGANISATIONAL VALUES
6 MANAGEMENT PROCESS
7 KNOWLEDGE MANAGEMENT SYSTEMS
8 PERFORMANCE MEASURES

influencing long-term organisational performance at a point in time. The dynamics underlying the movement of these factors are also important, as in fast-changing, complex situations achieving and maintaining alignment represents a considerable management challenge.

### The edge of chaos: where evolution is accelerated

From a complexity perspective, the wheel is also a way of showing which dimensions of an organisation are close to the frozen order represented by the centre of the wheel, and which parts are on or over the edge of chaos; the further from the centre the spheres (see Figures 4.9 to 4.20) connected by the dotted lines are, the closer to chaos they are. Every organisation follows its own unique evolutionary path, with the wheel variables moving in and out like the beat of a complex heart.

As shown in Figure 4.10, the path traced by an organisation's wheel profile indicates where the edge of chaos for that organisation is. Any move to push out a particular dimension of the wheel will push the organisation out if its traditional comfort zone and into a realm where it will experience cognitive turbulence. Equally, pushing a particular dimension of the wheel back in towards the centre will move it towards the ordered zone, where the degree of order will clarify issues and enable tighter structures to function.

Pushing all of the wheel variables out at once is liable to put an organisation into future shock or change shock, which may paralyse and/or harm it and its people. This should and can only ever be done in crisis conditions by those with exceptional experience in order to save the organisation. It is more likely that some of the wheel variables will need to move inwards as others are moved outwards, simply as a holding manoeuvre until the organisation is ready for changes in those variables held constant or moved inwards. This is typified by many transitions where an organisation is recentralised in a period of major change, in order to reintegrate some of the components that may have gone adrift.

There is a natural tendency for organisations to drift back into the ordered zone over time, as this is the lower energy state for the system and requires less work. New shareholders, fresh management, internal ambitions and initiatives, and external threats and opportunities work to counter this tendency and keep the organisation alive and responsive. It must be stressed that the edge of chaos carries risks, particularly that of resource and energy depletion.

This is why (apart from the fact that life is intrinsically messy anyway) a perfectly aligned wheel profile is never found. Organisations and individuals will always seek to minimise their effort, and they endlessly fine-tune their affairs so that they become more ordered. Yet being too ordered carries a cost: inflexibility and inability to adapt. This is why the evolutionary path of an organisation requires it to keep shifting the wheel variables to respond to changes in itself and its environment.

### Fullness: a measure of organisational development

The wheel of business evolution also measures the primitiveness or level of development of an organisation. The closer an organisation is to the centre, the more likely it is to have an organisational form shaped in the distant past. The organisation in Figure 4.11 is likely to have a fairly primitive command-and-control form, with little or no adaptive capability. Such brittle, authoritarian structures, like those in the former communist countries, fail when the heat is turned up inside and outside them. These structures must attempt at all costs to destroy any sources of change in or around them in order to survive, but the cost of doing so becomes unsustainable. Many modern organisations look a bit like this, particularly if they have been protected from real competition, as in some East Asian countries.

Some organisations are highly advanced, and represent new, ground-breaking ways of doing things. On the wheel of business evolution such organisations look like Figure 4.12 on page 126. Many of these

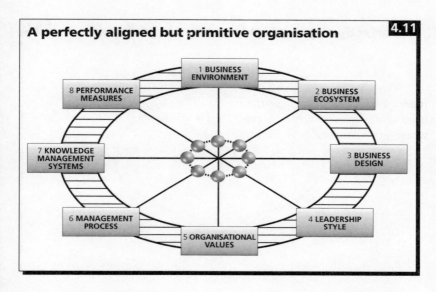

**A perfectly aligned but primitive organisation** `4.11`

organisations can be seen today in and around Silicon Valley, where intense competitive pressures ensure that organisational evolution is speeding up faster than anywhere else in the world. (However, none of them will be as perfectly aligned as the ideal organisation shown in Figure 4.9.) Such an organisation would have many of the following characteristics:

- Focused
- Future-driven
- Flexible
- Responsive
- Interactive
- Participative
- Knowledge-based
- Learning-centred
- Creative
- Bottom-up
- Visual
- Virtual

Few organisations have reached this advanced state. Although many are trying, probably over 99% of organisations today are closer to the

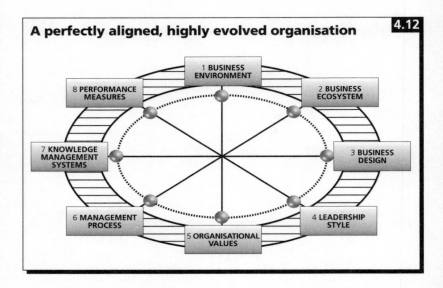

**A perfectly aligned, highly evolved organisation**  4.12

middle or inner circle of the wheel rather than the outer circle. The major management and leadership challenge of the next few decades will be to design and develop more adaptive, intelligent organisations, capable of handling the rapid transition to the digital, knowledge economy that is beginning to emerge from the remnants of the industrial age.

The wheel of business evolution is a useful tool in enabling executives to benchmark themselves and their organisations, and to ensure they are making the right moves in roughly the right sequence to transform their businesses.

### Wheel profiles: identifying types of organisations
Just as individuals are products of nature and nurture, their own genetic predisposition and the environment in which they have grown up, so too organisations are products of their nature and their environment. Individuals and organisations both have their evolution shaped by the forces of self-organisation and selection, but they are also capable of making conscious choices and learning. Psychological profiling allows the identification of distinct personality and character types, and one of the main uses of the wheel of business evolution is to enable the same kind of analysis of different kinds of organisational personalities.

The starting point for identifying the different kinds of organisations is to understand the balance or imbalance between the sources of change in an organisation. Some organisations may be driven to change largely by external conditions, and may spend most of their time in adaptive mode; for example, small fashion retailers or PC distributors. Other organisations may be operating to shape their environment in some respects; for example, high-tech start-ups or large multinationals, which dominate their niches during stable phases in the evolution of their industry or business ecosystem.

It is also essential to distinguish between different kinds of domains in which businesses or organisations seek to shape or adapt to their environment. A large multinational corporation may be capable of shaping the technical domain in which it has distinctive capabilities. For example, an oil and gas company may shape the future development of alternative energy sources, while having to adapt to changing social trends and political forces. Equally, large political or administrative bureaucracies may be capable of shaping the future of the programmes or institutions they are charged with, yet may have to adapt to technical and social changes around them.

The conclusion that can be drawn from this is that organisations are capable of shaping aspects of their environment when they command certain competencies and resources, but they must adapt in areas where they possess few or no distinctive capabilities or resources. Therefore, for a given organisation, it is important to understand the following.

- The nature and extent of change in its environment and industry or business ecosystem (external change drivers).
- The degree to which the organisation possesses some set of distinctive capabilities, competencies, resources and/or processes relevant to specific aspects of the external change drivers, which might enable the organisation to shape aspects of its environment (shaping organisational capabilities).
- Which aspects of its environment the organisation must adapt to, and how such adaptation co-evolves with the changes being generated internally by the organisation (shaper/adapter alignment).
- The nature and extent of change in the organisation, and what the sources of such change are (internal change drivers).

From the initial research into the wheel of business evolution, eight organisational types were identified, which fall into three categories.

SHAPERS

Shapers are organisations capable of shaping significant aspects of their environment, to the extent that they spend more of their time and effort in shaping than they do in adapting, and have a degree of success in the outcome. Shapers may occasionally lose their power, ambition or idealism and fall back into adapter mode, until they are reinvigorated by a new set of circumstances, a new purpose or a new leader.

ADAPTERS

Adapters spend most of their time and effort changing themselves to reflect changes in their environment. Although they may be quite creative in the way they adapt, they cannot be said to be shaping the agenda in their particular industry or business ecosystem. Adapters may occasionally have the opportunity to become shapers if they can gain some lead time on the changes in their environment, or they may lapse into reactor mode if there are few change drivers in or around them.

REACTORS

Reactors are generally resistant to change, although they may have an ambitious management team that attempts to make change happen. Reactors often become takeover or merger targets, or they simply go out of business. Some reactors may successfully defend their niche, and may become adapters if the forces for internal change and the effectiveness of the change effort are great enough.

## Detailed wheel profiles

This section shows in greater detail the profiles of some of the organisations involved in the original research leading to the creation of the wheel of business evolution. It must be emphasised that wheel profiles, like personality profiles, change over time, and that these profiles can only now be released into the public domain as they reflect the organisations involved as they were in 1991. Since then many of these organisations have undergone major changes, so their current wheel profiles are different. These profiles are meant to demonstrate how the wheel can be used in practical situations, rather than to comment on the organisations involved.

In understanding the organisations, it is also important to remember that they are products of their individual histories, as shaped by the forces of self-organisation, selection and choices they have made. Business evolution ensures that organisations and their environments will constantly be changing, in a mutual dance of co-evolution.

## Shaper profiles

POISED IDEALISTS: RANK-XEROX

Rank-Xerox is a joint venture between the Xerox Corporation and The Rank Organisation, set up in the early 1960s to distribute the then unique Xerox photocopying technology in the UK. During the period in which the Xerox technology was protected by patent, the organisation enjoyed unbridled growth. When the patent expired in the late 1970s, Japanese firms targeted Xerox. Canon and other large Japanese firms began to apply their techniques of miniaturisation and total quality to photocopying machines.

The result was that by the mid-1980s Xerox had lost a large part of its market share to the Japanese, and had responded with its own transformation programme centred on total quality management. This led to an organisation design focused on customer satisfaction, business process improvement and culture change. Many of the major business change and transformation approaches available in the late 1980s and early 1990s were launched by Xerox, and by 1991 it was beginning to regain some of its lost market share through more innovative products, improved product quality and customer service.

These forces were reflected in Xerox's wheel profile, which revealed the firm to be a poised idealist. It was poised because it had created the conditions in which major changes could be initiated and carried out in the organisation. It was idealist because it fully understood its transformation process and believed in its own ability continuously to improve the way it did things. As the then director of quality stated: "We believe that the main job of every manager in Xerox is to manage change."

So what do poised idealists look like as a wheel profile (see Figure 4.13 on the following page)? The rapid rate of change in Xerox's business environment and its business ecosystem are reflected in the location of the business environment and business ecosystem at the complex, dynamic and fragmented ends of these two spokes of the wheel. Poised idealists like Xerox develop flexible and responsive characteristics through open organic values and a pluralistic flexible management style. These characteristics may, however, be in tension with the rather conservative knowledge management and leadership styles in such an organisation. The idealistic values and pluralistic flexible management processes will unleash pressures for change, which the leadership style and knowledge management approach may not accommodate.

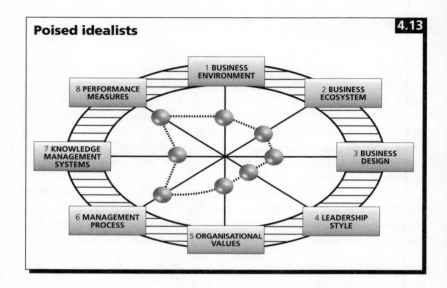

**Poised idealists** `4.13`

1 BUSINESS ENVIRONMENT

8 PERFORMANCE MEASURES

2 BUSINESS ECOSYSTEM

7 KNOWLEDGE MANAGEMENT SYSTEMS

3 BUSINESS DESIGN

6 MANAGEMENT PROCESS

4 LEADERSHIP STYLE

5 ORGANISATIONAL VALUES

Xerox qualifies as a shaper because it was able to renew its innovative capability in the face of the competitive threats around it and turn the situation around. It also displayed a great deal of foresight in how it went about changing itself and its markets, and eventually managed to accelerate the pace of change within itself to one which was at least equal to and in some cases greater than the rate of change in its environment.

ENTHUSIASTIC CHAMPIONS: WELSH WATER

During the late 1980s and early 1990s, the British government was in the process of privatising the water, electricity and energy industries in the UK. Welsh Water was one of two privatised water companies in this survey, and displayed markedly different characteristics from Southern Water Company, which was privatised at about the same time. Welsh Water chose an entrepreneurial route to create its new future, and Southern Water followed a more traditional route towards technical and service excellence.

Because of the conditions imposed on water companies, they were not allowed to grow at the expense of their investment in the underlying infrastructure of their businesses. Welsh Water decided it would increase its shareholders' returns by diversifying around its stable core business into new areas, such as hotels (located on the land it owned), engineering ventures, international water engineering projects and consultancy.

**Enthusiastic champions**

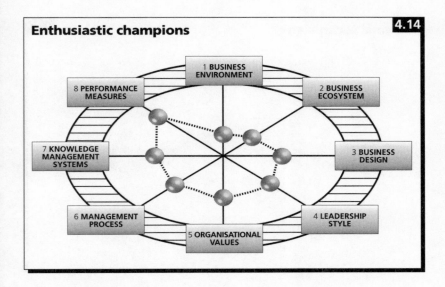

The environment in which Welsh Water operated its core business was stable, as it had a monopoly position in the supply of water to its Welsh customer base. The new business opportunities pursued by the company in diversifying away from its core business were characterised by much more competitive markets and a higher degree of risk. Changes in business design, leadership style and organisational values were driven by the ambitions of the senior management team to create a dynamic, profitable business.

There were, however, difficulties in gaining the relevant experience outside the core business, and in getting strategic alignment of all the different initiatives that were cascading down through the organisation following privatisation. Leadership style, organisational values and performance measures were all used as major drivers of change in the business, particularly as many of the last-mentioned were regulatory objectives imposed on customer service and rate of return. The redesign of management and business processes and information management systems were used to support these changes, with some success. The leaders of Welsh Water effectively shaped aspects of the environment around them, qualifying the firm as a shaper (see Figure 4.14).

RATIONAL TECHNICIANS: ICI FIBRES

ICI Fibres was a world leader in the production of synthetic fibres until

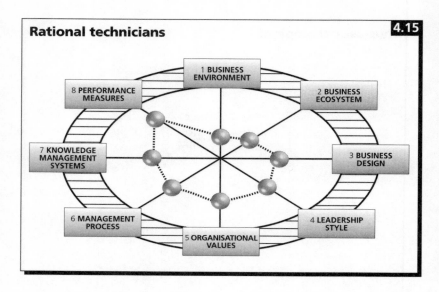

**Rational technicians** 4.15

the early 1980s, when changes in the General Agreement on Tariffs and Trade (GATT) resulted in developing countries being able to significantly undercut its prices. This commoditisation of many parts of the fibres business led to a major reassessment of the priorities of the business in the mid-1980s. Various change initiatives were launched at the beginning of the 1990s, including a total quality management programme and a re-engineering programme. Head office costs were slashed and the head office moved to Brussels.

By the early 1990s ICI Fibres was experiencing increasing turbulence in its business environment and major fragmentation in its business ecosystem. As the change wheel shows (see Figure 4.15), ICI Fibres was responding in a rational way by focusing on business process design, IT systems and performance measurements (for example, executive information systems). Although in the minds of the management team and the new CEO the technical problems facing ICI Fibres had effectively been solved, the neglect of leadership style, organisational values and management process resulted in an inability to make changes in other areas stick. This meant that the performance improvements that could have been realised through changes initiated in business design, IT systems and performance management were not delivered.

The challenges for rational technicians are, therefore, to create much greater understanding and ownership of change within the people in the organisation, using a leadership style that can create consistent organisational values. Despite these challenges, ICI Fibres underwent sufficient change to enable it to shape aspects of its environment.

## Adapter profiles

BALANCED GUARDIANS: PRUDENTIAL ASSURANCE

During the 1980s Prudential Assurance had begun the process of transforming from an organisation selling door-to-door life insurance and savings-related policies to a full-blown financial supermarket spanning investment, life, banking and pension products. The trigger for this change was the deregulation of the British financial services industry and the increasing competition from new products and business models, many of which are generated from the United States. Thus Prudential's business environment was becoming increasingly complex and dynamic, its traditional market-place was fragmenting and many new players were emerging in its ecosystem.

In the late 1980s and early 1990s, Prudential responded by entering new areas of business, such as pensions and investment management, and investing heavily in IT and management process redesign to facilitate its transformation. This process was only partially successful, however, because the leadership style, organisational values and performance measures had not been shifted sufficiently to support the major IT and management process investments. Moreover, Prudential had failed to think through the detailed business design implications of what was going on in its market-place (see Figure 4.16 on the following page).

As a result, although Prudential could be said to have adapted to some degree to the changes around it, its performance failed to reflect the efforts and investments made in changing the management team, the business portfolio and the IT systems. This is a classic problem with the balanced guardian profile, as the management and staff in such organisations are reluctant to take the risks that would enable them to learn how to change to support the changes going on around them. However, balanced guardians are cautious and seldom make major errors of judgment. As long as the changes in their environment are not discontinuous, they can cope. The real danger lies in radical change. During the late 1990s Prudential began to think more radically and opened a direct telephone and Internet-based banking service, Egg, and created some innovative new products.

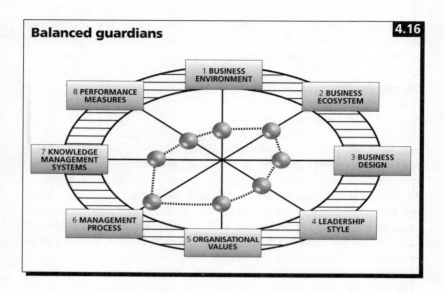

**Balanced guardians** `4.16`

PUBLIC INNOVATORS: CIVIL AVIATION AUTHORITY

The Civil Aviation Authority (CAA) has its origins in the various international agreements regulating air-traffic control. Since the second world war, the CAA has moved from being a purely military operation on the air-traffic control side to becoming a privatised business, which has invested over £400m in a new European Air Traffic Control Centre. The other part of its business, comprising the regulation of airlines and airports, was also transformed from a bureaucracy into a commercial organisation during the late 1980s.

By early 1990 the CAA had succeeded in putting in place the basic hygiene factors in a commercial business and had begun to focus on its customers. The considerable tensions in this process can be seen in the wheel profile (see Figure 4.17). Major changes in business design, management process, knowledge management systems and performance measures are reflected, but organisational values and leadership style had not changed significantly except for the CEO and a few of his main supporters. This resulted in some quite severe change blockages in the organisation and an extremely expensive overrun in the new air-traffic control facility, which even now is four years late and twice over budget.

This illustrates the real challenges of a public innovator, which revolve around the difficulties of making change happen in a highly structured, monopoly environment. Given what is currently known about business

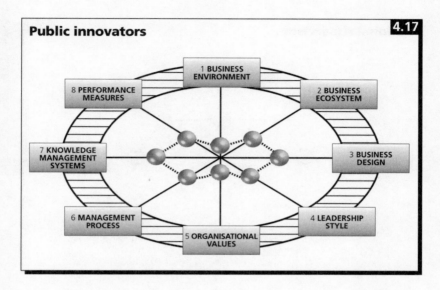

**Public innovators**

4.17

change and transformation, it is easier to see with hindsight where the CAA could have improved its change approach. However, it is clear that a much more systematic approach to change would have yielded economic benefits to the CAA and its stakeholders.

RATIONAL SUPERVISORS: J. SAINSBURY

Sainsbury was until recently the largest food retailing organisation in the UK. Founded in the late 1800s, the organisation had steadily grown under the leadership of the Sainsbury family to its position of pre-eminence in the early 1990s. By this time David Sainsbury had taken over as managing director and had started to change its rather autocratic style.

Sainsbury's competitors, particularly Tesco and Asda, were becoming increasingly aggressive in the early 1990s. Discount retailers such as Aldi, as well as food retailing by petrol companies, were beginning to eat away at Sainsbury's dominant market share. This could be seen in the increasingly complex, dynamic business environment and the greater fragmentation in Sainsbury's ecosystem in the change wheel (see Figure 4.18 on the following page).

David Sainsbury's efforts to introduce the cultural and management changes needed to help it compete, focusing on investing in information systems and organisational value change, can be seen from the wheel profile, where these variables have been pushed out. However, because of

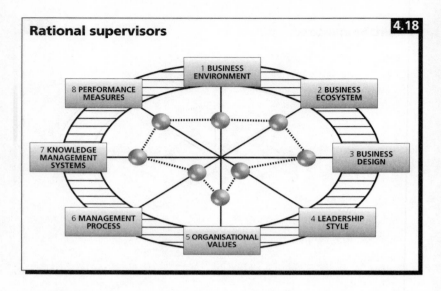

**Rational supervisors** 4.18

- 1 BUSINESS ENVIRONMENT
- 2 BUSINESS ECOSYSTEM
- 3 BUSINESS DESIGN
- 4 LEADERSHIP STYLE
- 5 ORGANISATIONAL VALUES
- 6 MANAGEMENT PROCESS
- 7 KNOWLEDGE MANAGEMENT SYSTEMS
- 8 PERFORMANCE MEASURES

the mixed messages the organisation was getting from the other members of the Sainsbury clan, the leadership style and management processes were not changed sufficiently to enable David Sainsbury to realise his new vision. Sainsbury has continued to be outmanoeuvred by its competitors and is in danger of slipping to number three in the retail industry. The culture of conservatism and an unwillingness to undergo self-examination, which bordered on arrogance, proved disastrous in the fast-changing retail environment of the late 1980s and early 1990s.

The real danger for a successful rational supervisor such as Sainsbury is that it becomes so well adapted to its niche in the environment that when change happens around it, it is both unable to recognise the signs and unable to act to make the necessary changes. No matter how much is invested in fine-tuning information systems, culture and performance measures, real change and its benefits cannot be realised because of an inappropriate leadership style and management processes. To sum up, Sainsbury has adapted in some ways (for example, by starting a bank and a new loyalty card), but these changes were made too late to reverse the competitive disadvantage the change wheel demonstrates in the lack of alignment of the key wheel variables.

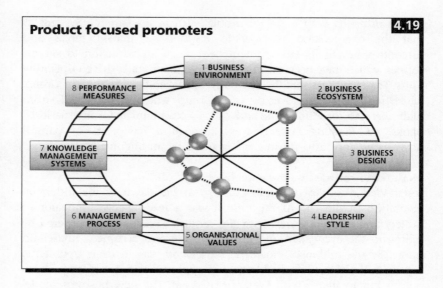

**Product focused promoters** · 4.19

*Reactor profiles*

PRODUCT FOCUSED PROMOTERS: BIS BANKING SYSTEMS

BIS Banking Systems was founded in the late 1970s in the City of London to commercialise back-office software for banks on IBM System 38 computers. The company experienced a decade of explosive growth, and its MIDAS package became the largest-selling international banking system. Initially, the company had the market to itself, but as it grew others encroached on its market share. The wheel profile in Figure 4.19 shows BIS Banking Systems's business environment and business ecosystem becoming increasingly complex, dynamic and fragmented during the late 1980s and early 1990s. The sales-led culture of the company, however, made it blind to the shifts in the needs of international banks and the changing competitive landscape.

The wheel profile indicates that apart from attempts to change the business design and leadership style of the business, the other four internal wheel variables remained unchanged and out of alignment with the external wheel variables. The operational fixed performance measures and functionally driven IT systems, together with the inward focus of the management processes and organisational values, led BIS Banking Systems to expand through diverse acquisitions at a time when it should have been focusing on reinventing its core offering.

The difficulty with a reactor profile, such as BIS Banking Systems, is that the organisation is slow to respond to market forces and discontinuities in its environment because of an addiction to success recipes, which have been reinforced by the functionally driven operating units. The result was that the company was taken over by the ACT Group, which itself was taken over by MISYS Group, which then merged MIDAS with KAPITI to consolidate the back-office software niche for international banks. BIS Banking Systems went through a few years of painful downsizing and restructuring as a result of its misalignment.

UNBALANCED CONSERVERS: JOSIAH-WEDGWOOD

Josiah-Wedgwood was founded in 1759 at the dawn of the industrial revolution in the UK. At the time it was a leading-edge innovator in pottery and ceramic wares. Over the centuries Wedgwood prospered by selling to the ever-expanding British Empire and became a household name. By the mid-1980s, however, Wedgwood was in deep trouble. Its captive colonial markets had largely disappeared and it was left with no option but to merge with Waterford Crystal. The new business model centred on creating a global giftware business based on the Wedgwood and Waterford brands.

A new management team was brought in and a major redesign of the combined business Waterford Wedgwood began. As the wheel profile in Figure 4.20 shows, however, apart from some changes of business design and leadership style, the other four internal wheel variables were left largely unchanged. This meant that major quality and re-engineering initiatives failed to have the impact they might have done if the organisational values, management process, knowledge management systems and performance measures had been aligned with the new style of operation and leadership.

The unbalanced conserver profile reveals an organisation that intends to change from a top-down perspective. The reality is, however, that the conservative organisation will resist attempts to change it, unless all of the key internal wheel variables are aligned to the external challenges facing the organisation.

The many change initiatives launched by senior management thus ran aground and failed to make any real impact. The outcome of this story is that after an initial period of difficulty in turning Wedgwood around, the combined Waterford Wedgwood brand began to reassert its power in the giftware market through innovative new marketing programmes. Gift ideas, personal accessories and new brands such as Rosenthal have

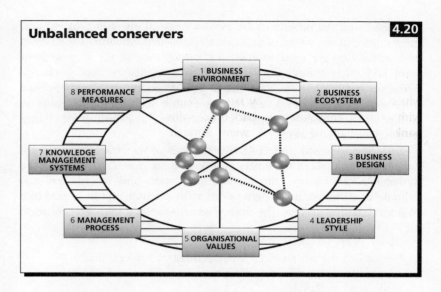

Unbalanced conservers · 4.20

substantially increased sales and profits, building on the design excellence of both companies. Market share and profitability are rising again. It is sad that because of the misalignment in the organisation it took so many years to achieve.

## Summary

Because it is such a complex task, business evolution is difficult to manage. The business evolution wheel is a useful tool for management teams and organisations that are becoming aware of the possibilities of applying the new sciences in their organisations, as it:

- provides a framework to put in context and calibrate the transition from industrial age to knowledge age approaches to strategic and operations management;
- enables a more informed conversation to take place about the role of complexity thinking and modelling approaches and tools in the organisational change process;
- facilitates the emergence of a coherent set of priorities and sequence of activities for change.

A wheel diagnosis is based on the outputs of structured interviews and workshops, in which the perceptions of a senior management team are calibrated, and the profiles of the various perceptions of the current and future states of the wheel variables are established. Structured interviews and workshops are used to elicit the perceptions of the management team and other stakeholders involved in a change process. A change dialogue emerges from the initial conversations triggered by the interviews and workshop, which can enable self-organising teams to surface and collaborate on specific items framed as priorities for change by the diagnostic process.

Once the personal and collective realities of the management team have been captured in the wheel as a basis for a structured, constructive dialogue about change, the management team and its advisers can validate or stimulate these perceptions with external inputs as part of a strategic learning process. The change wheel enables a management team to:

- establish the priorities for management of strategic and operational change in the business, and the role of new science inspired initiatives;
- co-ordinate and integrate the various change initiatives in an organisation;
- benchmark the progress made in change initiatives and capture the emerging lessons;
- balance the efforts made and resources devoted to change initiatives in accordance with their priorities and inter-relationships;
- link change initiatives tightly to the FutureStep strategic review process (see Chapter 5).

The wheel of business evolution describes a process in which an organisation seeks to adapt itself to an often supra-critical business environment, where maximum uncertainty exists and the variables being dealt with are unclear and the outcomes in the environment unknown.

There will be occasions where an organisation can harness the complexity and/or even chaos in its environment to generate new knowledge and shape aspects of its ecosystem to redefine the rules of the game. For most traditional players, however, the issues revolve around adaptation and how to align the key variables in their businesses to achieve adaptive agility and more effective frontline execution.

One of the key questions in the minds of the executives concerned will be: "What dimensions of our organisation and business should we seek to maintain in a sub-critical state, while we push other dimensions over the edge into supra-criticality?" In other words, how can we maintain an overall balance between the many facets of our business while poised on or near the edge of chaos when we need to change most rapidly? And when do we need to move that balance away from the edge of chaos in order to lock in desirable structural features and enhance our ability to exploit the position we have created in the ecosystem?

Ideally, an organisation should continuously self-organise and self-renew so that change is embedded in an ongoing adaptive and creative process and in its web of relationships in its ecosystem. Given the current state of knowledge and the ability of management teams of late industrial civilisation, however, change is still likely to be seen as discontinuous and to be managed as such. The business evolution wheel can be used for both continuous and discontinuous change processes. The difference in its operation will simply be a more rapid iteration and cycling through the different dimensions and the speed at which they change.

Lastly, the wheel is not concerned with providing the right answers. It focuses on gaps, misalignments and priorities, as well as the cross-impacts of the different dimensions of the organisation and its environment.

# 5 FutureStep: a new strategic management process for navigating complexity and generating innovation

IN THE CASE OF COMPLEX ADAPTIVE SYSTEMS, THEIR SCHEMATA HAVE CONSEQUENCES IN THE REAL WORLD, WHICH EXERT SELECTION PRESSURES BACK ON THE COMPETITION AMONG THE SCHEMATA, AND THOSE SCHEMATA THAT PRODUCE FAVORABLE RESULTS IN THE REAL WORLD HAVE A TENDENCY TO SURVIVE, OR BE PROMOTED, AND THOSE THAT ARE LESS SUCCESSFUL IN THE REAL WORLD HAVE A TENDENCY TO BE DEMOTED OR DISAPPEAR. IN MANY SITUATIONS, COMPLEXITY MAY OFFER A SELECTIVE ADVANTAGE.

Murray Gell-Mann, Director of the Santa Fe Institute[1]

### A new approach to strategic innovation

Adaptive enterprises should build in adaptiveness at three levels: their strategies, their organisations and their operations. This chapter explains how a new strategic management process, called FutureStep, can help companies integrate flexibility and responsiveness into every aspect of their activities. It is an approach to strategic management that has evolved through many years of practical experience with multinational organisations in several industries in Europe, North America and Asia. It is a modular tool, and parts can be used independently or as a complete programme for guiding strategic decision-making.

Organisations that have pioneered this kind of approach to strategic management include Shell, 3M, Hewlett-Packard, State Farm Insurance, Jardine Matheson, the British National Health Service, the US Department of Defence, British Telecom (BT) and Dutch Telecom. These organisations have experienced many benefits, including:

- enhanced organisational intelligence, shown by improved decision quality and accelerated organisational learning capability;
- greater clarity and robustness in strategic direction, with reduced risk;
- increased adaptiveness, speed and flexibility in responding appropriately to change;

- organisational design in which the shape or form of the organisation mirrors its function and embodies its own transformational capabilities;
- stakeholder alignment around a shared, sustainable model of the business ecosystem with which the organisation co-evolves.

The FutureStep process is aimed at enabling organisations to meet the challenges of navigating a complex and uncertain future environment, by helping them to evolve as complex, intelligent systems. It focuses on what an organisation can do in the present to increase its ability to operate in a sustainable way in the future. As outlined in Chapter 4, such activities are typically of two kinds.

- External: related to developing greater awareness and interactive foresight with the existing external environment, which may include attempts at prediction for those elements of the environment on which the organisation is particularly dependent.
- Internal: focused on internal structures, existing capabilities and self-generating creativity, which are largely independent of current circumstances and to some extent under the control or influence of the organisation.

In FutureStep, a strategic dialogue is established between the external and internal aspects of an organisation, helping it to develop and maintain a range of robust, relevant options, which match the complexity in its environment and are supported by its internal capabilities.

## The strategic learning process

FutureStep has three parts, which align with the stages in the strategic learning process outlined in Chapter 2. Although this process may at first appear to be linear, it is not; strategic management is a complex learning process, which has within it many non-linear and adaptive feedback loops. The convention of diagnosis, development and execution is, however, a logical and clear way to describe the key aspects of strategic management, and the way in which these activities contribute to navigating uncertain and complex futures.

The strategic learning process comprises four steps (see Figure 5.1 on the following page).

- **Scan.** At this stage the organisation takes stock of its recent

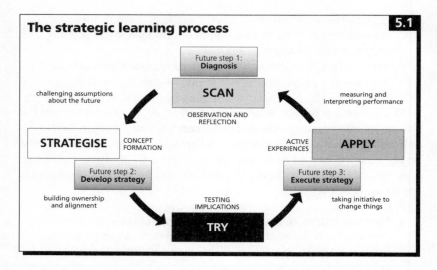

experience and uses a scan of itself and its environment to observe new patterns and reflect on their implications for the future. The scanning stage is critical, as it forms the basis for challenging assumptions about the future and generating insights into how value can be created in innovative ways. Such insights are generated through a process of "reframing", which is what happens when a new pattern is recognised by management, and a clash occurs between the new pattern and existing ways of understanding the world or a phenomenon. The stage is then set for a reframe, in which the clash between the old and new patterns is resolved through the emergence of a synthesis between the two. This stage is triggered by and managed through the diagnosis phase.

▨ **Strategise.** Based on the new insights generated during the scan stage, the organisation is able to develop and codify new ideas, concepts and approaches to create value for its stakeholders. Specific initiatives, projects and ventures can be conceived at this stage. These form part of the detail of the strategy development phase. A critical dimension of the strategy development process involves the building of ownership and alignment among stakeholders in the strategy process around the emerging features of the plan.

▨ **Try.** During this stage experiments and pilots are launched to test the ideas and initiatives generated during the strategy development stage. The aim is to try out some new things, through either simulation or real-world initiatives, and to learn from them. Then successful initiatives can be scaled up and unsuccessful initiatives can be reshaped or scrapped. This is an intermediate step between developing and executing strategy, setting the stage for full-blown execution of strategy.

◪ **Apply.** Working with the successful outcomes of the pilots and trials in the try stage, management can now commit resources to develop fully those initiatives worthy of backing. During this stage the measurement and interpretation of performance are essential to provide the feedback needed to learn the lessons inherent in the day-to-day experience of the organisation. This stage corresponds to the strategy execution phase of FutureStep.

The overall purpose of this strategic management process is to establish which strategic options or elements thereof are robust across the scenarios and use the most robust elements to develop a core strategic focus or theme. This is often described as a strategic intent. This new approach to strategic planning enables an organisation to:

◪ reinvent its business model, its business processes and its organisational structure to be able to deliver the strategic intent;
◪ understand the learning and development challenges posed by each scenario and by the organisation in delivering its strategic intent;
◪ identify the contingencies the organisation needs to be ready for in deploying its strategic intent, using a set of triggers driven by the scenario turning points;
◪ generate a compelling vision, which describes the future desirable state of the world the organisation will inhabit and how the organisation intends to help bring that future state about.

### How it works in practice

In different organisations these outcomes have been realised in different ways. For example, over a period of several years Hewlett-Packard has used FutureStep to help make key strategic decisions about different areas of its business, ranging from professional services to enterprise computing to personal computers to the extended enterprise. Glenn Osaka, a vice-president at HP, commented that:

> The FutureStep process has enabled us to rapidly mobilise various groups of stakeholders around different sets of strategic issues, and explore the complex array of possibilities and options in those situations. While enabling us to bring together what HP and its partners know about a situation, FutureStep has also helped us forge strong relationships and teams which have made it possible to act quickly on the strategic agenda which has emerged from the process.
>
> For me personally, I have found the process enables me to articulate my gut instincts about what the issues are and what we need to do about them, and share those issues with my colleagues in a creative, compelling way.

State Farm Insurance pioneered motor insurance in the United States in the early 1900s, insuring some of the first Model T Fords to come off the production line. Since then it has grown into the largest general insurer in North America, generating annual revenue of over $40 billion. During the 1990s the insurance industry began to change dramatically throughout the world. Unprecedented claims for natural disasters, new forms of competition and new technologies are changing the way the industry operates.

In 1996 State Farm decided to use FutureStep to test its strategy and develop new ways of developing strategy. Sharon Smoski, director of corporate planning, remarked:

> We looked at a number of different ways in which we could develop insights into the future of the financial services industry, and selected FutureStep because it appeared to combine the rigour of other processes we reviewed, with a high degree of pragmatic creativity which enabled us to engage our entire top management group to develop exciting new ways of looking at the real complexity of our business.
>
> The scenario development exercise was highly stimulating, and resulted in a fresh set of initiatives being taken once we had reviewed our strategic options using the strategic gaming and simulation module. The process was also enjoyable, with a strong sense of camaraderie emerging as the work progressed.

Jardine Matheson, founded 140 years ago, is one of the original Hongs (trading houses) in Hong Kong and currently generates over $10 billion in revenue. Jardine Office Services (JOS) was founded within the Jardine Matheson Group just over a decade ago to serve the needs of the corporate market in Hong Kong for office equipment, computing and telecommunications. It has since grown to a $500m business and is continuing to grow rapidly despite the Asian recession.

During 1998 JOS reached a point in its growth where several major strategic decisions needed to be reviewed, and it chose FutureStep from a number of options as the process it would use. As Steve Lo, managing director of JOS, said:

> JOS had recently made a major acquisition, and one of our key concerns was to integrate the two management teams through a new strategy for the combined business.
> FutureStep helped us align our management team around a new strategic thrust for JOS. We explored three main strategic options, and by testing them against scenarios for the world and Asian computing marketplaces we arrived at a robust strategic focus. It was particularly helpful to have thought through the implications of the Asian recession, and the process generated a level of strategic dialogue in our management team which has continued to enable us to examine our options together and spot the discontinuities in time for us to respond appropriately.
>
> I also personally noticed that the process was highly educational for all members of our management group, and has improved our ability to think strategically.

### Developing strategy

To apply FutureStep, it is useful to first get an overview of the three main phases in the process (see Figure 5.2 on the following page). These are subdivided into 12 modules, which can be used separately or as a full programme for strategy-making, and, typically, the process becomes cyclical as new challenges emerge. In this chapter the 12 modules are described in the sequence in which they would usually occur in a project.

It must be emphasised that strategy development is both a deliberate and an emergent process. Diagnosis, development and execution are often parallel processes that give rise to an emerging picture and set of moves, and often strategies are only recognised in hindsight. Nonetheless,

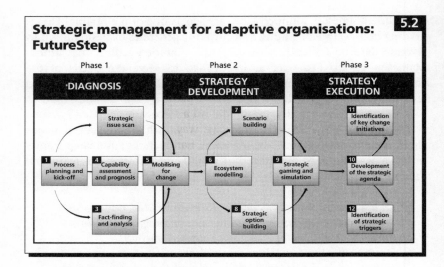

**Strategic management for adaptive organisations: FutureStep** — 5.2

the most valuable benefit of a strategic management process is that it creates and legitimises the space and time in which reflection and learning can be activated and codified, so that an entire organisation can benefit from and exploit crucial strategic capabilities and insights.

It may be popular to lament that in a chaotic environment, where complex adaptive agents do their own thing, management and planning are historical irrelevancies, designed for a linear age. Such a view would be mistaken, however. Only parts of the environment are chaotic, and only for limited periods, and living permanently on the edge of chaos is both disruptive and resource depleting. There are many patterns that repeat, even as we move from the industrial to the digital age.

Strategy and learning depend upon such regularities to function, and planning and management carried out in an adaptive style generates lead time for better decisions, economises on resources and catalyses a greater degree of coherence in an organisation. The key to such adaptiveness is the way in which strategy and planning are carried out. FutureStep emerged to fill the gap between brittle strategic management techniques and the need to navigate complex, uncertain environments, and it deploys complex adaptive thinking and tools throughout the process.

### Phase 1: Diagnosis
Initially, a set of diagnostic findings is developed as input for the external

and internal aspects of a strategic gaming matrix. The diagnostic process comprises four elements, together with an optional bridge to the strategy development phase.

- Module 1: Process planning and kick-off. The main stakeholders in the strategy process are engaged in planning the rollout of FutureStep in the organisation, and a variety of activities are then launched to get the process under way.
- Module 2: Strategic issue scan. The nature of the strategic context in which the organisation is operating (external environment) and the strategic challenges it faces are identified during the strategic issue scan.
- Module 3: Fact-based analysis. The nature of the current situation in the organisation and its environment can be established with the aid of evidence generated through traditional strategic frameworks and analytical tools.
- Module 4: Capability assessment and prognosis. The current capabilities of the organisation (its internal features) and the coherence or alignment between the external and internal aspects of the organisation are explored.

Diagnosis includes a variety of assessment methods for the business environment and organisational capability, together with classic strategy techniques for gathering evidence and testing hypotheses. The purpose of the diagnostic phase is to paint a rich and reasonably accurate picture of the organisation in its environment. This helps ensure that the strategy development process is working with fresh material that is relevant to the issues and concerns of executives. In this way deep and insightful knowledge and experience is captured in a format in which it can be analysed, shared, communicated and synthesised into effective strategy.

The strategic management process needs to be thought of not only as a knowledge-gaining and learning process, but also as a process of re-perceiving and reframing. High-quality strategic thinking is characterised by reaching different insights into the nature of the business environment and the opportunities for an organisation within that environment. Such insights emerge from the personal experiences of the members of the organisation and a process of experimentation, in which new ideas and business designs are tested in the market-place and from which the organisation gains valuable knowledge about what works and why.

The optional bridge to the strategy development phase is Module 5: Mobilising for change. This module is used when an organisation faces challenges in readying itself for change, which is often revealed in the diagnostic phase. The mobilising for change module catalyses and supports those stakeholders in the organisation who can make or break the changes that will come about during the FutureStep process.

### Phase 2: Strategy development

Strategy is developed using three core techniques to generate and test strategies through social and computer-based simulations.

- Module 6: Ecosystem modelling. The modelling of social, economic and business ecosystems is often a crucial input into the strategy development process. Such models are useful to represent and understand the current state of the strategic landscape in which the organisation is operating. Available modelling techniques range from systems dynamics to adaptive agent modelling; the latter is more effective for highly complex ecosystems.
- Module 7: Scenario development. Scenarios can be developed for an array of different environments or environmental features. For example, they have been used in military contexts to simulate real battlefield conditions, in healthcare to represent different landscapes in which the healthcare system might operate, and in telecommunications and computing to simulate the dynamics of complex economic and technological webs within a variety of business ecosystems. If ecosystem modelling has been carried out before scenario development, the scenarios can represent different states of the business ecosystems the organisation must navigate.
- Module 8: Strategic option development. This technique also includes real option approaches and can be used to develop a portfolio of options for an organisation, which can be mutually exclusive, complementary or path dependent.

The bridge between strategy development and strategy implementation is Module 9: Strategic gaming and simulation. Strategic gaming is the climax of the strategy development process, in which strategic options are tested for robustness and path dependence against a number of scenarios, using a combination of techniques including cross-impact matrices, swot, game theory approaches and adaptive agent modelling.

Linked sets of strategic moves emerge from Module 9, framed within a strategic focus that provides the coherence required to generate complex adaptive strategies as the organisation evolves.

## Phase 3: Strategy implementation

The third phase of FutureStep translates strategy into action in an adaptive way. In this phase the insights and conclusions reached in the strategy development phase are translated into a form in which the organisation can begin implementation, through the strategic agenda. The strategic agenda in turn gives rise to a set of strategic triggers and change initiatives.

◪ Module 10: Development of the strategic agenda. The strategic agenda, which operates as the framework for the execution of the strategy generated in Phase 2, is developed using a balanced scorecard or wheel framework (see Chapter 4). This enables the elements of the diagnosis (before) and the execution (after) phases to be compared and contrasted, so that the success of specific aspects of the organisation's strategy can be evaluated and important lessons learned. The extent to which strategies have created value for the firm and its stakeholders can also be assessed using this framework.

◪ Module 11: Identification of change initiatives. During the development of strategy, the need for changes in a variety of areas in an organisation is identified. This module translates these insights into specific change initiatives, which can range from internally focused things, such as a quality improvement or a culture change programme, to externally oriented things, such as customer satisfaction initiatives, new strategic alliances or new ventures. The strategic agenda is used to track progress in these initiatives, and to filter back the learning into the diagnosis phase in the next planning round.

◪ Module 12: Identification of strategic triggers. During the development of the strategic agenda, two kinds of strategic triggers are identified.
  • External. The key turning points identified in the scenario process (which lead to the evolution of the different scenarios) become the basis for the identification of triggers in the environment that must be scanned for and monitored. This enables the organisation to spot discontinuities and significant

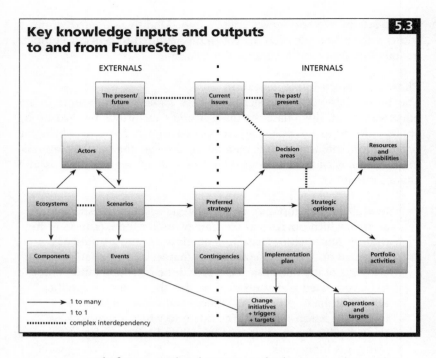

**Key knowledge inputs and outputs to and from FutureStep** `5.3`

events before or as they happen, and take appropriate action on each trigger.

- Internal. The key success factors for the strategic focus of the organisation developed during strategic gaming and simulation enable management to monitor their progress in implementing the strategic focus. Such triggers can be incorporated into a variety of balanced scorecards.

Figure 5.3 summarises the key knowledge inputs and outputs of the whole process, when fully implemented.

The next 12 sections, describing each module in more detail, focus on the practical issues involved in using the FutureStep process to develop adaptive strategies for an organisation, and on ways in which it can be successfully integrated into the management, planning and decision processes in organisations. The process continues to evolve as new challenges demand, although the core of it can now be regarded as best practice, as used by major corporations.

## Module 1: Planning for the strategic management process

In strategic management, as in most other activities, some initial planning is useful as to what the scope of the strategic management process is to be, and what kinds of issues are being addressed at what level. Module 1 deals with the activities required to modify, set up or operate the strategic management process in an organisation. Its objectives are to establish the following.

- Who the key strategic management process stakeholders in the organisation are (this should include, at a minimum, key board directors and senior members of the management team).
- The members of the team responsible for making a success of the strategic management process (this would naturally include any corporate or business unit strategic planning team, as well as the director responsible for strategic management, and could also include other functions such as IT, change management, human resources, training and development as well as business development).
- Specific project objectives for the strategic management process in the organisation.
- The likely stages of the project required to introduce FutureStep into the organisation.

An initial briefing meeting of the stakeholders in the strategic management process is advisable. This should be preceded by engaging stakeholders in conversation about what they see as the requirements for strategy development in the organisation, and what is needed to improve the strategic management process.

The strategy development process begins with a clear overview of the current situation, including:

- the current state of the organisation's purpose and strategy;
- the principal features of the business environment and how it is changing;
- major management and business processes;
- organisational design principles and structure;
- key people and roles in the organisation and their interfaces with and responsibilities towards the strategic management process;
- any frustrations and aspirations in the organisation in respect of the current strategy and planning processes.

## Potential participants in the FutureStep process 5.4

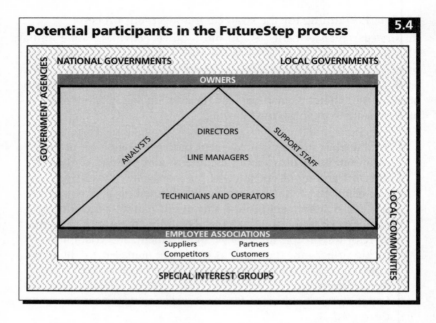

In considering who should be involved in setting up the strategic management process in an organisation, the cast of characters in Figure 5.4 may be useful. Some of the main deliverables produced during this stage should include the following.

- ◪ An overview of the current situation the organisation is in and what this means for how FutureStep is applied.
- ◪ A statement on the objectives, the role of the process and project, and likely stages.
- ◪ A list of stakeholders to consult and interview.
- ◪ Suitable environment and facilities for the strategic management process to be carried out.
- ◪ The members of the team required to launch the FutureStep project.

### Module 2: Strategic issue scan

The keys to shaping and/or adapting to a rapidly evolving, turbulent environment are as follows.

- ◪ To stay in touch with and remain appropriately connected to the networks of individuals and organisations that operate in or influence your organisation's environment.

◪ To be capable of generating and acting on powerful, value-adding insights into changing customer priorities, new technologies, regulations and market dynamics.

The purpose of the strategic issue scan is to refresh the knowledge and understanding of the strategy process stakeholders by taking an outside-in look at the organisation and its challenges and opportunities. The objectives of the strategic issue scan are to:

◪ establish an early understanding of the organisation, its themes, dilemmas and development challenges;
◪ understand the nature of the business ecosystem(s) the organisation operates in at an overview level;
◪ engage stakeholders in the strategic management process and understand their personal and collective concerns and agendas;
◪ provide an opportunity for stakeholders to talk and think freely and expansively about the organisation and the future, thus kick-starting the strategic dialogue which characterises excellent strategic thinking and management.

At the outset of the strategy process it is important to establish the issues that decision-makers and stakeholders believe are crucial to the future success of the business, and to identify trends, events and uncertainties that might affect the future of the organisation. This involves the following.

◪ Selecting stakeholders who can influence the future of the business, as well as experts or "remarkable people" who have an in-depth understanding of the relevant business ecosystem(s).
◪ Interviewing these stakeholders, remarkable people and experts in and around the organisation, using personal modelling techniques to map their knowledge and understanding of the issues they believe need to be addressed in taking the business forward.
◪ Creatively mapping the main themes that emerge from the interviews to highlight important features of the business model (or theory of the business), the environment in which the organisation is operating and the dilemmas that are driving the organisation to learn and develop.

The strategic issue mapping process takes place in roughly three stages.

*Stakeholder interviews*
This stage involves holding the interviews, capturing their output using modelling software, and then writing up and preparing personal maps for each interviewee. The interview process is built on personal modelling sessions in which interviewees are taken through a structured visual brainstorming process. This encourages the emergence of new patterns of thinking alongside the unearthing of current hypotheses about the relationship between the organisation and its environment. Some 20–30 mental models are usually constructed in this process, and then synthesised to establish key themes, dilemmas and development challenges in the organisation and its ecosystem.

In this module it is often possible to glimpse some of the theories of the business that exist in the minds of the stakeholders, and establish the degree of alignment between such theories. Some of the basic values of the stakeholders should also come to the surface, enabling polarities and possible dilemmas between them to be identified. The level of creative or destructive tension between the business as it is and the potential of the business should also become visible. The overall combination of such insights can then be combined into key themes, which are used to feed this information back to the executive group.

At the start of the interview process the focus should be on two main activities. First, agree a list of interviewees. Some interviewees may be chosen on political grounds because it is important to include all stakeholders who could make or break the strategy process. Second, define the trigger question for the interviews, which should be based on the major strategic concerns of the organisation as perceived by the senior management group. Trigger questions can vary widely, depending on the nature of the challenge an organisation faces. Examples are as follows.

◨ What do you believe are some of the key issues for Royal Dutch PTT in developing and growing its business between now and 2002? (This question was used in 1992 to start a major review of the business development strategy for the recently privatised organisation.)
◨ What do you see as some of the key issues arising between now and 2001 which will influence the success of alliance between Hewlett-Packard and Microsoft in developing NT as a premier

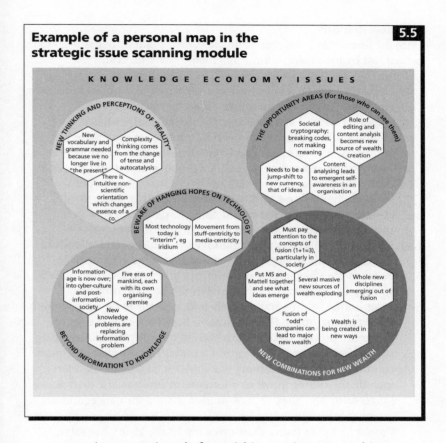

**Example of a personal map in the strategic issue scanning module**

**5.5**

enterprise computing platform? (This question was used in 1998 to generate scenarios and options for HP in its enterprise computing business.)

▧ What do you believe are the major forces and players shaping the future of the financial services industry, and what do you see as the key issues in State Farm's strategy between now and 2002? (This question was used in 1996 to start a review of State Farm's strategy.)

Figure 5.5 is an example of a personal map from an anonymous interviewee.

### Interview analysis

Once the interviews have been completed, four main activities need to be carried out by the project team implementing the process.

- Conduct a theme analysis using a variety of techniques to identify emergent patterns in the issues raised by interviewees.
- Prepare a natural agenda. Once the theme analysis has been completed, it is possible to develop a model of the business within its environment. This shows the direction in which the organisation is heading, given the current mindset and priorities in the business and the forces operating in the interaction between the business and its environment. This is the natural agenda, the strategy that would come to pass if no further intervention were to be undertaken.
- Identify axioms, dilemmas and divergences. The natural agenda forms a default strategy, to the extent that there is agreement between the stakeholders on priorities and issues. Within such a strategy lie axioms: rules that govern the behaviour of the organisation and its stakeholders and are held to be true by the management group. There is always, however, some degree of difference among stakeholders, even at the simplest levels, giving rise to divergences in the natural agenda. The simplest and most common divergences among stakeholders or alliance partners include the degree to which shorter-term profit is favoured above longer-term measures such as market share dominance; and the extent to which investments in high-risk, high-return investments should be made rather than investing in the lower, but safer, returns available in the core business. Such dilemmas can represent profound differences in values and opinions among stakeholders, and need to be worked through using dilemma modelling techniques to avoid major disruptions later on in the strategic management process.
- Select telling quotes and write a story. The last activity in the analysis of the interviews is the preparation of a story that articulates the natural agenda, axioms, divergences and dilemmas to the stakeholders, using quotes from the interviews to bring the story to life. Such a story is capable of recounting how the organisation got to be where it is today, and the choices it faces going into the future. It should also capture some of the personality and culture of the real organisation. Arie de Geus, a

former head of Shell Group Planning, likes to call this the "mirror" for the organisation to look in and see itself for the first time.

In complexity terms, this story becomes the equivalent of John Holland's complex adaptive system developing a model of itself, so that all of the autonomous agents in the organisation suddenly begin to share a common history, identity and starting point for the future, which act as a frame for their decisions and actions. This is the first step in enabling an organisation to become intelligent: to develop self-awareness and understanding of the whole of itself in relation to its environment.

### Feedback to stakeholders

When the natural agenda story and all its components have been completed, it is essential to bounce the penultimate output off the stakeholders holding the positions of greatest difference, as well as some lying towards the centre of the natural agenda, to test the robustness and authenticity of the story. Once this is complete, it is useful to set aside an afternoon to present the natural agenda and all its components to the important stakeholders and any other influential players involved, allowing them to digest the findings before agreeing what the implications are for the next stages in the strategic management process.

It is also essential to maintain the involvement and goodwill of those interviewed and to get the stakeholders to agree how and when it is best to provide feedback to them. Again, this will depend to some extent on the politics of the situation, and the reaction of the stakeholders to the natural agenda and all its components.

The outcomes from the strategic issue scanning stage include the following.

- Shared issues: initial issues and concerns, which may previously have been hidden, are brought out into the open and discussed.
- Clearer, creative strategic thinking: personal models for each interviewee are produced, which help clarify and synthesise their thinking about strategic issues.
- Paradoxes, dilemmas and gaps: the strategic issue theme analysis highlights gaps in strategic thinking in the organisation.
- Corporate natural agenda: a shared natural agenda for the company forms the frame within which further strategic thinking and dialogue can be developed.
- Shared language: some new terminology and language, which will

be used through the rest of the project, is generated and codified.

## Module 3: Fact-finding and analysis

Although the strategic issue scan is able to get at the perceptions of insiders in the organisation as well as some remarkable external perspectives, there may still be a lack of well-documented evidence about the business and the world in which it is operating. The purpose of fact-finding and analysis is as follows.

- To ask important questions about the issues and themes that have been raised in the strategic issue scan.
- To generate hypotheses about these issues and themes, which can be tested through the gathering of qualitative or quantitative evidence.
- To gather the evidence required and analyse it from the perspective of both the questions and the hypotheses, and look for new angles or patterns that might emerge during the course of the investigation.
- To apply appropriate strategic and operational frameworks to present the evidence and highlight the key messages that emerge.

A crucial part of business strategy involves mapping the strategic landscape in which the business in focus is currently operating, so as to address whichever aspects of the landscape are most critical to the future success of the organisation. The objective of fact-finding and analysis is to answer whichever of the following questions (and any others that emerge as important) appear to be most relevant, given the themes that emerged from the strategic issue scan.

- What is the nature of the market-place and its segmentation? What are the profit and growth characteristics of the segments? How are the market and customer priorities changing?
- Who are key partners and potential partners on the demand and the supply sides of the business?
- What role do the different parts of the business play in the value chains and networks they operate in? Which business models appear to be most appropriate for each of these roles, and how co-dependent are they?
- What is the competitive positioning of the business and its offerings, and who are the major competitors (both product specific and generic)?

- What is the business's total value proposition? How competitive is it? How might it be improved?
- What is the nature of the business networks the business currently operates, and how do they contribute to the total value proposition?

There is an exceptionally large array of input material for fact-finding and analysis. Entire courses in marketing, business strategy, competitive intelligence and operations research are devoted to the subject, and the limitations on what can and should be gathered in the way of data should be set by the cost/benefit trade-offs between different analyses.

The most important qualitative input into this stage is the strategic issue scan, which provides some focal points for the analysis and assists in making judgments as to which analyses should receive greatest emphasis. Fact-finding and analysis follows the basic sequence of the scientific method, which in strategic terms translates to the following.

- Questions. Ask the right questions to explain or predict the phenomenon the company is investigating. Be guided by the issues and concerns emerging from the organisation and its decision processes.
- Hypotheses. Generate some hypotheses to explore the possibility space around those questions, as economically as possible. Use the axioms from the natural agenda to generate the initial rule-set of hypotheses. (Hypotheses are essentially rule-like, and framed as: "if ..., then ...".)
- Testbeds. Select real-world testbeds in which evidence can be gathered to confirm or disprove the hypotheses. Ensure these testbeds are representative of the population or ecosystem that the company is seeking to understand.
- Framework. Construct a research framework and methods for sampling and interpreting the evidence gathered.
- Research. Carry out the research, gather the information, process it and present it in formats that allow the hypotheses to be tested.
- Answers. Formulate answers to the original questions based on the lessons learned from the entire fact-finding and analysis process.
- Communicate. Communicate the findings to the principal constituencies that may have an interest in them, especially those that need to be swayed by evidence.

Fact-finding and analysis should lead to a much clearer picture of the business and the strategic landscape in which it is operating. Many of the issues and concerns raised during the strategic issue scan should have been clarified, and the FutureStep project team should now be in a position to begin either the capability assessment or/and the strategy development phase with confidence.

## Module 4: Capability assessment and prognosis

The strategic issue scan, together with fact-finding and analysis, provides a solid baseline from which to begin strategy development, but there may still be unanswered questions about the ability of the organisation to meet the challenges and exploit the opportunities presented to it.

The purpose of the capability assessment module is to determine the organisation's principal development challenges in the light of the strategic issues it faces. The wheel of business evolution and other balanced scorecard frameworks can be used at this stage to provide a powerful framework to organise, synthesise and manage the new knowledge being gained through the strategic learning process. They can also be used to analyse the actions, organisational changes and strategic moves that will need to take place during and after the diagnostic and strategy development phases.

The objectives of the capability assessment module are as follows.

- To understand the nature of the organisation and its environment in terms of the eight sectors of the wheel of business evolution or some other balanced scorecard framework.
- To contrast the strategic challenges the organisation faces with its capability to meet these challenges.
- To establish the priority areas for change in the organisation.

All that has been learned so far through the diagnostic process should be viewed as a potential input to this stage, as well as any other relevant strategic and operational data. The corporate natural agenda and the research findings from fact-based analysis are good starting points. Whoever develops the diagnosis should ensure that they build on relationships with those who have already been interviewed or consulted to explain the purpose of this stage of the work.

A list of interviewees should then be agreed, and decisions taken on which interviews should be carried out to face-to-face and which could be done through a questionnaire.

The capability assessment and prognosis module has three components.

### Gathering evidence

The first step involves conducting interviews (using the wheel), to assess the strategic profile of the organisation. Examples of such strategic profiles, including Xerox, ICI, Prudential, the Civil Aviation Authority, Sainsbury and Wedgwood, are given in Chapter 4. An abbreviated version of the wheel of business evolution questionnaire is set out in Appendix 4.

### Interpreting the evidence

Once the wheel questionnaires have been completed, gathered and analysed, any apparent areas where information appears to be missing can be identified and further investigations carried out to fill those gaps. Some of the main things to look for at this stage include the following.

- Personality. Spotting which kind of organisational personality the business has.
- Sources of energy or motivation. Does the organisation get most of its energy or motivation from the outside (is it extraverted, like Xerox) or does it seek most of its energy or motivation from within (is it intraverted, like Sainsbury)?
- Modes of gathering information. Does the organisation search mainly through its senses for information (like Citicorp and TSB Bank), or does it generally seek information by trying to grasp the essential patterns (like Wedgwood and Virgin)?
- Basis for decisions. Does the organisation rely primarily on analysis for reaching its decisions (thinking, as do the Civil Aviation Authority and IBM), or does it rely primarily on feelings and values for its decisions (feeling, as do 3M and Hewlett-Packard)?
- Style of operation. Does the organisation prefer to conduct its affairs in a planned, orderly, controlled way (judging, as do insurance companies like Prudential), or does it prefer to carry out its business in a flexible, spontaneous way (perceiving, as do creative businesses such as advertising)?
- Sources of change. It is important to understand the balance or imbalance between the sources of change in the organisation. Some organisations may be driven to change largely by external conditions, and may spend most of their time in adaptive mode

(for example, small fashion retailers and PC distributors). Other organisations may be operating to shape their environment in some respects, including high-tech start-ups or large multinationals, which dominate their niches during stable phases in the evolution of their industry or business ecosystem.

◪ External change drivers. What is the nature and extent of change in the organisation's environment and industry or business ecosystem?

◪ Internal change drivers. What is the nature and extent of change in the organisation, and what are the sources of such change?

◪ Shaping organisational capabilities. Does the organisation possess some set of distinctive capabilities, competencies, resources and/or processes relevant to specific aspects of the external change drivers, which might enable it to shape aspects of its environment?

◪ Shaper/adapter alignment. Which aspects of its environment must the organisation adapt to, and how will such adaptation co-evolve with the changes being generated internally by the organisation?

### Diagnosing and communicating the results

Once the evidence from the questionnaires and other sources has been interpreted, an assessment of the priorities for change in the organisation should be documented and communicated. The first step is to present a diagnosis to the project team members and agree with them the implications for the project. Then it is advisable to agree when and how to feed back the diagnosis to the interviewees and other stakeholders in the strategic management process.

The following are some of the outcomes that a capability assessment diagnosis can provide.

◪ An understanding of priorities for change in the organisation, supported by a set of facts, figures and opinions.

◪ A recognition of these priorities by key stakeholders.

◪ A change template for the later process, which contains the initial settings for the key external and internal variables in the organisation to enable the management team to:
  • prioritise the various programmes and initiatives for strategic and operational change in their business;
  • co-ordinate the various change initiatives in the organisation;
  • benchmark the progress made in these change initiatives;
  • balance the efforts made and resources devoted to change

initiatives in accordance with their priorities and
interrelationships;
- link change initiatives tightly to the strategic review process.

## Module 5: Mobilising for change

This stage of the process can be used in at least three different ways.

- If the current challenges for the organisation and its capabilities
  are widely shared and understood, then mobilising for change can
  be used instead of the diagnostic phase 1 as a prelude to the
  strategy development phase 2.
- If, after the capability assessment stage, it is clear that strategy
  development will suffer from a lack of interest or a resistance to
  change owing to cultural or political forces in the organisation,
  then mobilising for change is an essential next step before moving
  into strategy development.
- At any stage in the strategic management process when blockages
  to change or confusion arise among the stakeholders, mobilising
  for change is a useful approach to clarify the change agenda and
  priorities.

The purpose of mobilising for change is to prepare the key
stakeholders in the organisation for the strategy development process, so
that the maximum amount of creativity and enthusiasm is available in
the development of strategy. Mobilising for change can also help to
clarify and consolidate the learning and knowledge gained in the
diagnostic phase, and to provide a powerful kick-off for strategy
development and the later implementation phases.

The objectives of mobilising for change are to establish the following.

- Consensus among the stakeholders in the strategic management
  process on the challenges the organisation faces and the means
  available to develop the capabilities to meet those challenges.
- A broad agenda for analysis, decision-making and change in the
  organisation.
- First-cut plans, timescales and resources for the FutureStep process.

If the diagnostic phase has been completed, all of the outputs from
this phase should be made available to the participants in mobilising for
change. If mobilising for change is being used as a prelude to the strategy

development phase, then relevant evidence of the need for change, and activists for change, should be involved. Because of the political pressures surrounding this particular activity, the project team needs to ensure careful stage management of mobilising for change, so that outcomes are clear. Hence the design of this stage is crucial.

Mobilising for change revolves around facilitated planning and goal-oriented problem-solving sessions, and comprises three strands of work.

### Current state and challenges of the organisation

The results of the diagnostic phase or any other relevant evidence (if the diagnostic stage has not been done) must be synthesised by the project team. This activity culminates in:

- a presentation by senior members of the management team on the organisation, its products, people, markets, and their perception of its challenges; followed by
- a presentation by the FutureStep project team on what the interviews in the diagnostic phase (by personal modelling or the wheel of business evolution) actually showed, as expressed in the natural agenda, axioms and dilemmas.

### Overview of the strategy development and implementation phases

A presentation on the strategy development and implementation processes and their benefits should be preceded by a thorough review of the way in which FutureStep should be applied in the organisation.

### Examination of constraints and next steps

The specific constraints on reaching the goals stakeholders seek for the organisation through the FutureStep process can be examined used the goal-oriented problem-solving approach. Discussion and agreement on how to proceed, including priorities, commitments and timescales, should then occur, based on the solutions identified during the goal-oriented problem-solving exercise. The principal outcome from this stage is agreement or at least clarity among stakeholders about the following.

- Perceived critical issues and emergent themes inherent in creating a robust future for the organisation, that is, a clear statement of the "problem situation".
- Obstacles to change and sources of resistance to change, and how these and any other constraints should be overcome or dealt with.

◪ The issues and challenges facing the organisation on which there exists some degree of consensus about the changes required and solutions available.

◪ An agreed overall project plan, and identified responsibility holders for the main stages of and activities in the FutureStep process.

## Module 6: Business ecosystem mapping

As outlined in Chapter 4, the purpose of business ecosystem mapping is to enable a senior management and/or strategy development team to manage their organisation's learning process about the past, present and future states of their organisation and its environment. Within the structure of the strategy development process, ecosystem mapping can be used as follows at several stages during strategy development.

◪ To document the current state of knowledge about the shape and structure of the current business environment (the baseline strategic landscape).

◪ To establish how future strategic landscapes might evolve, and what the elements of such landscapes would look like (the future strategic landscape maps).

◪ To understand how the component value networks operate in both the baseline and future strategic landscapes, and how different competitive and co-operative games evolve in these networks (the value network game analysis).

These three applications of ecosystem mapping provide snapshots of what the company has learned at each stage of the strategy development process. They are designed to generate different sets of possible outcomes from the present. The baseline and future strategic landscape maps enable the company to:

◪ guide the strategy development process with realistic input;
◪ review the completeness of the work done at each stage in developing strategic options and scenarios;
◪ benchmark what has been learned in the strategy development process.

The inputs into ecosystem mapping include all of the material developed during the diagnostic phase, and in particular the following aspects of the material captured in the personal modelling, wheel of business evolution and fact-based analysis stages.

- The components of the ecosystem and major players, and whether there are any intense centres of co-evolution driving the ecosystem's trajectory.
- The interrelationships between the components, major players and their respective strategic positions.
- How the business in focus fits into the ecosystem.
- Trends and zones of interest in the ecosystem, including answering two questions: what is the structure of the business ecosystems in which the business's networks reside, and how are they evolving? What other business ecosystems compete directly or indirectly with the business's ecosystems?

To ensure a reasonably accurate description of the strategic context of the firm within the ecosystem, a careful choice of external experts will add depth and richness to the emerging picture. These industry and subject-matter experts should be properly briefed to ensure a contextual fit of their material.

It is also essential to ensure that all participants in the strategy development process are working from the best available information. There are a number of iterations to developing a model of the business ecosystem in which the organisation is operating.

- First, develop a baseline ecosystem model using the material listed above under inputs. It is easiest to map the flow of value through the ecosystem by using the left-hand side of a whiteboard as the supply-side and the right-hand side of the whiteboard as the demand-side, and then mapping the interactions among players on the left and right and in between.
- Next, use arrows to map the principal flows and relationships between the different components and players in the ecosystem. Look for intense centres of co-evolution, which might be driving the pace of development of the ecosystem. At this stage it is essential to establish which relationships on the map are complementary or symbiotic and which are competitive; that is, where do the capabilities and offerings of the players act as complements or substitutes for each other?
- Where there are strong competitive or substitution effects between

groups of players or ecosystem components, it is possible that the company is dealing with competing ecosystems. The relationships between firms straddling these competing ecosystems should be mapped especially carefully, as such firms often control key gateways between the ecosystems. Look for signs of "co-opetition", that is, firms that compete with each other on one front but act as allies on another. Such complex relationships need to be carefully handled and well understood.

For each business ecosystem being mapped, it is useful to determine which stage in its life cycle each ecosystem is in. As explained in Chapter 4, ecosystems typically go through four generic life-cycle stages: pioneering, expansion, maturity and renewal. These stages also correspond to the stages of the evolution of markets.[2]

A useful and rapid way of developing ecosystem models is to run one or more facilitated workshops, covering the following areas.

- A definition and example of a business ecosystem.
- Presentations and awareness-setting by invited experts.
- Creating an early version of the organisation's total value chain and the value network surrounding this value chain.
- Mapping on to this value network the population of the ecosystem with player types, examples and their interrelationships, showing complements, substitutes, collaborators, competitors and co-opetitors.
- Capturing and mapping the implications of the main trends in the ecosystem in focus.
- Fleshing out in further detail possible zones of interest, particularly gateway co-opetitors and intense centres of co-evolution.
- Capturing the model, and distributing it for comment and further enrichment to the main strategy stakeholders, as well as external experts who could not be part of the process.

These elements can be repeated where necessary as many times as is required to truly understand the ecosystem(s) in focus. The outcomes from the ecosystem modelling stage include the following.

- The ecosystem model, expressed as both a map and a supporting text description.

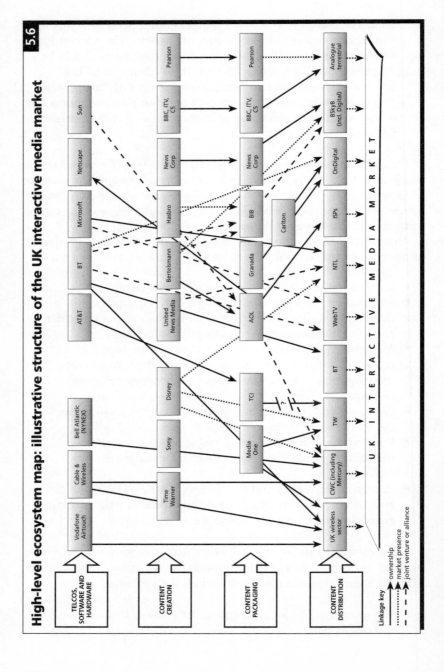

**High-level ecosystem map: illustrative structure of the UK interactive media market**

◪ A picture of the patterns of evolution of the ecosystem, including how it emerged from the past and possible future states it might evolve to.
◪ A clear description of the current role of the organisation in the ecosystem, and what its principal relationships and unique contributions in the ecosystem are.
◪ Possible areas for portfolio evolution.
◪ A shared new language, which can be used to discern patterns that might be critical to the future of the organisation.

Some examples of high-level ecosystem maps are shown in Figures 5.6 and 5.7. It is now possible to map the evolution of the ecosystem(s) through the scenario process, and to explore some of the options for the organisation to co-evolve with the ecosystem(s) it participates in.

## Module 7: Scenario development

Having developed a diagnostic profile, a baseline ecosystem model and strategic options on the way forward for an organisation, it is time to look ahead and discern the multiple possible shapes of the future through the "future fog" surrounding an organisation. Given that the future is both unpredictable and uncertain, it is important to remember the following principles in developing scenarios.

◪ Relevance to the business. Scenarios need to be highly relevant to the situation an organisation is in. This means ensuring that all relevant aspects of the organisation's business ecosystem are addressed in scenarios. Only relevant scenarios are capable of being credible to executives and thereby engaging their deepest assumptions about the future.
◪ Stimulating learning. Scenarios must act as catalysts for organisational learning. They therefore need to be sufficiently challenging to be capable of stretching mindsets, enabling individuals to reframe their current assumptions about the future.
◪ New ways of working together. New knowledge and new ways of seeing things imply changes in relationships and ways of doing things. Scenarios must be capable of bringing new knowledge and ways of thinking into the organisation, and the scenario process must stimulate collaborative dialogue where new ways of working and thinking together are explored.

# High-level ecosystem map: the Microsoft security ecosystem

5.7

| Segmented value chain | On person devices 1 | End-user device security 2 | Transport security 3 | Premises security 4 | Security management 5 | Directories and trust authorities 6 | Content security 7 | Transaction management 8 | Credit assurance 9 | Government policy 10 |
|---|---|---|---|---|---|---|---|---|---|---|
| **Services** A | | | Solution providers, systems integrators | | | | MSFDC | CyberCash | | |
| **Software** – Apps – Tools – OS B | Atally, Spyrus, Datakey / PCSC Workgroup | | | Network Associates | Microsoft | VeriSign | Cylink / Cylink, Frontier, BBN, HP, TIS | | | |
| **Hardware** C | | | Cisco | ICSA | | | | | | |
| **Standards** D | | | | | W3C, IETF | | Internet Mail Consortium / Cylink | OBI / SET Workgroup | | |

**VALUE ELEMENTS**

Microsoft ecosystem member

Where across the economic web are the strongest value creation opportunities?

172

The purpose of the scenario development stage is to build relevant, stretching scenarios of the environment and business ecosystems in which an organisation operates or might operate. Such scenarios are designed to test the strategic options available to the organisation beyond their limits and generate new information in the process of strategic gaming and simulation. Scenarios are thus the equivalent of flight simulators, in which different designs or organisations can be destruction tested. But there is one difference: scenarios also highlight opportunities and evolutionary dynamics in the complex socio-economic and technological webs in which post-millennial businesses operate. There are two kinds of scenarios.

- Ecosystem scenarios, which model the different possible future states of a business ecosystem(s). Ecosystem scenarios are essential when dealing with complex, dynamic ecosystems to capture actionable insights. They are also useful if the organisation is seeking to understand disruptive technologies or similarly complex phenomena.
- Generic scenarios, which model the dynamics of the key features of the environment of an organisation. Generic scenarios are useful if the environment is anywhere on the range from simple stable, through simple dynamic to complex stable.

The objectives of the scenario stage are as follows.

- To build an understanding of how the forces in the ecosystem may behave and interrelate in the future.
- To establish and define a small number of plausible scenarios, each portraying a different view of future.

During the diagnostic phase, and ecosystem modelling, a large number of assertions, insights and hypotheses about the possible future shape of the business environment and the ecosystem will have emerged. All of these are useful in the scenario development process, which benefits from the input of as many divergent and unusual perspectives as possible. If there is a time in the strategy development process to be creative and out-of-the-box, this is it. This is why organisations as diverse as Shell, IBM and General Motors deploy a vision network of remarkable people who bring challenging perspectives to bear on the mindsets of the senior management group. It is essential to involve as many of these kinds of people as possible in the scenario development process.

If ecosystem mapping has not been done before scenario development, it is important to find and brief good external experts, who can provide a fresh perspective on the organisation and its environment.

Scenarios are developed in a process that usually reaches its climax in a two-day workshop, as outlined below.

### Establishing zones of perceived uncertainty

Participants in the scenario building process are asked a trigger question to describe what they see as the driving forces in the environment that could influence the future of their industry or business ecosystem. These driving forces are displayed on a whiteboard and tracked on computer software designed for the purpose. Once the display is complete, the attractors for the individual forces emerge through a clustering process. Each cluster is then labelled, and the consequent cluster titles are used to examine the relationships between the clusters of driving forces. Relationships are mapped using arrows and keywords to describe the interaction between clusters of driving forces.

### Mapping tracks to multiple futures

The output of the previous stage is a dynamic map of the principal forces operating in an organisation's business ecosystem. This is then used at a high level as a logic diagram to check for consistency when building scenarios. This map also contains the predetermined elements, driving trends and uncertainties that are the raw material used to build scenarios. Uncertainties that are critical to the future of the organisation become the turning points leading to different scenario outcomes.

To start the process the uncertainties are separated from the other driving forces and mapped on to a force field, where the criticality and uncertainty of each are evaluated. The uncertainties that are most critical and uncertain are then used as the core set of critical uncertainties from which the turning points between the scenarios can be generated.

At this stage, complexity and chaos theory are being used to generate information through the deliberate creation of chaos in the minds of the participants in the process, although at a subconscious level. The rigour of the process and the skill of the facilitators are critical to the successful conclusion of this phase, as uncertainty often generates a high degree of anxiety in those experiencing it.

Turning points can now be generated by using a technique that enables participants to imagine different kinds of outcomes from each area of critical uncertainty. These outcomes are defined as different future states of each critical uncertainty, which can be qualitative and/or quantitative, depending on the nature of the variables inherent in the critical uncertainty.

To identify the core part of the scenario skeletons, which emerge later in the process, synergistic combinations of flips, flops, flaps and/or fleps are then identified (the terms used here are derived from circuit-board design). The logic of how these different outcomes form turning points then needs to be established to build scenario skeletons. The minimum number of skeletons required is two and the maximum is four. It has been established that human brains are not sufficiently challenged by one scenario, even if it is different from the default scenario in the organisation, but they find it difficult to handle more than about four alternative scenarios at once.

### Building multiple scenarios from trends and turning points

Scenario skeletons then need to be built, using the logic of the turning points to identify those predetermined elements and driving trends that are relevant to the logic of each particular scenario skeleton. Story lines for each scenario skeleton are then created, much as a movie director, writer and designer would work together in establishing the basic plot line of a story for a film. The plots must, however, obey the logic of the driving forces map and be plausible and relevant to members of the organisation, otherwise they will be rejected by the corporate immune system as science fiction.

It is advisable to appoint a champion for each scenario, who can co-ordinate the work of a team of people in and around the organisation to research and scan the business environment in general and the organisation's business ecosystem in particular for supporting evidence. This can be used to flesh out their specific scenario skeleton into a fully fledged story, complete with scenic backdrops, significant characters or players and a dramatic script, which describes the logic of the scenario through the unfolding of a series of events according to the underlying plot line described in the scenario skeleton.

The more vividly this "filming" activity can be carried out the better. The use of multimedia and other resources is often highly effective in helping the organisation members involved to identify with, and be entertained by, each scenario. Visual aids such as newspaper clippings, diagrams, drawings and charts are important ingredients in developing a story for each scenario. They can then be put together in a scenario book for the participants.

Each scenario should also be mapped to demonstrate the business ecosystem consequences of the scenario logic. This involves taking the baseline ecosystem map and showing the ecosystem's migration path over time to the future strategic landscape described by each scenario. Specific issues that should be addressed include:

- the market segments of interest in each particular scenario;
- the kinds of customer value propositions offered;
- the specific products and services that comprise these offerings;
- the strategic architecture of the organisation in its value network, including key business processes;
- the technologies, partners (demand and supply side) and competencies that are required;
- the resource implications for the business ecosystem of each scenario;
- the competitive dynamics in each scenario.

It is important to remember that the organisation in focus in this exercise should feature only as a minor part of the ecosystem map, as the purpose of the map is to provide an outside-in perspective. The components of the scenario development should include:

- definition and example of a scenario;
- review of the business ecosystem model, together with presentations by industry experts or remarkable people;
- identification of driving forces, drawing on trends as well as stable and unstable components;
- creation of 2–4 alternative futures using the method outlined above;
- naming of the scenarios, their comparison and review of futures;
- creation of scenario timelines and fleshing out with driving trends and predetermined elements.

Of course, there is a limit to how much can be done in the two or so days of a workshop, so the outputs of the workshop are effectively skeleton scenarios. The work of fleshing out the skeletons into living stories of the future, which can engage an audience, has to be done afterwards. Scenario-building teams are thus usually put to work after the workshop to develop the skeleton scenarios into full-blown scenarios, including presentation material and multimedia to bring them alive. The scenario development stage has several important outcomes.

- ◪ Scenarios in a form that can be presented to, and entertain, an audience.
- ◪ Critical events, roles, players and turning points to alternative futures in each scenario.
- ◪ Themes common to all the scenarios, including an analysis of the deep structure underlying the scenarios, which is a synthesis of the baseline ecosystem and driving forces models.
- ◪ Timelines suggesting the speed and timing of events in each scenario.

Scenario development is a powerful process for challenging and stretching the mindsets of the senior management group in an organisation. It can be enough to lead to major breakthroughs in the way in which the business environment, ecosystems or industries are perceived by senior management, and to potential reinvention of the industry or ecosystem and changes in the rules of the game.

The most powerful application of scenarios, however, lies in their use within the strategic gaming and simulation stage described in Module 9 below. This framework enables the specific consequences of particular strategic moves to be examined, and enables the organisation to build a powerful repertoire of patterns of strategic moves centred on a core strategic thrust. Figures 5.8 and 5.9 on the following pages show some scenarios developed for a healthcare business.

## Module 8: Strategic option and business model generation

Strategic choice is a prerequisite for the longevity of any organisation. The history of business is littered with the corpses of organisations that failed to maintain sufficient strategic options. Such organisations literally run out of time, resources and options. The best time to develop strategic choice is before troubled times arrive. Strategy is most powerful when creating a future, not when dealing with one that is happening already.

It is difficult for successful organisations and management teams that "stick to their knitting" to appreciate the value of strategic choice. In delayered, downsized organisations, executives focus more than ever on the detail of getting things done in a leaner, faster, better way. Although this is necessary for immediate results, quick-results myopia puts the organisation at serious risk in the medium to longer term. Strategic options are critical to building in the flexibility and robustness in any organisation, and are thus an important part of the core strategic management process.

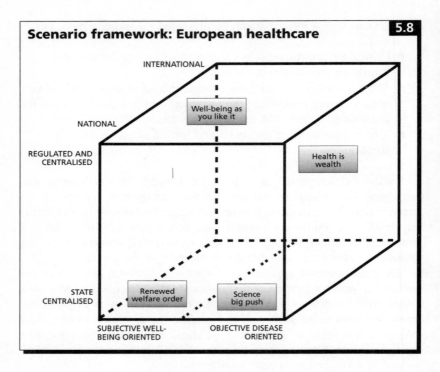

**Scenario framework: European healthcare** 5.8

The purpose of the strategic option stage is to generate distinct and/or complementary strategic options and business models. The objectives of generating business models and strategic options for an organisation are as follows.

- ⬛ To establish consensus on what the current business model (or business idea) is.
- ⬛ To generate a set of distinctive strategic options and sub-options suitable for the business of the future, which are accessible from the business model of today.

Any and all material developed during the diagnostic phase and business ecosystem modelling phase is relevant to the internal state or configuration of the organisation, and is essential input to the development of strategic options. Information about the resources, infrastructure, competencies and capabilities of the organisation, together with historical information about its evolution and its current state, form

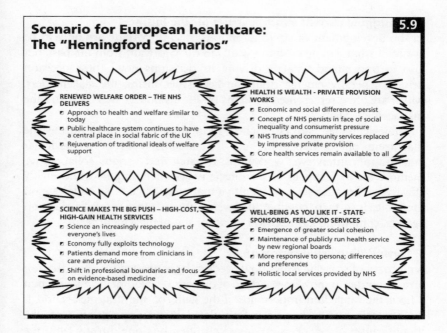

**Scenario for European healthcare: The "Hemingford Scenarios"**
5.9

**RENEWED WELFARE ORDER – THE NHS DELIVERS**
- Approach to health and welfare similar to today
- Public healthcare system continues to have a central place in social fabric of the UK
- Rejuvenation of traditional ideals of welfare support

**HEALTH IS WEALTH - PRIVATE PROVISION WORKS**
- Economic and social differences persist
- Concept of NHS persists in face of social inequality and consumerist pressure
- NHS Trusts and community services replaced by impressive private provision
- Core health services remain available to all

**SCIENCE MAKES THE BIG PUSH – HIGH-COST, HIGH-GAIN HEALTH SERVICES**
- Science an increasingly respected part of everyone's lives
- Economy fully exploits technology
- Patients demand more from clinicians in care and provision
- Shift in professional boundaries and focus on evidence-based medicine

**WELL-BEING AS YOU LIKE IT - STATE-SPONSORED, FEEL-GOOD SERVICES**
- Emergence of greater social cohesion
- Maintenance of publicly run health service by new regional boards
- More responsive to persona; differences and preferences
- Holistic local services provided by NHS

the initial mosaic picture of the organisation. It is also possible that the business is unfolding according to a previous design, or imitating a well-known competitor or role model, so executives should be alert to what is happening to those ideas in practice.

Based on the original interviewing and facts-based analysis, the current business idea can be used as a starting point for this stage of strategy development. There are five main steps in creating a set of powerful strategic options for the organisation.

### 1. Describing the current theory of the business

The process of developing strategic options should begin with an analysis of the current theory of the business. This enables managers to understand the driving forces that got the organisation to where it is now. Why has the organisation been successful, and what has kept it there? Or, if the organisation is experiencing difficulties, what made the difference between the successful state and the current difficulties? A good description of the theory of the business enables managers to build strategic options that are rooted in current reality, and to be aware of those elements in the history of the business that should form part of the core identity of the business.

## 2. Identifying current strategic issues for the business

In the development of strategic options, it is important not only to be aware of what the organisation wants to carry forward from the past, but also to understand what is driving its decisions now. These decision drivers generally emerge from the key issues facing the stakeholders, which are often represented by items on the agenda of the board and the management team.

Strategic issues can be elicited in a number of ways during the diagnostic phase, depending on the circumstances of a particular organisation. Interviews, workshops, research and various collaborative methods are available to map strategic issues, including new and highly effective techniques such as cognitive mapping. Once these issues are on the table, it is then possible to develop them into a strategic decision agenda, containing key decision areas for the management team.

## 3. Formulating key decision areas

A given set of strategic issues now needs to be converted into key decision areas, in order to move to the stage of options development in a way that reflects the range and importance of the items on the strategic agenda. If the strategic agenda has been formulated in an appropriate way, the identification of key decision areas can often be done directly from the strategic agenda categories. More often, however, further work on the strategic agenda items is required to translate these items into genuine areas for decision rather than a mere laundry list of action items. The latter outcome indicates that either the management team has not yet come to grips with the things that are truly strategic in their business, or the elicitation of the issues was superficial.

Once the key decision areas have been formulated and the management team is satisfied that the list of areas is complete, it is then possible to generate tactical options in each decision area. These tactical options are used as the raw material from which strategic options are generated later in the process.

## 4. Generating tactical options in each decision area

The word "decision" derives from the Latin word meaning "to cut off". Thus when a decision is made options are usually cut off or reduced in number. Not all decisions are irrevocable, although most decisions limit the choices available to an organisation.

A prudent manager therefore considers as many options as is feasible within a given window of time before making a decision, thereby reducing the risk that a snap decision may commit the organisation irrevocably to a path or direction from which there is no return. Tactical options thus not only form the basis for the generation of strategic options; they also ensure that managers do not rush into important decisions blind or partially sighted, and that a wide range of options is considered, including obvious options and lateral creative options.

What often happens in organisations is that choices between different tactical options are made using political rather than objective criteria. Particularly where there is time pressure and stress, managers select the option that appears most familiar and in their own best interests, rather than the best option from the organisation's point of view.

All managers also have their complex adaptive and hidden agendas, which they are pursuing alongside and sometimes in conflict with the formal organisational agenda. It is crucial that tactical options are selected which:

- offer best overall advantage for the organisation, rather than merely being good for one of its parts;
- align with other tactical options to produce a coherent direction and minimise conflict between such options.

### 5. Synthesising strategic options

To combine options in such a way as to exploit their synergies, managers are led through a clustering exercise where they are asked to identify synergistic tactical options. A consensus of the management group or team is then developed to ensure that the clusters of options are in fact coherent and internally synergistic. To develop clusters of tactical options into strategic options, further thought must be given to the following.

- The strategic thrust of each cluster. What are the strategic consequences of pursuing this set of options?
- How easy would it be to implement each cluster of tactical options?
- To what extent would the thrust involve radical change for the organisation?

Once the full nature of each cluster has been explored, a narrative description of each option should be developed and a title selected. The set of strategic options is now ready to be tested against the scenarios described in Module 9. The strategic option generation process usually culminates in a two-day workshop covering the following.

◪ A review and confirmation of the current business idea.
◪ Agreement on critical issues and decision areas.
◪ Development of ranges of tactical options to address each decision area.
◪ Build-up of strategic options through synergistic combinations of the tactical options.

The outcomes of the strategic option generation stage include the following.

◪ A definition of the current business, its value propositions, capabilities and stakeholder motivators.
◪ A set of decision areas driving the current senior management agenda.
◪ A viable set of 3–4 alternative full-scale strategic options, each made up of sub-options that each address one or more of the decision areas.

The strategic option generation process is in itself valuable, and in some strategy processes forms the highlight of activities. However, the real power of the strategic options is the way in which they come to life and evolve when they are played out during the strategic gaming and simulation exercises of Module 9.

## Module 9: Strategic gaming and simulation

Complexity theory (and experience of life) teaches that although the future is likely to be unpredictable in detail and specific content, there are broad patterns that may recur over time in human relations. Such archetypal patterns are what complexity modelling and strategic gaming are specifically designed to detect, predict and/or create.

Although it is not possible to eradicate uncertainty or prevent things turning out contrary to desires or expectations, it is possible to navigate and manage complexity. Complexity can be managed to the extent that it can be rationally understood (cognitive strategies). If individual cognition is insufficient, it is possible to use human and computer networks intuitively to process complexity and uncertainty (social computing strategies). The FutureStep process builds on both cognitive and social computing approaches to manage complexity.

Strategic gaming and simulation enable management teams to focus on the strengths and weaknesses of a variety of strategic options, and genuinely to get to grips with the way in which these options interact in different ways with different kinds of futures. In this stage, the different strategic options developed in Module 8 are tested for robustness and reality, during a business scenario cross-impact matrix workshop. The ultimate purpose of strategic gaming and simulation is to enable the key business and management stakeholders to do the following.

- Identify the strategic direction and options that appear to be most robust and desirable in the different possible futures the business might face.
- Articulate a renewed vision of the desired future business ecosystem from the organisation's perspective (where we want to be).
- Generate a robust statement of strategic intent, which says clearly how the organisation is going to get to where it wants to be and embodies the learning from the cross-impact exercise.
- Define some of the pathways that would enable the organisation to influence its business ecosystem to move towards the desirable future state. This can include combinations of strategic moves.

The main inputs to the strategic gaming and simulation stage are the scenarios and strategic options. Because the strategic gaming and simulation stage is the high-point of the strategy development process, it must involve the stakeholders. Involvement works best if they come prepared to champion either a scenario or a strategic option. Champions should be thoroughly briefed to extract the maximum benefit from their participation.

### Simulation modelling

The building of strategic simulation models to simulate the evolutionary process can be an exceptionally powerful way of gaining non-obvious, counter-intuitive insights into the characteristics of a strategy and the worlds that it must navigate to survive, thrive or perish. In such simulations, strategic options and business designs are tested for robustness in the different landscapes envisaged by the scenarios, using adaptive agents and modelling approaches based on game theory or systems dynamics.

Simulation modelling is a powerful tool, but on its own it does not have the power of strategic gaming to engage the strategy stakeholders in a voyage of discovery through the strategic landscapes in which they may one day have to operate.

### Strategic gaming

The most powerful way to gain human insight into and learning from the interaction of the strategic options in each scenario is to engage the strategy stakeholders in a strategic gaming process. This process is all the richer for the simulation modelling work done alongside and in support of it, but stakeholders must interact with and learn from each other, as well as renegotiate their relationships, so a live process is required.

This live process builds from the preparation and rehearsal of the strategic options and scenarios by champions from among the senior management group. The only way in which they can engage mentally and emotionally in the landscapes of the future is to try living in them, implementing the strategic options that are available to the firm. Gaming is thus a way of refreshing and testing the mental models and mindsets of senior management, getting at some of their most cherished assumptions about the world, their business and each other.

The climax of this process is a three-day facilitated workshop, which includes the following.

- Rich, multimedia-supported story-telling about each scenario and the features of each strategic option.
- An evaluation of each option in each scenario (this stage links strongly with the simulation modelling process, as computer simulations can be compared with gaming outcomes if required).
- A review of the capabilities needed for survival in all scenarios (robustness).
- A review of the features of the strategic focus that may emerge from the options, and the complementarity, mutual exclusiveness and/or path dependence of the strategic options.
- A trial run in developing a coherent vision and strategic intent for further testing in the organisation.

The key aspects of strategic gaming and simulation are discussed below.

### Testing strategies for robustness

Following the presentation and story-telling around the options and scenarios, a cross-impact (or evaluation) matrix is set up to represent the intersections between the options and scenarios, as shown in Figure 5.10. As the participants in the strategy development process go through the cross-impact matrix cells, testing the robustness of each strategic option, they are learning lessons at three levels.

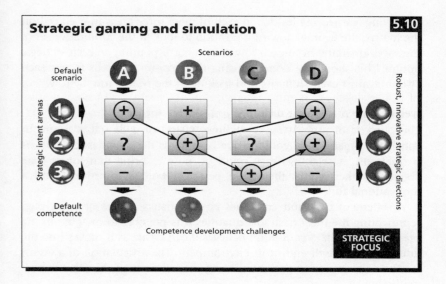

- Outside-in strategic landscape dynamics. Each cross-impact cell contains important messages about the way in which each strategic option interacts with the strategic landscape depicted in the scenario. Using a variant of the SWOT method known as SWOTI (strengths, weaknesses, opportunities, threats and interesting), participants are encouraged to build a dynamic model showing the impact of the scenario on the strategic option in the particular cell being considered. These outside-in lessons define what the impact of the strategic landscape on the strategic option is, and what the landscape looks and feels like when attempts are made to implement the strategic option.
- Inside-out value network responses. Depending upon the nature of the strategic landscape in each cross-impact cell, the organisation may choose to structure its value network differently to orchestrate the maximum possible beneficial response to the particular landscape.
- Robustness messages. Having evaluated the outside-in and inside-out messages of a particular landscape and the responses that could be orchestrated, executives are then in a position to ask: what key elements would make the strategic option more or less robust in this particular scenario?

Having learned the lessons in each of these three areas in each cell on the matrix, the team is now in a position to look at the cumulative set of messages emerging from each row of cells corresponding to each strategic option. This should be done by using the cross-impact cells to test each option against each scenario, and looking at the results row by row.

### Articulating a coherent vision of a desirable future

The purpose of articulating a coherent vision of a desirable future in which the organisation could thrive is to focus the organisation and its partners on those things they could do now to bring that future state about. In other words, the vision performs both a directional and a motivational function.

A statement of vision embodies characteristics, values or principles, representing the most desirable qualities it is possible to imagine in the present, which the organisation believes it can create as it moves into the future, both in itself and in its environment. The articulation of a vision for the organisation is generated using the columns of the cross-impact matrix by:

- defining what learning and development challenges the organisation faces in each cross-impact cell;
- identifying the core competencies and distinctive capabilities the organisation would require to compete successfully in each scenario, whatever strategic option was being pursued;
- understanding in what kind of world the organisation would be most successful, given its current distinctive capabilities, and the lead time and resources required to develop new capabilities;
- defining the kinds of actions and thinking that could help create the kind of future in which the organisation could make its greatest contribution.

During the course of building scenarios and using them to test strategic options, participants usually gain strong impressions about the desirability of each scenario. The diversity of the human race means that it is also usual to find different people who prefer different scenarios, even within the same company or management team. There is often, however, some consensus within a group as to which world they prefer as a whole, which is a good starting point for developing a vision.

The vision material developed by the participants ties in closely with the inside-out lessons learned in the cross-impact matrix, which provide signposts as to how the organisation would need to orchestrate itself and its value network to realise the vision.

## Developing strategic focus

A strategic focus comprises the unique combination of offerings, capabilities and markets that the organisation believes will provide the most attractive returns in the short to medium term. The strategic focus emerges from the strategic gaming exercise as a combination of the vision for the organisation and the most robust strategic option.

The strategic focus is the starting point for developing a statement of strategic intent, which articulates how the organisation will realise its vision. Individuals and organisations share the common intention to survive and continue or extend themselves through time and space. What expression of strategic intent will result in the fruition of this intention?

- To be the leading player in the industry?
- To make a return on investment of 18% on revenue of $10 billion by 2005?
- Or will to be the best in xyz line of business suffice?

Unfortunately, such simplistic statements of exhortation and ambition do not provide sufficient information to generate intelligent action; effective self-organisation cannot come from such simple expressions. A statement of strategy must become a statement of design through which the principles, processes and practices of an organisation are developed. These statements must represent the whole as seen from any location in the organisation. It is important to note that statements of strategy should not imply anything about the future, even though they provide a blueprint and conceptual schema from which the future will be created. Strategic intent is a statement of design for creating a desirable future (stated in present terms). The ideal purpose of the statement of strategic intent is to provide for every member of the organisation and its principal business partners:

- a theory
- an understanding
- a structure of interpretation, or
- an orientation to the world.

Each individual, on interpreting a particular strategic intent, will look at what is going on in his or her environment and be able to make choices that are aligned with the choices and actions of others. Each individual will be able to count on others to take actions that will result in self-organising alignment, often without communication.

An effective statement of strategic intent embodies sufficient ambiguity to generate creativity and enough clarity to evoke common understanding. In other words, the statement of strategic intent should contain only a few elements and requires active interpretation to make sense of it. If the statement is too complex, however, it will be difficult to translate into immediate action and could result in implementation chaos. Some examples of simple yet clear strategic intent include the following.

- Komatsu: "Surround Caterpillar" (or "Maru C" as it became known in Japanese)
- NEC: "Develop/integrate communications and computers"
- Disney: "Keep it clean, keep it friendly, make it a real fun place to be – and make sure that it is that way for employees as well as guests"
- Hewlett-Packard: "Improve the results people get at work and in the home through innovative information technology"

It must be emphasised that although the development of such simple yet powerful statements is one of the principal outcomes of this stage, in practice the process of getting to such a statement has to be tackled bottom-up, working from a great deal of detail rooted in the lessons learned from the cross-impact evaluation process. It is also essential that such statements of strategic intent are fully fleshed out with the requisite level of detail to enable a management team to have a shared model of what the implementation implications are.

The outcomes from the strategic gaming and simulation stage will include the following.

- A coherent vision: an agreed proto-vision for the organisation, which can be fleshed out into a fuller picture with the involvement of the key stakeholders in the organisation.
- Opportunities, threats and contingencies: a wider understanding by the key players of the opportunities and threats that have to be planned for, and the contingencies that can serve as the first point for developing scanning triggers.
- Strategy simulation models, which can be used to demonstrate the

interaction of different strategies within a variety of environments.
- Strategic focus/intent: the proposed way forward for the organisation, including the strategic focus and statement of strategic intent.
- Strategic moves: depending on whether the strategic options were mutually exclusive, complementary or path-dependent, a set of strategic moves comprising agreed chosen parts of the original strategic options can also be derived from the exercise.
- Robustness of core strategy: more robust strategies and sub-strategies, and agreement on no-hopers.

Once the robustness messages, vision and strategic intent have been digested, the organisation should be ready to move into implementation mode to deliver the strategic intent. Three further critical outputs of the cross-impact matrix should be taken forward to guide the future evolution of the organisation.

- Contingency triggers identified in the scenarios should be designed, integrated into the scanning process and then activated in the planning process.
- Performance measures implicit in the strategic intent should be formalised and then integrated into the decision processes of the organisation.
- The campaigns, programmes and initiatives required on the strategic agenda of the senior team to deliver the vision and strategic intent should be fleshed out and given milestones before being integrated into the planning process.

Before this can happen, however, the full organisational significance of the revitalised strategic intent and the vision must be understood, together with the implications this has for organisational change. The senior team should deal with these issues before it can move on and engage the rest of the organisation in a dialogue based on the work done in the first two phases of the FutureStep process.

## Module 10: Development of the strategic agenda

Once a strategic intent has been formulated, the organisation can begin to move coherently in a specific direction. A well-formulated strategic intent is the starting point for developing a strategic agenda and a business design, incorporating the essence of that design around which:

- a clear set of strategic objectives can be formulated (one of the principal objectives will include strategic positioning within the business ecosystem);
- the organisation and its value network can be aligned to harness energy and commitment;
- distinctive capabilities and competencies can be identified and built;
- relevant markets and segments can be defined;
- resources and infrastructure can be captured and committed;
- strategic architectures and business processes can be designed and implemented;
- a variety of strategic options can be nurtured, providing the basis for the flexibility required in an uncertain and rapidly changing environment.

These items in themselves are both outcomes and processes, and ends and means. They represent the essential elements required to create value in a competitive world. These seven elements interact as a system, so that any business design that emerges from a strategic intent lacking one or more of them will fail. Equally, even if all seven elements are present, but are not mutually reinforcing, it is probable that the business will not realise its full potential.

The objectives of developing the strategic agenda include the following.

- To develop accurate maps of the business landscapes and ecosystems in which the organisation is operating. These should have a sufficient level of detail to enable the positioning of the organisation in its value network, and the moves of the organisation and its collaborators and competitors, to be captured.
- To define and agree on the direction and high-level core strategies that will actually be followed by the organisation within these landscapes and ecosystems.
- To complete the "after" picture of the capability assessment carried out in Module 4, and to use it to identify which new or improved capabilities the organisation needs to carry out the strategic intent.
- To sketch a preliminary business design, which can deliver the strategic intent within the capabilities the organisation has available or can develop or access.

◪ To gain an initial understanding of which key initiatives are required to make the strategic intent and vision happen through these capabilities.
◪ To put in place a strategic scorecard, which the senior managers and the organisation can use to track progress towards the vision and objectives of the organisation and to learn from.

Once the material generated from strategic gaming and simulation is recorded and disseminated to key strategy stakeholders, the principal inputs required to develop the strategic agenda are as follows.

◪ The vision and strategic intent statements developed in Module 9, as well as a summary of the principal insights and learning points from the strategic gaming and simulation.
◪ The capability assessment developed in Module 4.
◪ The ecosystem maps developed in Module 6.

The process of developing a strategic agenda has five principle stages.

### Business landscape and ecosystem maps
The lessons of strategic gaming and simulation are used to describe the following.

◪ Business landscapes. These are generated from the predetermined elements and driving forces in the scenarios. Headings such as political, economic, social and technological can be used to classify the different forces operating in the strategic landscape if this is required. The goal is to pin down elements that are fixed in the strategic landscape, or are moving in predictable directions.
◪ Business ecosystems. Based on the strategic landscape and value network response descriptions generated during the cross-impact workshop, it is now possible to describe the different possible ecosystems or states of the current ecosystem in which the organisation might need to operate. This description also details the types of games being played in each ecosystem, who the players are, and which role each of them plays in the ecosystem. It is now possible to begin to describe the moves that the organisation needs to make to enable it to realise its vision and strategic intent.

## Strategic direction and core strategies

To define and agree on the direction and high-level strategies that the organisation will actually follow, the key strategy stakeholders must have the opportunity to review, comment on and revise the vision and strategic intent to their mutual satisfaction. This is an important part of the process, and failing to do this could lead to lack of ownership of the outcomes of the entire strategic management process.

Thus there needs to be plenty of healthy debate, and the proto-vision and strategic intent should ideally be discussed at all levels in the organisation. Communications forums should be arranged, and the implications of the proto-vision and strategic intent outlined and discussed.

Once ownership of the proto-vision and strategic intent has been embedded in the management group and the organisation, it is necessary to flesh out both the vision and the intent by making the following elements of the strategy more explicit.

- The key markets and value propositions for each market.
- The distinctive capabilities needed for each value proposition, and in which areas the firm will be making a unique contribution through its own innovation trajectory, and in which areas the partners, allies and/or co-opetitors of the firm will be bringing their own unique contributions to the value proposition.
- The competencies and resources necessary to make the strategy work.

At this stage it is often useful to run a workshop in which these tasks are carried out, along with the use of a matrix to highlight the essential processes required to develop and deliver sustainable customer value in each key market.

## Capability assessment: part 2

It is now important to assess whether the organisation is equipped to carry out the strategic intent. Does it have the capabilities and characteristics required? This step starts with the capability assessment developed in Module 4, which is now the "before" picture of the organisation's capability. Both the proto-vision and the strategic intent will place new demands on the organisation, and it is essential to ensure that it is able to meet these demands. There are four areas to check.

◻ The critical success factors (CSFS) for the vision. That is, which factors are critical to ensuring that the vision is realised? For example, Hewlett-Packard's vision of making people's lives easier and more fun at home and at work through information technology requires HP to be a partner of choice for the best high-tech companies in the world, including Microsoft, Nokia and a host of Internet portal and service providers. Another CSF requires HP to be one of the lowest-cost but highest-quality manufacturers in the world.

◻ The core capabilities required to deliver the strategic intent in each area, and the business processes required to harness these capabilities and convert them into customer benefits and long-term customer satisfaction.

◻ The relevance of particular processes to specific CSFS. This is achieved by putting the CSFS along the top of a matrix and the key business processes along the left-hand side. Then use the matrix to test processes against CSFS to find the relevance of particular processes to specific CSFS, and to gauge the strength or state of the process relative to the requirements of the CSF.

◻ The statement of capability requirements. Using the analysis carried out on CSFS, capabilities and relevance of processes, complete the "after" picture of the capability assessment carried out in Module 4 and use it to identify which new or improved capabilities the organisation needs to implement its strategic intent.

### Business design

In this step the strategic management and senior management teams sketch a preliminary business design that can deliver the strategic intent while meeting the requirements for success in the landscapes and ecosystems the business will operate in. The form a business takes will depend on the three fundamental design principles required if it is to be designed for intelligence. These are covered in greater detail in Chapter 3: flexible operations, creative structural tension and customer pre-eminence. Many off-the-shelf business and organisational designs are available for specific types of situation and function. These can be used to improve the way things are done in an organisation.

During business design, the strategy wheel elements of leadership style, organisational values, management processes and knowledge management (see Chapter 3) should be evaluated to ensure that these softer aspects of the organisation are aligned to the changes taking place in the strategy and the business design.

At this stage financial business models can also be produced for the first time to assess the viability and attractiveness of the business design(s), but great care must be taken not to throttle promising new ideas through pseudo-rigorous financial analysis.

### Strategic scorecard

The last step in creating the strategic agenda requires the management team to put in place a strategic scorecard, which the key players in the organisation can use to:

- track progress towards the vision and objectives of the organisation; and
- trigger learning reviews and capture strategic lessons learned during the implementation of the new strategic intent.

Some of the main issues in developing and applying effective performance measures for the strategic scorecard are as follows.

- Are the measures appropriate to the vision and strategic intent?
- Do they measure the strategic dimensions of the business design?
- How well are performance measures integrated with the value and cost drivers in the business model?
- Do the management processes make extensive use of current performance measures?
- How good is the organisation at using performance measures for the purposes of improving control and accelerating learning?
- How extensive is the use of the major performance measures at different levels in the business?

The principal outcomes from the stage during which the strategic agenda is created are as follows.

- A widely shared vision and strategic direction for the organisation.
- A clear statement of the preferred strategy and sub-strategies to be followed, expressed in terms of both the components of the portfolio and the distinctive capabilities and competencies required.
- The main themes and assumptions of the strategy.

- A reinvigorated business design capable of delivering the strategic intent and vision.
- An initial view of the initiatives required in delivering the strategy.
- The apparent risks and contingencies involved.

## Module 11: Identifying and implementing key changes

Having developed a strategic intent and begun the process of developing a dialogue based on the strategic agenda outlined above, it is now essential to induce change in the organisation so as to begin to deliver on the new vision and business design. This is achieved by building on the work done in developing the strategic agenda, and translating the strategic agenda into specific projects, programmes, initiatives and actions that enable the organisation to move forward towards its vision.

As there are many different approaches to change and transformation in organisations, some of which will be not be suitable for all organisations, the initiators of the process must choose what they consider to be the most appropriate approach for the organisation. It is also important to assemble those who can actually make change happen, and to ensure that the reasons for change are clear to all involved in the strategic management process.

The main objectives for this stage of work are as follows.

- To gain consensus on the areas and mechanisms of change needed to introduce and implement the strategy.
- To build a high-level set of integrated change plans, using trials, pilots and experimentation wherever possible to gain flexibility and adaptiveness in the way in which the organisation changes itself.
- To gain commitment to the changes required from all the stakeholders. It is essential to be able to identify the three main change constituencies – change champions, change resisters and the apathetic – and formulate different strategies to influence each appropriately.

The inputs to this part of the process are the vision and strategic intent developed during strategic gaming and simulation and the strategic agenda material developed during Module 10. There are several steps in identifying and launching changes or transformation in an organisation.

## Identifying change initiatives

The way to identify key change initiatives is to start by considering the distance between what the organisation is now and what it wishes to become, as revealed in the vision and strategic intent. To navigate towards a changed corporate destiny the organisation needs a change compass to guide it. The simplest way is to begin by assessing the distance between where the company wants to be and where it is at the moment, and establish the criteria that describe:

- the successful future state the organisation will be in when it achieves its vision (the success criteria); and
- the key success factors that will enable the strategic intent to deliver the vision (the success factors).

These success criteria and success factors form the bottom row of a matrix, which will be used to evaluate how far the organisation has to go to meet these criteria and influence these factors (see Figure 5.11). The left-hand column of this matrix contains the major business processes that the business design of the organisation requires. Each dimension of the wheel of business evolution must be addressed in making change happen effectively. In each of these eight dimensions (depicted as the column headings of the change grid) clear change processes must be designed to establish the key success criteria in the change process for the organisation as a whole.

Equally, change goals for each of the principal business processes or functional areas (the row headings in the change grid) must be set so that progress can be measured and mid-course adjustments made. These change goals are set in the spirit of provisional hypotheses, and are thus much more flexible than traditional goals. Their purpose is to guide, inspire and provoke learning, not to reward, punish or constrain achievement.

## Managing the change process

The way in which change is managed and measured is an important part of the change management process. Six steps are crucial to doing this well.

- What are the current issues generating the need for change in the organisation as perceived by senior management? As perceived from the middle-out, and bottom-up? What issues do customers and suppliers have with the organisation?

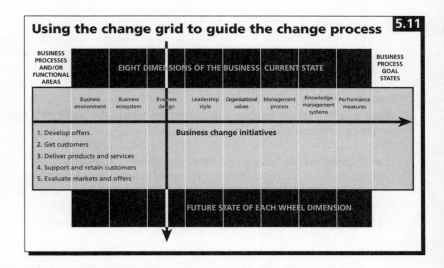

# Using the change grid to guide the change process 5.11

- Using an organisational diagnostic process, such as the wheel of business evolution, does a review of what the key stakeholders believe align with what senior management perceives to be the issues? What additional issues and divergent views does this raise?
- What information does senior management require to translate its initial strategic synthesis into a functional model from which a new organisation can be designed? Principally, what are the change options and constraints? What needs to be redesigned and how should it look? Which key stakeholder groups should be aligned with the direction of change? How can their support be enlisted?
- What approaches to change will work in this particular organisation? (The wheel diagnostic provides much of the necessary information.) How should the change process be designed to harness the energy and knowledge in the organisation given its current situation?
- As the organisation goes through the change process, progress should be assessed against the benchmarks established using the wheel of business evolution and mid-course adjustments made. Change processes are at heart learning processes, and the goals set at the beginning of the change process should be reviewed as it proceeds.
- The last stage in each cycle of change is a re-evaluation of how

successful the change process has been, together with a fresh diagnosis of which new things should be changed given the emergent and unexpected changes going on in and around the organisation.

### Setting up change initiatives

Much of this stage is run in workshops, in which the following topics would be covered.

- ◼ Briefing on challenges and the organisation's responses.
- ◼ Briefing on the organisation's wheel of business evolution profile, then completion of questionnaires on the present and future state of the organisation.
- ◼ Highlighting of transformation challenges and the sequence in which they must be addressed.
- ◼ Brainstorming resolution of gaps between problem areas and solutions, given the constraints. Goal navigation (reverse fishbone) techniques work well here.
- ◼ Testing the options for change against the competitive landscape and scenarios developed during strategic gaming and simulation. How do they align with, and support, key strategic moves and the strategic focus of the organisation?

The key change stakeholders need to agree on responsibilities, the approach to corporate transformation to be used and the milestones for ensuring that progress is on track.

### Making change stick

How does the senior management team make change stick, ensuring that the effort put into the initial processes results in a culture of permanent, beneficial change where key managers see their primary responsibility as being real change leaders?

In initiating the change process, it is necessary to consider to what extent change should be brought about top-down, middle-out or bottom-up (see Figure 5.12). Specific areas in and around an organisation will vary in their need to change, and such changes will also need to be orchestrated by the centre. The characteristics of successful top-down change include the following.

- ◼ Analysis of organisation and need to change

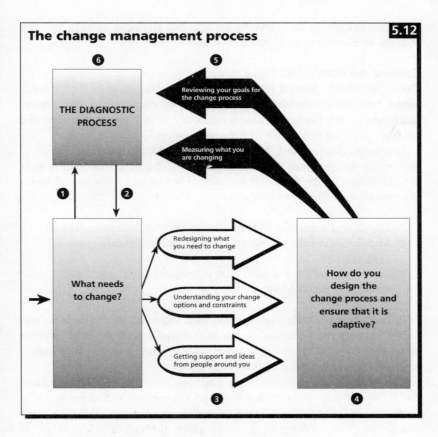

**The change management process**  5.12

- Creation of shared vision and common direction
- Separation from past and sense of urgency
- Strong support for leadership role and political sponsorship
- Clear, achievable implementation plan
- Development of enabling structures
- Honesty, involvement and communication
- Reinforcement and institutionalisation of change

Middle-out and bottom-up change should follow any top-down change process, and should be initiated at much the same time. The strategic focus and strategic agenda must be interpreted by each part of the organisation involved in the change process to ensure alignment between the top-down, middle-out and bottom-up changes. The key to strategic dialogue is to evolve in parallel the dialogue agenda and the changes to existing management processes.

### Evolving the strategic dialogue

Once the strategic agenda has been developed and some of the thinking about how to design the business and the organisation for greater intelligence and flexibility has been done, it is time to broaden the strategic dialogue to the rest of the organisation.

Learning, change and transformation come about as a result of intelligent dialogue resolving the problems of the past and dealing with the challenges of the future. Management teams can initiate and guide strategic dialogue in three ways.

- Top-down, where the agenda is managed by the senior team.
- Middle-out, where the agenda is managed by middle management.
- Bottom-up, where the agenda is managed by managers and workers at many levels.

They can choose which combination and sequence of methods to use, depending on the situation of the organisation and the management team, the strategic intent and vision, and the implications for change, given the strategic synthesis that is emerging.

The wheel of business evolution diagnosis is an important element in the judgment that must be made about the timing and sequence of a combination of top-down, middle-out or bottom-up dialogues and change processes. Dialogue can take place through a wide range of personal interactions and group processes, from intimate conversations to large assemblies of people in convention halls or lecture theatres.

The basic principles of communication, human psychology and cognitive science apply to these interactions and processes. For example, the complexity of the dialogue between two individuals can be high, as they can focus exclusively on the messages they are sending each other at a variety of levels. A CEO addressing a company rally, however, has to limit the messages to simple points that can be put across easily. There is little room for ambiguity or uncertainty at this level of communication.

To be useful, different means of intervention require different kinds of personal interactions and group processes. For example, a radical change in the business processes of an organisation or a total review of its strategic direction could not be brought about by a succession of one-to-one conversations; too many people would need to be involved and it would take too long. Either a broadcast approach would be used initially (only really justifiable in a crisis), or a series of group and team events would be needed to build the necessary grassroots support for the change process.

The principal outcomes from the change initiative stage of FutureStep include the following.

- There should be consensus among the key stakeholders on the changes needed and the sequence by which they will be activated.
- A skeleton set of plans to deliver the strategy should be in place.
- There should be a clear and shared view of the risks and issues associated with the implementation of change in general, and also in respect of specific initiatives.
- A portfolio of actions to mitigate risk should be available and understood by those responsible for implementing the change. This should include pilots and trials, where possible, to increase the flexibility of implementation.
- Responsibilities for implementation should be unambiguous.
- Timescales and milestones should be set, agreed and used to monitor progress and carry out learning reviews as change progresses.

## Module 12: Strategic trigger identification

The last three critical outputs of the strategic agenda that need to be taken forward to guide the future evolution of the organisation are as follows.

- Contingency triggers identified in the scenarios should be integrated into the scanning process and then activated in the planning process.
- Performance measures implicit in the strategic intent should be formalised and then integrated into the decision processes of the organisation.
- Campaigns, programmes and initiatives required on the strategic agenda of the senior team to deliver the vision and strategic intent should be fleshed out and given milestones before being integrated into the planning process.

The main objectives for the last stage of the FutureStep process include the following.

- To identify triggers for strategic decisions and actions.

- To designate responsibility for checking for the triggers.
- To ensure that the campaigns, programmes and initiatives generated and launched during the course of the strategic management process are monitored and reviewed, and that learning about what is happening takes place.

The strategic agenda and change initiatives, together with the contingencies generated in the scenarios, are the principal inputs into the identification of strategic triggers. Before running a workshop to finalise scanning and monitoring, it is important to understand thoroughly the detail of the strategy and how it might ideally be played out.

Monitoring strategic progress and scanning the environment are two of the most important tasks of the senior managers in an organisation. To ensure that the most appropriate strategic triggers have been identified for both progress monitoring and scanning of the environment, it is useful to run a workshop covering the following.

- A confirmation of the high-level objectives of the company through the chosen strategy.
- Base-case measures of progress.
- Scenarios as a prompt of what might happen, and hence what triggers to look for.
- Strategy redefined as a series of options.
- Triggers to decide whether or not to take up the options.
- Consolidation in terms of who will measure what, using what, how often, recorded where, to prompt what.

The last set of outcomes from the last stage of FutureStep should enable managers to stay on their toes and keep their organisation poised and nimble. These are as follows.

- A set of success measures – a dashboard – by which to steer the company, its new strategy and the transformation.
- An identified set of triggers.
- People responsible for monitoring and informing on the scanning criteria.
- People charged with setting up the management information systems necessary to handle the information and link it with other forms of management systems, such as budgeting or executive information systems.

# 6 The future of the e-conomy

## The challenge

BUSINESS IS GOING TO CHANGE MORE IN THE NEXT TEN YEARS THAN IT
HAS IN THE LAST FIFTY.

Bill Gates, *Business @ the Speed of Thought*[1]

SOMEWHERE OUT THERE IS A BULLET WITH YOUR COMPANY'S NAME ON IT.
SOMEWHERE OUT THERE IS A COMPETITOR, UNBORN AND UNKNOWN,
THAT WILL RENDER YOUR BUSINESS OBSOLETE. BILL GATES KNOWS THAT.
WHEN HE SAYS THAT MICROSOFT IS ALWAYS TWO YEARS AWAY FROM
FAILURE, HE'S NOT JUST BLOWING SMOKE AT JANET RENO. HE KNOWS THAT
COMPETITION TODAY IS NOT JUST BETWEEN PRODUCTS, ITS BETWEEN
BUSINESS MODELS. HE KNOWS THAT IRRELEVANCY IS A BIGGER RISK THAN
INEFFICIENCY. AND WHAT'S TRUE FOR MICROSOFT IS TRUE FOR JUST ABOUT
EVERY OTHER COMPANY. THE HOTTEST AND MOST DANGEROUS BUSINESS
MODELS ARE OUT THERE ON THE WEB.

*Fortune Magazine*, July 12th, 1998

## The solution

AN ORGANISATION'S ABILITY TO LEARN, AND TRANSLATE THAT LEARNING
INTO ACTION RAPIDLY, IS THE ULTIMATE COMPETITIVE ADVANTAGE.

Jack Welch, chairman, General Electric

THE OLD COMMON SENSE WAS AN UNDERSTANDING OF CAUSE AND EFFECT
IN THE COMPLICATED WORLD OF DISCRETE EVENTS. THE NEXT COMMON
SENSE IS A DESCRIPTION OF CAUSE AND EFFECT IN A WORLD OF
INTERWEAVINGS.

Michael Lissack and Johan Roos, *The Next Common Sense*[2]

This book suggests that the seventh wave economy offers unprecedented
opportunities, and unparalleled risks and threats, for businesses of all
kinds. Against this backdrop it has been argued that what constitutes
success in the knowledge economy is very different from, and in many
ways opposite to, those things which make for success in the industrial
age economy. Thus as the world changes the old common sense no

longer works, and new perspectives, frameworks and tools are required.

## Developing organisational intelligence to manage complexity

Howard Sherman, founder of Midas Mufflers and several other highly successful businesses, and his partner Ron Schultz, explain forcefully in their book *Open Boundaries*[3] that:

> *Business success or failure in today's world is essentially cognitive success or failure. Cognitive has two equally significant meanings: 'to know' and 'to beget'. Taken together these two meanings suggest that all birth is an awakening to knowledge. To know and to generate are inseparable.*

Sherman and Schultz focus on the way in which innovation can be accelerated by operating businesses as complex adaptive systems. There are several important threads in their argument, centring on the way in which ways of thinking, metaphors and the language used both limit and generate the possibilities people can entertain and generate in their businesses. The authors describe a world of ideas in which the competitive edge for business lies in being continually on the lookout for "non-linear adjacent possibilities".

What this means in layman's language is that the next set of market-spaces will be those in which businesses can thrive by pushing the edges of what they are currently doing, especially by co-evolving with other players. This can stretch an organisation's capabilities to deliver successful offers into these markets.

This theme echoes the central idea of Bill Gates's book *Business @ the Speed of Thought*,[4] that in the emerging web-workstyle and web-lifestyle, electronic systems-based intelligence is enabling people to "manage with the force of facts". Gates emphasises that the fast flow of good information, actionable data, is the lifeblood of any organisation. Through the implementation of a digital nervous system businesses are able to get to market first, empower their people and take big risks. The key to doing these things successfully lies in raising the corporate IQ, so that better decisions are taken more often by more people in an organisation.

In another book,[5] Suzanne Kelly of Citicorp and her co-author Mary Ann Allison delve into the implications of complexity for organisations, with the focus on what self-organising human systems are capable of within the constraints of today's major corporations. Using an innovative model of how dysfunctional behaviour arises in the largely formal systems of major organisations, Kelly and Allison show how to break out of these dysfunctional patterns. This allows organisations to evolve from unconscious self-organisation within rigid power hierarchies to adaptive, open systems consciously co-evolving with their environment. The key to this evolution lies in how the informal systems and processes in the organisation are used to catalyse change, and the way in which leaders and teams generate creative and self-organising dynamics to carry the organisation towards higher peaks of fitness.

Tom Petzinger, who has spent 20 years analysing business for the *Wall Street Journal*, is one of the most fluent and encyclopedic authors on the subject of complexity in business. In his book *The New Pioneers*,[6] Petzinger shows how the greatest source of wealth generation in the knowledge economy is coming from small and medium-sized businesses, the most successful of which are those operating according to the principles of complexity management, whether intuitively or deliberately. Through hundreds of cases, Petzinger describes how organisations as different as Amazon.com, Charles Schwab, Avedis Zildjian, Du Pont, Great Harvest Bakeries, Koch Industries, City Soft, Gateway, Monarch Marketing, Mercedes Credit, the New Philharmonia Orchestra and LDS Hospital exemplify the spirit of the third-millennium economy, and the principles of complexity.

## Towards the "connect and create" organisation

What will it be like to work in, manage or lead the organisation of the future? Will there be some basic, recognisable kinds of organisations, or will their shape and form have multiplied into many exotic varieties?

Those who rose to the top in industrial age organisations were generally suited to monarchic autocratic or charismatic leadership styles. Such leaders centred on tradition, and saw their primary role as ensuring the preservation of the status quo, with only minor tweaks around the edges being allowed when change was required. Contrast and compare General Electric's Jack Welch around 1980 and IBM's former leader John Akers with John Chambers of Cisco, Percy Barnevik of ABB and Carly Fiorina of Hewlett-Packard. Leadership used to involve "winning the battle", with the leader as chief prophet and general rallying the troops around a narrow mission. In contrast, in the seventh wave economy, leadership revolves around designing adaptive frameworks and processes, within which hunter-gatherer knowledge workers can spot adjacent possibilities and develop the capabilities and partnerships to exploit them before the window of opportunity closes.

The leadership style best suited to the third millennium is democratic, facilitative and future-focused. Gone are the command-and-control organisations celebrated in Dilbert cartoons. The focus on hierarchy and conservatism in Dilbert-space is driven by basic survival needs, rather than the urge to create and colonise new frontiers and opportunities. In the latter context leaders nourish the roots and catalyse frontline entrepreneurship, forming coaching and mentoring relationships with their staff. Compare how AT&T used to be run in the 1980s and early 1990s with how Steve Case of AOL and Jeff Bezos of Amazon now run their organisations.

Strategy in seventh wave businesses is developed around shared purpose. It is concerned with aligning visions, creating options, generating scenarios and launching pilots and experiments in market-spaces. As shown in Chapter 2, prediction, forecasts, plans and rigid programmes are simply non-adaptive and too slow for the connected, blurring economy. The stakeholder focus shifts from return on investment (ROI), profit and physical or financial capital to long-term economic value-added (EVA) and net future opportunity (NFO), where resilience and longevity are achieved through a focus on intangible forms of capital such as intellectual assets and human capital. The kinds of organisations required to deliver promises to customers and stakeholders are very different from those with which we are familiar.

The evolutionary successors to command-and-control organisations are those that connect and create. Such organisations are future-focused. Their organisational mindset and values emerge from a participative process. In the industrial age organisation, values were shaped by the power hierarchy and imposed top-down. Management processes had tightly controlled structures with strong negative feedback loops to control deviations. The central mechanisms used by those in power to map territory, retain control and encourage the workforce were plans, budgets, security, promotion, status and money. In the knowledge age organisation the unwritten rules of the game (or "the way things are done around here") are generated through learning processes, which result in flexible, evolving sets of context-sensitive rules.

The central metaphors for this kind of organisation are associated with brains, organisms, cultures and ecosystems, rather than the machine, warfare, family and tribal metaphors of the industrial age. To connect and create, the management processes in knowledge age organisations revolve around distributed entrepreneurial learning processes grounded in shared purpose and values. Instead of a narrow, top-down emphasis on the need to provide specific skills driven by task-defined needs, knowledge generation and management in third-millennium businesses focus on bottom-up, competency-building processes, which encourage creativity and the emergence of new categories and models.

The rigid operational measures imposed top-down in command-and-control organisations are replaced by new approaches to performance measurement, characterised by systems such as the balanced scorecard. This enables flexible strategic measures to evolve in the digital and human nervous system in the organisation. Intranets, extranets and e-business software packages provide powerful tools for the development of distributed performance measurement processes, which enable what is important to evolve in real time with the organisation and its environment. Examples of connect-and-create organisations are becoming increasingly easy to find. They range from South West Airlines, BP-Amoco, parts of Citigroup, Koch Industries, Sencorp, Semco and Monsanto in traditional industrial age sectors, to St Luke's ad agency, Sun, AOL, Amazon, Lucent, Cisco, Hewlett-Packard and Sony in the knowledge economy.

The human race has always used stories to store complex knowledge and transfer it to future generations. In the knowledge economy, technology has become the campfire around which people tell their stories. Art, music, movies and other forms of expression have also become essential to describe and represent experiences that are hard to put into words.

Yet this focus on technology limits us to descriptions based on information and bandwidth, rather than meaning and coherence. Organisations are complex adaptive social and cognitive systems constructed by individuals, each of whom has their own ideas, opinions, values and perspectives. Our interpretation of who we are, and what is important to us, is critical in determining when, where, how and with whom we interact, work and play. Such insights are fundamental to managing teams, leading organisations, developing new offers and shaping communities, whether onland or online. Complexity-based management is at the same time a mindset, a movement and a method, all of which require the creation of contexts within which people can make sense of and act effectively in their own worlds.

To develop greater organisational intelligence to manage complexity, there are three essential ingredients that managers need to understand in order to "connect and create":

- Using a complexity mindset and methods.
- Managing the connections in and around the organisation.
- Enhancing the seven cognitive faculties which enable the organisation to apply its intelligence.

## The complexity mindset

Meaning is not something individuals possess, or something that is transferred from one person to another. It is made moment by moment in human minds. In the real-time, online economy, shared meaning is what holds organisations and communities together and enables them to function effectively. The human race is also remarkable for the fact that it makes meaning not only within individuals, but also in teams, organisations and societies.

For organisations, however, there is no guarantee that the coherent thought and action will take place automatically. Self-organisation and change in and around organisations ensure that perfect alignment will never occur, and that things will always be somewhat messy and inefficient. A complexity mindset helps to bring some order to this situation. It is based on several simple principles.

- Collaborative processing. No one of us is as smart as all of us. Trying to deal with complexity on your own is extremely difficult. Individuals need to use their networks and sharpen their team learning skills so that they can collaboratively process complexity into bite-sized chunks and deal with them effectively. Organisations should take full advantage of collaborative technologies and environments, where rapid acceleration of collective thinking and agendas can occur, and many options can be tested and selected in real time.
- Recombination and repurposing. Organisations should encourage play and creativity to facilitate the combining and recombining of the knowledge, resources and process building blocks in the organisation and its partners, especially in the development of new offers and delivery capabilities
- Continuous experimentation. In the world of e-business there is much less time to develop complex plans and forecasts. Companies should use the power of the new technologies to

launch real-time pilots, much as IdeaLab does when researching a new Internet business proposition. It simply creates a website and starts selling the new offer to see how many people click on it and buy it. This kind of real-time, online market feedback is the most valuable information a company can have.

◪ Coherent language and imagery. Businesses should use powerful, appropriate metaphors and images, and tell stories in ways that promote coherence and alignment in the organisation. Summarising basic operating principles into "the ten commandments" or the "seven core values" is an essential part of this process.

◪ Guiding perspectives. These enable those engaged in the business of the organisation to take meaningful actions, and to integrate their own sense of identity and purpose with that of the organisation.

◪ Strategic insight and foresight. Strategic insight encourages readiness and agility in an organisation by co-developing rich insights into the way that a business landscape is evolving. The process generates multiple hypotheses about where such evolution might take things, and how the company might shape or adapt to them. Although it is impossible to predict the exact nature of the future, it is possible to gain some sense of its general shape through such insights.

A complexity mindset, though necessary, is not in its own right sufficient to enable an organisation to master complexity in the seventh wave economy. A set of methods that apply the principles of complexity thinking is needed to enable managers to get to grips with the complex adaptive systems they are immersed in from day to day. The approaches and methods developed in Chapters 2–5 and the appendices should be deployed as required. Using a complexity mindset and methods will work most effectively in an organisation that is internally and externally connected. In such an organisation learning and adaptation happen with the right level of connectedness, and intelligence can be applied through a variety of cognitive faculties at each stage in the management process.

## Managing the connections

How can organisations become more intelligent in the connected economy? When describing the operation of learning in the mind of an individual, it is possible to point specifically to the networks of neurons in the brain and body making new connections, and changing the strengths of older connections, as the learning process unfolds. In an organisation, however, it is networks of relationships that learn. These relationships can be human or artificial, but they all rely on symbol systems such as language to establish relationships and communicate with each other.

People in organisations are able to establish contact and communicate remotely as well as locally, using a variety of communications and collaborative technologies. Whatever the nature of such contact and communication, however, language of some sort is essential for its establishment. Thus, unlike networks in living organisms or other complex adaptive systems, an organisation does not rely on physical contact to establish relationships and communicate.

Despite these differences between individuals and organisations, there are still fundamental principles that apply to becoming more intelligent in both domains.

- Speed and quality of learning. The learning cycle in an organisation needs to operate as fast as if not faster than those of its partners and competitors, at a similar level of quality. In other words, the right issues need to be discovered and addressed, and good enough decisions taken in each decision area to ensure that the organisation is moving ahead with sufficient speed in the right direction.
- Just enough connectedness. Just the right level of connectedness between an organisation, its peers and its stakeholders is essential for it to learn and become more intelligent. If an organisation is over or under connected to any particular group of players or stakeholders, then the judgment of the organisation will be biased or flawed.
- Quality and bandwidth of connections. If an organisation has poor connections with the principal stakeholders in its network, then its learning and intelligence will suffer. Quality connections include high bandwidth, enabling the rapid exchange of useful information and the building of shared knowledge in strategic areas. Similarly, the quality of connections inside an organisation is a crucial factor in its success.
- Rate of change in the connections. As the world changes, so too must the connections in and around an organisation change to reflect this. To make the right strategic moves, an organisation

must change its internal connections as well as those between itself and its stakeholders, at least as fast as the changes going on in its value web and environment.

To ensure that knowledge flows across these connections, and that intelligent decisions are arrived at, an organisation will need to develop its cognitive faculties.

## Seven cognitive faculties to cultivate

Organisations need to ensure that they are developing the collective mental muscles to react to and shape their environment. This is important at the operational, managerial and social levels, and means that as well as having individuals with the faculties described below as part of the management team, the management processes of the organisation must enable managers to:

- consider all factors surrounding important issues and decisions;
- generate creative options and offers for the organisation continuously;
- understand the systemic consequences of actions and programmes in and around the organisation;
- analyse and assess problem areas and opportunities;
- resolve dilemmas created by different options, power groups and value systems in the organisation;
- consider many different kinds of future scenarios, to ensure the organisation remains open to change and opportunities;
- explore ways of overcoming constraints preventing the achievement of goals;
- arrive quickly at good enough decisions which balance fact-based evidence and intuitive judgment.

To carry out these cognitive activities effectively, successful managers and entrepreneurs need to possess one or more of seven cognitive faculties.[7] Each of these must be developed and applied to navigate complex issues in any organisation. They also play an important role in ensuring that each module in the FutureStep process (described in Chapter 5) is properly enabled with the requisite strategic thinking skills.

- Perception
- Creativity

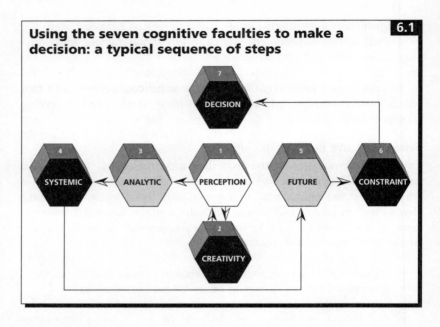

**Using the seven cognitive faculties to make a decision: a typical sequence of steps** `6.1`

- ◪ Analysis
- ◪ Systems thinking
- ◪ Future thinking
- ◪ Constraint identification
- ◪ Decision

A typical way in which the seven cognitive faculties are used in decision-making is shown in Figure 6.1. There are, however, many more combinations of these faculties. When combined with the 12 different kinds of intelligence,[8] together with the large variety of situations in which they may be used separately or in conjunction, the number of ways in which the seven faculties can be used approaches infinity. A decision-sequence scenario using all seven of the cognitive faculties might be as follows.

PERCEPTION
While playing a game of golf, Scott Chambers, chairman and founder of E-Tech, heard from a friend about a new competitor, Webstar Technologies. Apparently, Webstar had just made his friend's company an offer on their new product, which appeared to be more advanced and much cheaper than anything in E-Tech's product range, using a

technology he had never heard of. Chambers immediately called his strategy director and asked him to get as much information as he could on Webstar. He also insisted that they "consider all factors", and use this as an opportunity to test whether E-Tech's technology was falling behind. This really was an opportunity to apply the helicopter view for which Chambers was famous among his colleagues.

The ability to perceive situations and people comprehensively and appropriately lies at the heart of the leader's job: to get people doing the right thing well. The ability to perceive things differently is also a cornerstone of the entrepreneurial mind, enabling business builders to see opportunities and take risks that their more conventional colleagues do not. Steve Jobs, co-inventor of the Apple microcomputer, and Bill Gates, founder of Microsoft, are good examples. Both of them perceived opportunities that IBM, Xerox and most other major computer companies did not. The faculty of perception can be developed in many ways, such as wide reading, travel, new experiences and mixing with unusual people.

### CREATIVITY

The chairman used this new development to think again about what real customer benefits his company was offering, and whether they could deliver more value some other way. He used some De Bono lateral thinking[9] exercises and a hexagon braindump,[10] putting himself in the customer's shoes, to generate some tough questions for the board about the way they currently thought about E-Tech's business and its customers.

Creativity, the ability to rearrange familiar elements into different patterns, which may add more value to customers and stakeholders, drives successful innovation in business, and often goes hand in hand with entrepreneurship. The creative faculty can be stimulated through exposure to the arts, sciences and creative people.

### ANALYSIS

E-Tech's strategy director got his team together and briefed them on "project red alert". The chairman's list of tough questions had challenged them all to think again about their business concept. First, they needed to get all the information they could on the new competitor and its technology. Second, they reviewed their scans of the business environment to see if there were other signals that might fit with this new development. Third, they accelerated a customer research programme, adding questions to test some of the hidden assumptions about what their customers really wanted.

A month later analysis of the results highlighted that Webstar's new product now accounted for 7% of market share, and that 13% of E-Tech's customers had switched to the new competitor in the previous year. The new technology used by Webstar enabled it to charge 10% less than E-Tech for a better product.

Analysis is the ability to create knowledge out of information using the left-brain intelligences (factual, linguistic, mathematical) within the frameworks required in specific disciplines. Learning a new discipline through training and education is the best way to develop the analytical faculty. The analytical faculty is essential for all directors, as exemplified by the psychometric tests applied to most executive job-seekers nowadays. It is, however, seldom a distinguishing faculty because of its ubiquity.

SYSTEMS THINKING

The operations and research and development teams were called in to help do some modelling of how E-Tech could change the way it operated to counter Webstar's threat. There appeared to be two options: stay with its existing technology and re-engineer the operation to reduce costs; or get hold of the new technology being used by Webstar and ditch its own manufacturing process. Both options had many different implications.

The red alert project team first developed a soft systems model[11] for each option to illustrate how manufacturing cycle times, costs, customer delivery, sales volumes and pricing would be affected by re-engineering or introduction of the new technology. They then used this to create a computerised simulation model[12] to show how E-Tech, its suppliers and customers would cope with each option. It became clear that the introduction of the new technology option was far superior in the long run, but that E-Tech would be at great risk if Pacific Rim competitors flooded the market and the company was unable to maintain its quality and service levels owing to a lag in retraining factory workers and customer service people in the new technology. Unfortunately, neither of these two possibilities could be predicted with any certainty at that time.

Systems thinking, the ability to see things as a whole (or holistically), including the many different types of relationships between the many elements in a complex system, characterises many of the world's leading executives.

FUTURE THINKING

The board insisted that the red alert project team prepare a scenario evaluation of the two options. The board could then experiment with the implications of the new technology for product and service quality, customer satisfaction and market share, and the possibility of Pacific Rim competitors flooding the market in the next year. Before it could make a decision, it would have to find out whether E-Tech could afford to take the riskier option with a higher payoff, or whether it should stick to its knitting and re-engineer. The board needed to know what critical success factors would make each option succeed or fail. The chairman also wanted to know whether E-Tech could go for both options as a "one-two punch".

The exercise revealed that the new technology option appeared to be the most desirable in both scenarios. It also revealed that the probabilities of the Pacific Rim competitors entering the market in the next year were higher than previously thought. The pure re-engineering option would yield clear short-term advantages in both scenarios, but it would cripple E-Tech in the medium term if it failed to slipstream the new technology into the re-engineering programme.

Future thinking, the ability to see how the future might differ from the past and present, is probably the most crucial of the seven faculties for a manager. It relies upon a specific brain function known scientifically as "prospective memory", which enables a variety of "action queues" to be built up in an individual or organisation.[13] A specific action queue, such as "Run out of the emergency exit in case of a fire", is triggered by a specific event – a fire. Equally, a strategy (an organisational action queue) to "Open a branch office in China" could be triggered by the offer of a joint venture in China. The way to develop future thinking is regularly to create new personal and organisational options, and evaluate them against different possible futures by asking "what-if?" questions. This helps avoid the dangerous condition of "corporate one-track mind".[14]

CONSTRAINT IDENTIFICATION

The critical success factors for the new technology option were identified. One of these factors was that highly skilled technicians were required, but only two were available in the country. Furthermore, there appeared to be lead times of over five months on the supply of the new technology, which would give Webstar an unacceptable lead. There also appeared to be potential staffing problems involved in the re-engineering option. The red alert team and the board used a goal navigation and reverse cause effect thinking to establish where the problem areas were in each option, how they interacted, the potential solutions that existed or can be invented, and how long they would take to complete and at what cost.

Constraint identification, the ability to foresee possible constraints on actions or plans, evaluate their impact and overcome them, is fundamental to organisational survival. Critical thinking is a form of constraint thinking, where the emphasis is on what is wrong with a plan or action. The analytical and creative faculties are often harnessed at this point to work out a way of overcoming the constraint. De Bono calls this "black-hat" thinking.[15]

DECISION

After three weeks of intensive effort, the red alert project team was in a position to present its findings to the board. The constraint identification exercise enabled it to find several solutions to the risks posed by the new technology option, while creating a way of doing some immediate re-engineering to limit the short-term damage being done by Webstar. The board had become convinced of the need to deliver a "one-two punch", as Chambers had suggested, and was keen to back the new technology slipstream strategy put forward by the project team. The internal and external political consequences were examined, action plans were drawn up, task forces selected, and the tools and techniques required for major changes in the business model were identified and acquired.[16] Chambers was delighted in the payoff from E-tech's new strategic management process, which would ensure it remained at the forefront in its field.

Decision, the ability to make sound judgments and take good decisions on behalf of stakeholders and the organisation, based on competent political evaluation, relies on the decision faculty. This in turn relies on the other six faculties, and will often fail if decisions are based on poor perception, lack of creativity, inadequate analysis, failure to view a system as a whole, inadequate future-proofing and failure to recognise real constraints. The best way to develop the decision faculty is to make many decisions, with the obvious caveat that each decision should benefit from the use of the appropriate cognitive faculties wherever possible.

## Complexity management methods

Organisations straddle two fundamentally different types of systems: human activity systems, which are complex, evolving and intelligent; and infrastructural systems, which in comparison are complicated, stable and dumb. The evolution of an organisation is driven by the codification and abstraction of its business and management processes into components of

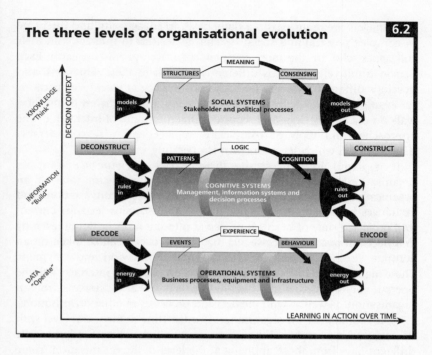

**The three levels of organisational evolution**  6.2

its infrastructure. These phenomena are more commonly known as automation and business process design or re-engineering. At a higher level and over longer timescales, webs of firms and their environment co-evolve, leading to changes in the structure of entire industries and economies.

This happens at three levels, and two kinds of interfaces connect these three levels, as shown in Figure 6.2. Complexity-based tools and techniques are beginning to act as key components in each of these interfaces. Although many approaches to complexity and e-business treat all systems as having similar dynamics, it is important to distinguish between operational, cognitive and social complexity.

In Figure 6.2 physical systems are at the bottom, people and intelligent (or cognitive) systems are in the middle, and organisations and social systems are at the top. The big difference between physical and human systems is that human systems have intentionality, or direction. By understanding the processes by which data are converted to information and information is converted to knowledge, it is possible to identify when and where companies should be using different kinds of interfaces to manage the complexity surrounding them.

Managers are required, on a daily basis, to engage with and intervene in complex physical and social systems, as well as to interact with their colleagues who are the most complex cognitive systems on earth. Each person intuitively responds differently to each of these situations, and develops different messages for each constituency at each level, because, for example, a press release is fundamentally different from going for a walk on the factory floor and requires different modes of interaction. The approaches and tools of complexity management vary considerably depending on which level a person is operating at.

It is useful to look at the three levels in Figure 6.2 from an organisational perspective. The middle level is the sum total of an organisation in action, at which critical management conversations and exchanges take place. A variety of information systems feed the current and projected state of business processes into the organisational learning and decision-making processes, so that key decisions can be taken on an accurate fact-base, combined with managerial intuition and judgment. These management, information and decision processes interface with the operational infrastructure, business processes and systems in an organisation, as well as with the decision processes of other organisations.

At the same time, an organisation is interacting at the social level with its stakeholders and political processes, which obey fundamentally different laws from those applying at the level of the organisation. There the interfaces are likely to be with social institutions, such as the media, the courts, regulators, governments and government ministries, corporate boards and annual general meetings, together with the edifice of corporate governance.

## Operational systems

The sensors and effectors in e-businesses are increasingly real-time, online, interactive and fact-based in their approach. The newer computerised business and management systems for industrial age corporations, such as SAP, BAAN or Oracle, and the e-commerce applications for Internet businesses, generate massive amounts of data or facts. The people and infrastructure operating the core business processes in an organisation are continually encoding such facts through their physical experience of day-to-day events and the behaviour of other people and systems.

Infrastructure encodes experience in the form of machine memory, and people encode their experience in the form of patterns in neural networks. Data are consumed during the physical process and information is produced. Experience is translated into patterns that obey various kinds of logic and are describable as information.

The human brain encodes 11m bits of data ten times per second, of which between 8 and 56 bits/second ends up in our conscious awareness after being filtered. This means that most learning is subconscious. This kind of physical learning involves imprinting or conditioning, and results in implicit knowledge. Much of organisational life and human culture operates at this implicit level of encoding, creating hidden assumptions and knowledge. It is at this level that is possible to describe the digital nervous system of an organisation, or organisational reflexes, where the right things are being done in the right way, and exceptions are handed up to the next level to be dealt with.

## Business processes

Of course, in the seventh wave economy this industrial age approach is already severely defective; not only is it slow and conservative, it also lacks sufficient bandwidth to process the complexity of the knowledge age economy. A new way of managing businesses on the ground has evolved: process and network management. The beauty of processes is that they can be customer, not internally, focused and even internal links between processes can be focused on internal customers. Processes integrate activities and information across functional, product and market areas in an organisation, and provide a stable base on which to plan information systems, people and operational requirements.

A simple map of the business processes required to thrive in the knowledge economy is set out in Figure 6.3 on the following page. Each of these processes has several attributes.

- The speed of the process, for example, the average time taken to gain a new customer, deliver an order or respond to a customer query. The cycle time of the business is made up of the sum of all the times of all its core processes. Faster cycle times can result in improved profitability and greater market agility.
- The net profit and economic benefit of the process (some processes generate revenue much greater than their cost), for example, the order to cash process generates much of the revenue in most firms, with low costs. The support customer process is often quite expensive and seldom generates immediate revenue. In the longer term, however, this process generates customer loyalty, and its impact is on customer retention and lifetime customer

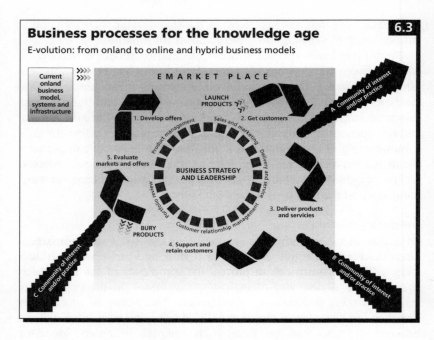

**Business processes for the knowledge age** — 6.3

E-volution: from onland to online and hybrid business models

value, which is economically more powerful than simply collecting cash.

- ☑ The operational systems and people requirements of the process. Each process draws on different aspects of the business's systems and infrastructure as well as different skill sets. The value of a process is a direct function of how well such diverse inputs are converted into value-adding outputs for customers and other stakeholders at every stage.
- ☑ The strategic value of the process. The information gathered in a process can be vital to the survival and growth of a business. Processes such as offer development and market understanding can make the difference between success and failure in the medium term. Certain processes may also hold the key to the competitive advantage of a business; for example, outstanding delivery processes are the secret of much of Amazon's success.

It is important here to distinguish between the business process re-engineering, total quality management and process-based thinking and methods that evolved in the late 1980s–early 1990s and the processes required for the knowledge era. Although powerful in their own right, these methods require significant adaptation to the knowledge economy and the e-commerce, Internet-based business environment. Similarly, software provided by firms such as SAP, BAAN, Peoplesoft and Oracle, which promises to deliver a digital nervous system to firms, automating and informating their basic business processes, is not sufficient either. Such enterprise resource planning (ERP) approaches are not particularly flexible, and all of the firms involved are scrambling to upgrade their offerings for the e-business world. In the future there are likely to be many more adaptive agent and value web based approaches for business process management, providing highly flexible and adaptive ways of running e-businesses.

In the online world, hundreds of new packages have grown up to provide real-time online solutions for doing business over the web. E-commerce software providers such as Xinet, IBM, Broadvision, Lotus Domino, Open Market, Netscape, Oracle, Microsoft and Commerce One are competing hard to generate a lead in this increasingly competitive market. An illustration of some of the product functionality already available is shown in Figure 6.4 on the following page.

In the e-business age, flexible strategic measures of success, which evolved middle-out and are distributed across the key areas of a business, are crucial to survival. In such an environment, business processes must be plugged into real-time online performance management systems to report on and evolve the right set of performance measures. Business processes continually generate information, which can be data-mined and evaluated as to its implications for the firm and its stakeholders. Various pieces of software are now available to generate real-time adaptive feedback and learning from business processes. Strategic enterprise management modules are being produced by most of the large ERP vendors, and they promise to deliver what the executive information systems of the early 1990s failed to deliver.

Such systems will be useful to executives who require instant overviews of what is happening in a business. They will also act as a powerful learning and communication tool for managers, helping them find new ways to improve their business performance. The management processes developed in this way should enable executives to sort what is mission critical from what is humdrum and unimportant, and to escalate key issues into the next level of cognitive processes in the organisation.

## E-business technology platforms 6.4

| Portal server technologies | Call centre | ITV support | | PC support | PDA/phone | Other services |
|---|---|---|---|---|---|---|
| Componentised middleware/glue | Channel integration | | | Common business objects | | |
| E-customer technologies | Catalogues | E-shop | | Wallets | Micro billing | Payments processing |
| Community and commercial technologies | Mktg and campaign systems | Personalis-ation services | Intelligent search services | Intelligent decision services | Decision support systems | Workflow/ case / Dynamic publishing |
| Management and planning | Back office administration | Systems administration | Planning | | Reporting and analysis | Profiling and data mining |
| Business process technologies | Data models | | | | Data integration | |
| Communications | Media product and content information/rules | | | Rules, tables (knowledge) | | Customer information |
| External technologies | Linkages | | | e-mail, chat, bulletin board | | |
| E-new business and e-procurement technologies | ISP | In-portal alliance partners | Off-portal alliance partners | Trading community | Content providers | Technology providers / Advertisers |
| General management | Finance | HR | | Marketing | Alliances/legal | Strategy |

## Business design

In the age of e-business, most organisations will be structured as versatile innovators driven by adaptive processes. Much of the productive capacity of such organisations will be distributed across many enterprises, forming value webs with key business partners and stakeholders. Several different kinds of business designs are emerging in the connected economy, as illustrated in Figure 6.5. In the experience economy, you are what you charge for. A variety of business models have been generated which illustrate the various ways of earning revenue.

CONTENT-BASED MODELS

- ◪ Content creators, for example, CNN, CNBC, Dow-Jones and Reuters provide news and share prices and Forrester.com generates e-commerce business analysis.
- ◪ Content packagers, for example, FT.com provides a searchable index of many different business reports from many different companies.

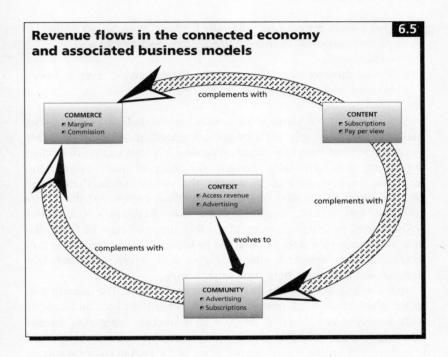

**Revenue flows in the connected economy and associated business models** `6.5`

CONTEXT-BASED MODELS

- ☛ Search engines, including some of the best-known names on the web such as Yahoo, Lycos, Excite.
- ☛ Portals, for example, Freeserve. In the UK the advent of free ISP/portal services has forced many portals to examine new funding mechanisms apart from access revenues.

COMMUNITY-BASED MODELS

Communities have emerged in many areas, wherever a common interest is shared. Examples include Motley Fools, iVillage, BizProLink and NetNoir.

COMMERCE-BASED MODELS

This category has provided one of the widest ranges of business models, including the following.

- ☛ Aggregators, for example, Chemdex provides a comprehensive list of laboratory supplies bringing suppliers together.

◪ Auctioneers, for example, eBay, the first person-to-person online auction company, deriving revenue from posting fees and commissions.

◪ Virtual category killers, for example, eToys, deriving revenue from margins on products sold.

Consumers in the physical (or onland) world walk into a shopping mall and find what they want by going to the shop or department that stocks the kind of item they require. Whether it is toys, clothes or kitchen appliances, they physically navigate the store or mall using signs, directions and memory as guides. In the online world, there is no physical world to navigate, only a user interface, comprising the screen, keyboard and mouse. Consumers are now navigating a cognitive environment, in which clues to where they are, and how to find what they want, are on the screen or marked by sounds. Almost everything they interact with is designed, and their eyes and minds are needed to navigate, without much help from other senses.

In the online world, the store exists only in the mind. The departments in the physical store are now experiences, rather than specific locations with products and services for sale in particular categories. Understanding how value-adding experiences are created in this hybrid world of onland and online environments is one of the keys to business success in the 21st century.

The basic laws of business success will still apply, however. A business will need a clear and attractive range of value propositions, which are delivered through a set of distinctive capabilities, enabled by a competitive resource base, infrastructure and outstanding core competencies.

What will be different in the evolving competitive landscape is that businesses will need to develop strategy using a variety of complexity-based methods, ranging from fitness landscape simulations to combinatorial experiments and adaptive strategy processes. Success will depend on the ability to navigate and adapt to rapidly evolving business landscapes.

## Leadership style

In the flat, comparatively democratic organisations that are gradually becoming the norm, leaders must know how to motivate their people by showing them the way and demonstrating that they are future-focused and heading in the right direction. If they do not, the organisation's talent will simply move on.

This style of leadership will draw heavily on the visionary and learning leadership models developed by people such as Warren Bennis and Peter Drucker. It will also succeed by creating an environment with values and behaviour that are attractive to those who work in it (and to those who deal with the organisation), and which is mindful of the complexity in which it exists.

### Organisational values

Increasingly, organisational values will be formed participatively, embodying evolving sets of context-sensitive rules, which are highly flexible in their application. The trends of moral individualism and community miniaturisation mean that all organisations need to be capable of supporting shifts in values to enable members of an organisation to respond to different contexts.

### Knowledge management approaches

Information systems and knowledge management approaches will provide considerable competitive advantage to organisations that are capable of using them to develop distinctive capabilities. Instead of the top-down approaches of the 20th century, knowledge management will operate through distributed learning processes grounded in shared purpose and values. In other words, knowledge management will become much more entrepreneurial and less corporately focused, as web-based technologies rapidly accelerate the speed at which new ideas can be tested and taken to market.

This approach is championed by the successful credit card and financial services company Capital One, where the job descriptions for staff focus on the number of experiments they are able to generate, and the rate at which they can take successful new offers to market. Using this data-mining-driven, highly iterative approach, Capital One has grown dramatically at the expense of traditional credit card providers, as it is able to focus on niches of a few hundred people and their needs. As Jim Donohey, Capital One's chief technology officer, has said, the goal of Capital One is to have tens of millions of customer segments, with one customer in each.

The emphasis in successful e-businesses will therefore be on a bottom-up, competency-building approach, enabling the formation of new categories and models, rather than merely gathering data around existing ways of viewing the business. Just as Amazon, eBay, e-Trade and Yahoo have rewritten the rule books in creating new kinds of business models, with very different value propositions from anything that existed before in the onland world, so players in the knowledge economy will have to reinvent their offers regularly. Knowledge management techniques are thus crucial to survival.

A variety of techniques are emerging, many of them drawing on a rich heritage of existing management methods. For example, accelerated learning approaches and creativity techniques are now being applied in an online environment. New web-friendly software, based on computer-based training methods, enables just-in-time know-how to be delivered to knowledge workers when and where they need it, via the web or on CD-ROM. In the creativity arena, the latest versions of Idons-for-Thinking, Idea Fisher, Imagination Engineering, IdeaPro and many others are available to accelerate brainstorming and the generation of new ideas.

Creativity techniques, by their very nature, embody complexity and evolutionary principles as they evolve through the three stages of:

- generating divergent ideas (for example, brainstorming);
- finding new patterns emerging from the ideas generated (emergence and pattern recognition); and
- selecting or building on the best ideas (convergence) to take them to implementation.

Intelligent agent-based programmes, as developed by firms such as Intelligenesis, with its Webmind product, and Autonomy, with its range of knowledge management products, enable users automatically to:

- aggregate and organise all internal documents (such as e-mails and presentations) and external information (such as news feeds and websites) into easy-to-navigate directories;
- categorise and tag all documents, presentations, articles and web pages based on the actual ideas in each piece of text, and insert hypertext links to other relevant material;
- access relevant information through easy-to-navigate directories or natural language queries;
- profile users based on the ideas in the text they read or write, and then identify colleagues with relevant skills and knowledge;
- route information to those most likely to be interested, including delivering personalised information that helps employees keep up to date with industry and competitive developments.

Lastly, complexity-based knowledge management techniques will need to align with the organisational requirements for innovation, especially the fact that most major breakthroughs are generated in peripheral isolates. Peripheral isolates are groups that are cut off from the mainstream of thinking in a particular area or discipline but are sufficiently connected to reinvent a discipline or invent new technologies and methods, which are then taken up by the mainstream again. The invention of personal computers, the Internet and other major technologies are all examples of ways in which socially peripheral and comparatively isolated groups of scientists, engineers or programmers invented something radically different while tinkering at the edges of traditional disciplines.

## Beyond methods

In the knowledge economy, most of the new forms of wealth are being generated through value webs. For a value web to function, it is essential that a radius of trust is established between the players in the web. The trust between the members comes in many different versions, as different kinds of players validate each other according to different criteria, depending upon their role in the value web. For example, Hewlett-Packard's Enterprise Solutions Group trusts Intel to produce the new 64-bit Merced chip, which will power a range of new HP products. HP also trusts Microsoft to produce the high-performance Windows 2000 (or NT5) server software, which will fully exploit the features of the Merced chip.

However, HP expects Intel to sell the Merced chip to other players, and it knows that Microsoft will be delivering Windows 2000 globally to all NT and Windows users. What matters to HP is that by collaborating with Intel and Microsoft it is gaining valuable knowledge and building a powerful reputation in the market-place for cross-platform enterprise computing capabilities. HP also continues to build a wider radius of trust, making it easier to do business in its chosen value webs and creating more options.

Other than the radius of trust, the most important asset an organisation can build is not physical or financial capital but social capital. Social capital creates high levels of trust in and around an organisation. Such trust tells people not only that the organisation will deliver on its promises, but also that it is a rewarding organisation to do business with in the longer term. Economic hubs, such as Silicon Valley and Seattle Forest, and financial centres, such as London, New York and Tokyo, thrive on a high level of social capital. This creates an environment in which more risks can be taken and promotes more ways in which these risks can be reduced through the network of relationships in the system. In short, social capital creates more options, encourages diversity and fuels economic growth. Like communities, however, social capital takes time to build, and requires the right ingredients.

## A helicopter view

In conclusion, to recap the principal messages of previous chapters:

### 1. Understand the drivers of the e-business economy

In Chapter 1 the principal message was that the sources of complexity and uncertainty in the new business environment can be understood, and that businesses must understand and master complexity to survive and thrive. The chapter explained how the age we are entering is a product of seven major evolutionary waves, where technology emerges as the major driving force behind social and organisational evolution. The 12 drivers of the e-business economy together with the six forces of business and technological evolution provide powerful frameworks to help map the new business environment.

Appendix 1 provides more background on the origins and basic principles of complexity science and how a complexity perspective on management and organisations is different and adds value.

### 2. Understand the new definitions of success in an e-business world

Chapter 2 looked at what it takes to be successful in a complex, rapidly evolving world, contrasting conventional success recipes with the new drivers of success in the knowledge economy. The messages and frameworks in Chapter 2 include the nine basic principles of complexity (self-organisation, emergence, non-linearity, memory, adaptability, being, identity, conscious learning and coherence) and the three aspects of organisational evolution (co-evolution, adaptive agents and internal models).

These basic concepts set the scene for an overview of how organisations evolve in complex business ecosystems through the process of strategic dialogue. Strategic dialogue relies for its success on strategic learning, a process that can be initiated and maintained using the five rules of complexity management. Appendix 2 explains in more detail how to apply the principles of leadership in the third millennium.

### 3. Learn from current complexity applications

Chapter 3 investigated a variety of complexity management applications in four main areas: managing and changing organisations; strategic management; information systems; and operations management. It shows how complexity management is being applied in many major organisations.

The main lesson in Chapter 3 is how rapidly businesses are taking up and applying complexity-based ways of doing things. Complexity-based techniques and technologies are becoming the next source of competitive advantage.

### 4. Understand the key evolutionary challenges

Chapter 4 demonstrated how to use the wheel of business evolution framework to consciously manage the evolution of a business. The alignment of the external forces operating on an organisation with the internal capabilities, processes and competencies of the organisation, is seen to be the key to successful business evolution. Each of the eight segments of the wheel framework is based on research using the diagnostic questionnaire in Appendix 3.

Some basic lessons about managing organisational evolution were derived from the wheel of business evolution, and illustrated through eight case studies of three different kinds of adaptive strategies: shapers, adapters and reactors.

### 5. Use the right tools and methods to make things happen

Chapter 5 sets out a series of strategic management tools known as the FutureStep methodology, an approach developed with and for organisations operating in the digital economy. The tools and methods involved should ensure that a widely shared vision is created, enabling a business to evolve in a robust strategic direction, which is clearly articulated and understood at all levels in the organisation and by strategic partners. The modules in the process also ensure that:

- the major capabilities, competencies and resources required to deliver on key facets of the company's strategic direction are in place and aligned;
- the changes needed in and around the organisation are identified and initiated; and
- this all happens in an accelerated fashion.

Appendix 4 describes the role of scenarios in business evolution in more depth.

Appendix 5 explains the new language that is emerging to describe business evolution in the knowledge economy.

Lastly, there is a short list of further recommended reading on complexity management and the new sciences.

## Pioneering opportunites

These are exciting and risky times. As individuals, we have an unprecedented opportunity to shape the course of history and the nature of the seventh wave economy and society that we are entering. This book will, it is hoped, provide valuable insights into what is driving the evolution of this new world, as well as some essential tools and frameworks to act on these insights. Developing foresight into what impact these e-business drivers will have on all organisations is the major strategic challenge for the 21st century. As Tom Petzinger puts it in *The New Pioneers*:[17]

> *Today's pioneers have embarked on a new frontier, some in search of riches, some in search of freedom, all in search of the new. Unlike the West of old this frontier is not one place. It is a frontier of technologies, ideas and values. The new pioneers celebrate individuality over conformity among their employees and customers alike. They deploy technology to distribute rather than consolidate authority and creativity. They compete through resilience instead of resistance, through adaptation instead of control. In a time of dizzying complexity and change, they realise that tightly drawn strategies become brittle while shared purpose endures. Capitalism, in short, is merging with humanism.*

# Appendix 1
# A brief primer on the new sciences, complexity and organisations

## The roots of complex systems thinking

The breakthroughs in classical science that followed the publication of Newton's *Principia* in 1686 catalysed a series of technological advances that spawned the Industrial Revolution. Such advances also lead to unprecedented social, economic and political change, while providing an intellectual framework for economic theory and inspiration for early management theorists. Although classical theory has served us well in its time, the science of complexity is creating a new understanding of the world, and of social and economic systems, which highlight the deficiencies of the linear and simplistic classical theories.

Complexity science was one of the major scientific breakthroughs of the 20th century, providing managers with the opportunity to use new metaphors, frameworks, tools and models to develop strategies and organisational designs that emphasise intelligence, learning, flexibility, creativity and adaptiveness. It can be defined as follows:

> *Complex systems research (or "complexity science") is the study of the properties, behaviour and evolution of complex biological, computational, technological and economic systems (termed "complex adaptive systems"). It builds inter alia on the mathematics of chaos, catastrophe and genetic algorithm theory that describe non-linear systems, and integrates findings from evolution and cognitive science which describe the emergence of life and intelligence. Complexity is not a single discipline, but a process that represents the sharing of ideas, method and experiences across a number of fields. The resulting synthesis has generated a powerful set of theories, tools and models that can provide important insights into the complex realities of organisational development, business strategy and economic change.*[1]

Recent research suggests that complexity, life and intelligence arise at the boundary between order and chaos, where complex systems are both stable enough to store information yet evanescent enough to transmit it, and hence be spontaneous, adaptive and alive. Complex adaptive systems (CAS) grow complex structures and environments, which are adaptable, resilient and capable of generating perpetual novelty. They do, however, often lack efficiency, predictability, controllability and immediacy. At their best, complex adaptive systems:

- are self-generating and self-organising;
- thrive on individual choice and spontaneous creativity;
- are robust, capable of stability and also self-renewal; and
- are capable of developing and displaying intelligence.

Complexity theory was developed from the idea that simple rules (structures, principles), with a design or grammar, are the source of the greatest variety and flexibility in the universe. The theory has been demonstrated and further developed by experiments made possible by highly elaborate computer simulations. The message is quite clear: survival is contingent on a design that balances the forces of an ecology in such a way that a stable base identity is created – an identity with enormous flexibility in its specifics and applications. Such an identity is generated in the interaction between an organisation and its environment, and shaped through the strategic management process.

## From the big bang to the knowledge age

The universe and the world of business appear to operate on principles of scientific chaos and complexity. These principles include the possibility that the universe as a physical system is poised at the "edge of (scientific) chaos (not "randomness")". Together with entropic principles driving the universe towards heat death, there are also negentropic forces feeding on this energy, giving rise to life and ways of making a living. Life and business exhibit these same principles, operating at or near the edge of chaos, obeying power laws revealing avalanches of extinctions in everything from species to languages to firms.

### The biosphere emerges from the remnants of the big bang

Biologists and archaeologists say that life began some 3.5 billion years ago in the primordial oceans. One of the main features of the emergence of life was autocatalysis: a process whereby sets of chemicals in clay minerals created self-sustaining chain reactions leading to the first unicellular forms of life, the prokaryotes. Complex chains of reactions are a characteristic of every form of life in existence today, as well as the biological ecosystems and social systems of which we form a part. (The origins of life are beautifully described in Stuart Kauffman's *At Home in the Universe*, which also includes many other insights into the natural world.[2]) We live in an autocatalytic universe in which, wherever we find energy, the challenge is to stop things reacting with each other rather than to start reactions.

A further startling feature of the universe, and of life, is that the whole system appears to exist on the edge of chaos, a form of bounded instability in which small perturbations in a system can generate large effects. Again, to observe this phenomenon, energy of some kind has to be available. From the distribution of the size of quasars, to the distribution of the size of avalanches in a sand-hill, a "power law" is in operation, in which there are fewer large events or phenomena and many smaller ones. This is also an uncanny echo of this law in Pareto's law, which points out that 80% of wealth is generally in the hands of 20% of the population – the 80/20 principle.

Because of the autocatalytic nature of living systems operating at the edge of chaos, all of the order around us is actually the result of a phenomenon called self-organisation. In other words, natural and human environments contain order because biological or socio-economic forces and entities self-organise into forms of order which, in retrospect, appear designed. The eye has spontaneously emerged several times in evolution in different phyla, yet it would appear to be too complex simply to have emerged from a process of self-organisation and evolution. It did, however, although it took 3.5 billion years to do so.

Self-organisation can take place only in a state of bounded instability (or, as the complexity theorists call it, the edge of chaos), and generally results in the resources in a system being reorganised into new patterns. We are all familiar with these states of bounded instability: a merger or acquisition, a tense relationship that threatens to end in separation or divorce, a change of government, a change in the CEO or board of a company, and so on. What does this mean in practice?

Non-living physical and chemical systems generally settle down into an orderly state of lowest energy (all fires burn out, all ice melts at room temperature into water, which drops to the ground, rain falls from the clouds and settles to the lowest level it can as groundwater, and so on). Living systems, however, go the other way: while alive they generate movement and energy, feeding off the energy dissipated by other systems, whether non-living (such as the sun) or living (such as plants and animals). The same is true for organisations and businesses: to survive they must engage with other living systems in a flow of energy, matter and information, and add more energy (or value) than they take out of the flow, otherwise they go bust.

Self-organisation enables complex adaptive systems to emerge at a variety of levels in the natural and socio-economic worlds. Once complex adaptive systems come into being they can do one of two things.

- Remain in the same form. For example, the original forms of life, the prokaryotes, did not change for the first billion years of their existence, until they had generated so much oxygen as waste product that the eukaryotes began to emerge from mutations and self-organisation. The eukaryotes were capable of surviving on oxygen, and led to the multicellular life forms we are familiar with today. (The original prokaryotes still live on in our cells today and are known as mitochondria.)
- Evolve, which is what started happening when multicellular life forms began proliferating across the surface of the planet. Since then evolution has not stopped, and it is now taking place in many ways: biologically, technologically, economically and socially.

Evolution of any kind goes through three stages: first it generates variety through self-organisation and mutation, which is then selected by interaction with the environment. Those variations that succeed through many successive generations then generally become fixed; for example, the size and connectivity of the human brain is two to three times that of any other species, because this feature has become locked in through its success over many generations. Other variations in homo sapiens, for example, the tail, have not proven successful through successive generations and are now left as relics in our bodies with no function (the coccyx bone at the base of the spine, which used to be our tail, for example).[3]

Once the complexity of a group of interacting biological or socio-economic entities reaches a certain point, complex natural or business ecosystems emerge, in which co-evolution starts to dominate the way in which the evolutionary process happens. Although most evolution has been painted as Darwinian (selection of the fittest and strongest individuals or species), we now know that through a process of mutual accommodation there is a great deal more of symbiosis and co-operation between species than there is competition. Such co-operative processes then lead to the emergence of natural networks and hierarchies, in which the sharing of resources and specialisation of roles can take place.

## Out of the biosphere emerges the sociosphere

The social world humans inhabit is a product of our origins as "wise apes". Our tribal and territorial nature emerges from several million years of evolution in which we survived and evolved as a result of our ability to work together in small groups, developing and sharing tools, know-how and the products of our hunting and gathering. Networks and hierarchies are essential features of being a wise ape. Hierarchies enable the sharing of know-how, resources and tools. Networks provide a stable structure in which long-term commitments can be made and enforced, while also recognising the different developmental levels, needs and responsibilities of members of the tribe.

From tool-making and use, humans eventually found ways of generating surpluses, resulting in the impetus for trade, leading to the emergence of a complex sociosphere. In the sociosphere, humans found that complex cognitive functioning and language were critical enablers of their way of life as a species, because socialisation into a culture, specialisation in specific roles and tasks, education and training to support socialisation and specialisation, and innovation all involve complex communication, technical and social skills.

Each stage of evolution builds on the stages that have gone before. For example, all of the properties of the biosphere carry through to the sociosphere: autocatalytic networks; self-organisation in zones of bounded instability; the emergence of new levels of system out of earlier components of more primitive systems; and complex ecosystems in which entities co-evolve with each other.

## The sociosphere forms the basis for the technosphere

Complex tool-making and use, combined with trading, eventually led to the establishment of specialised factories where production methods (whether making steam engines or building the Model T Ford) enabled the realisation of economies of scale. These allowed the creation of even greater surpluses in industrial economies and, for the first time in history, sufficient abundance, giving humans enough resources to live on without having to contemplate scarcity.

Once production methods became sufficiently advanced, they could produce machines for calculation and communication, which, along with published media and notebooks, became the first mind-tools to be mass manufactured. Mind-tools and the science of management began to co-evolve, so that the industrialised methods of control that evolved from the factories of the industrial revolution began to be used to increase productivity and control over everything from factory output to railroad schedules. Such technologies afforded powerful tools to synchronise, concentrate and automate the activities of industrial society.

In the 1950s and early 1960s, once the age of abundance had begun, command-and-control management gradually gave way to a slightly more *laissez-faire* form of motivation known as Theories Y and Z. Human beings were assumed to want to achieve in work and simply needed to be motivated to develop their full potential. Technologies and mind-tools were transformed during the subsequent few decades to become tools of liberation, as Apple depicted in its "1984" ad in which an Apple Macintosh breaks the hold of the cloned "big brothers".

The story is not yet complete, of course, and in the complex adaptive knowledge economy many radically new forms of organisation and ways of doing business will emerge. So what does all this mean for understanding, learning from and managing complexity?

## The complexity perspective on management

In the seventh wave, at the beginning of the second renaissance, policymakers and executives are undergoing a transformation in their perceptions about what it means to lead and manage. This transformation is being brought about by the need to manage in more complex, fast-moving environments, in which the old rules of the game no longer work and views of the world require reframing. The way in which we view the world is a function of both who we are and what we are capable of seeing. The choices we make and who we become result from the interaction between how we understand the world and what we do with that understanding in specific situations.

### The old rules of the game

The traditional perspective of management (which was dominated by a form of scientific logic known as positivism) makes a number of fundamental assumptions. For example, traditional management theory and practice assumes the following.

◿ Objective truth is "out there", and facts are independent from their observer. Thought and action are viewed as separate events in a linear cause and effect relationship, where thought precedes action, and where most strategies are rationally thought through and deliberately programmed to achieve their objectives. Knowledge precedes and defines action.

- Much of the task of management revolves around the analysis of what needs to be done, and then the programming of the actions to achieve the goals identified together with the management of these actions, using established rational decision-making frameworks.
- Language is a precise tool, and the more precisely it can be used the better. (So positivist traditionalists favour exceptionally precise but artificial languages, such as mathematics and statistics.)

Positivists generally come from the pure sciences, and disciplines such as engineering, computing, accountancy and mathematics, where the proponents of this approach can justify it through its delivery of theories and technologies that are practically useful. Positivism is the driving force behind modernism and modernisation, and the rational, analytical approaches to management.

To understand the difference between the complexity perspective and the traditional perspective, it is necessary first to establish what are the old rules of the game. In the traditional perspective on management, a number of fundamental assumptions are made.

- Equilibrium is assumed to be the norm, and the strategist's job is to find ways of maintaining corporate equilibrium through planning approaches and systems, even when organisations and markets are known to be complex adaptive systems operating far from equilibrium.
- Predictability and control: we work in areas and ways in which we can attempt to predict the future and control most of the aspects of our destiny. We may even know what we do not know, but what kills businesses is what we do not know we do not know. How do we deal with uncertainty?
- Choice and intentionality: we assume that with enough information and a rational planning process we can make logical choices and deliver on the intentions we set ourselves. Our plans and budgets have a bad habit of coming unstuck with monotonous regularity. What does strategic choice mean in a complex, uncertain, far-from-equilibrium, fractal world?

◪ Best way of doing things: we believe that there are recipes that will guarantee success, if we can just find them and make them stick. We use these recipes as alibis when things go wrong, and then reach out for the next fad. Surely there must be a way to escape this vicious circle of "initiativitis"?

In the old rules of the game, investments and commitments were made, then implemented. To ensure these commitments were successful, any perturbations that were perceived as having negative consequences for such investments or commitments were damped down. The commitments were measured in terms of business cases, project plans and budgets, and any deviations from plan were called variances, which were generally to be avoided.

The traditional approach assumed that any variances were caused by, or were the fault of, someone. Elaborate procedures were thus set up to measure performance, so that variances could be associated with individual behaviour. Random positive variances (good luck) resulted in rewards for superior performance, but recurring negative variances were associated with demotion and blame, and eventually dismissal.

At its extreme, the traditional approach to management results in a Dilbert-like world, in which the entire organisation is seeking ways to improve its image with least effort, while finding appropriate scapegoats to blame when things go wrong. This is a cruel Darwinian world, in which the ends justify the means and no one can be trusted for long. Given the success of the Dilbert series of books, a great deal of the traditional approach to management must still exist.

The lens of traditional thinking generally results in one of three outcomes.

◪ Explanation. If the system is genuinely linear with clear cause and effect relationships (for example, many mechanical, electrical or simple chemical systems), it is possible to explain the behaviour of the system fairly accurately using the traditional perspective. It must be emphasised, however, that such situations and systems are the exception rather than the rule in life.

◪ Ignorance. It may not be possible to recognise or comprehend patterns in what appear to be chaotic, random or simply unfathomable systems or phenomena. This leads to a failure to generate understanding or knowledge and a loss of potential opportunities, or a failure to recognise potential threats. For example, before the disciplines of psychology and cognitive science developed, the mind appeared to be a complete mystery because of its profound complexity and non-linearity. Similar examples abound throughout history, where simple solutions are prescribed to complex problems without any reliability of outcome, from weather (the rain dance) to healthcare (the witchdoctor) to economics (the forecaster) to astronomy (the astrologer).

◪ Oversimplification. Highly complex phenomena may be oversimplified using linear cause and effect models, leading to incorrect and even dangerous conclusions, especially when the side-effects or phase transitions of the system or solution that is being modelled are an issue. This happens a great deal in any new area of science, where obvious cause and effect relationships are easily spotted, and only in the longer term do side-effects become apparent. Thalidomide and DDT are two examples of the damage over-simplistic models can wreak in medicine and agriculture, leading to deformed babies and ecosystem destruction respectively, although they were both at first deemed safe. Genetically modified crops could be another example.

## The interpretivist (or post-modernist) perspective on management

The often accurate perception that the traditional, positivist perspective on life had severe drawbacks, despite its success in creating new technologies and worldviews, caused a reaction to positivism, which can be briefly summarised under the label interpretivism. Ever since Plato disagreed with Aristotle, who some would claim to be the father of positivist thought, the reaction to positivism has often resulted in an equally extreme set of views. From the early existentialists to post-modernists such as Derrida, interpretivism alerts us to the extent to which we construct our own reality and deconstruct the realities and "texts" of others.

In the mainstream interpretivist view of management several assumptions are made.

◪ Subjective truth is "in there", and nothing can be stated that is independent of the observer. All perception and cognition is simply an interpretation of what is going on, rather than a form of "truth", so one interpretation should not be privileged over another.

- Thought and action are inseparably intertwined, and people construct their own selves, meanings and futures through action. Knowledge is only possible after action, and even then it is open to doubt.
- Management is a performing art in which creativity and interaction are critical, enabling new meanings, visions and ideas to emerge from a diverse array of elements. In this world little can be planned, as the surprises and shocks of the new are a daily occurrence, and the best that can be achieved is messy adaptation or creation.
- Language is seen to be inherently ambiguous, lending an element of surprise to conversations and keeping space open for dialogue and creativity. Reality is seen to be a personally and socially constructed phenomenon.

Interpretivists often have backgrounds in the arts, languages and social sciences, and disciplines such as philosophy. Entrepreneurs and people in professions such as psychology and change management also share some of these assumptions. Interpretivism is the *zeitgeist* of the post-modernist and visionary or transformation schools of management.

The new sciences create a bridge between positivism and inter-pretivism. Positivism can be reframed as an attempt to view the world through predefined categories, in which the semantic network in the left brain is used to categorise and count things, and then to form relationships between them and explanations about these relationships. Positivism is thus a top-down approach to the world, relying on pre-existing categories and frameworks to interpret, explain and act upon phenomena. It is most useful when the world is stable and linear, so neat categories can account for and explain everything to our satisfaction.

Interpretivism can be reframed as an attempt to view the world through a multifaceted set of lenses, deploying, for example, metaphors and systems-thinking type approaches to free us from the tyranny of pre-existing categories. In this way of viewing the world the more intuitive, right-brained visual network is used, allowing us to tap into emotional intelligence and memory as well as mental intelligence. Interpretivism is thus a bottom-up approach to the world, attempting to build up patterns from discrete sets of phenomena, and to understand the changing dynamics of these patterns. In this way new categories can be invented which transcend the old. Interpretivism is most useful in a rapidly changing, non-linear world, in which past patterns and categories are out of date and of little use in understanding the present or future.

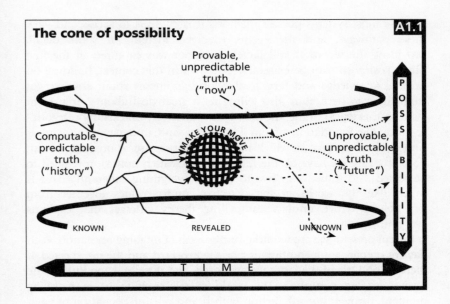

**The cone of possibility**

A1.1

Provable,
unpredictable
truth
("now")

Computable,
predictable
truth
("history")

MAKE YOUR MOVE

Unprovable,
unpredictable
truth
("future")

POSSIBILITY

KNOWN            REVEALED            UNKNOWN

TIME

*Evolutionary thinking*

The lens of complexity enables a powerful new way of thinking about complex phenomena: evolutionary thinking. Based on the new sciences, evolutionary thinking powerfully deploys positivist and interpretivist approaches through an understanding of the way in which computable, predictable truths emerge (in the form of "the past" or "history") from the unprovable and unpredictable truths surrounding us (in the form of "the future"). To understand how this works, it is necessary to think differently about time.

In the centre of Figure A1.1 there is a circle labelled "make your move", which lies midway between two convex lines that slope away, to the left into the past and to the right into the future. The area between these two convex lines represents the set of available pathways from which you could have arrived at your present state, and from which you may evolve from your present state into a future state that is presently unknown. The "you" being described could be at whatever level of description you are operating, from the individual to the social, or even the sub-atomic through the microcellular to the galactic.

On the left-hand side of the diagram are sets of solid arrows depicting the different pathways that may have been involved in your getting from a prior state in time to now, and the state you are in at this moment.

Because most systems possess memory, it is possible to access and view these pathways, and the events involved therein, in some detail, providing the record is still largely intact or was captured in the first place. Positivism can be extremely powerful in this context, building on existing knowledge and facts to develop hypotheses about how we got from there to here, thus also telling us a great deal about our present state. In this world of the known we can safely rely on existing categories to form the foundation of our knowledge and understanding. Unless some part of the record, which may reveal a surprise, is missing, we can be pretty sure we have all the relevant facts, which now simply need to be sorted into a theory or two to explain everything coherently. This is much like the world of the detective, putting clues together from available evidence until a compelling theory emerges that explains everything.

In the present, we are working in a context of ongoing revelation. Each day we prepare for a combination of the expected and the unexpected. If there is too little of the latter we are bored, and if there is too little of the former we are perturbed. The world reveals itself to us moment by moment, through our interaction with it and our interpretation of what is actually going on. The present is a strange place because we are required simultaneously to look back at the past and project our understanding of the past into our expectations of the future, and to consider that the future may hold as yet unknown truths that we have not yet discovered. Evolutionary thinking requires that this tension be maintained as much as we can bear, in order to create as many options as possible in the face of uncertainty while retaining as much of our capability from the past to act as swiftly as we can whenever required.

On the right-hand side of Figure A1.1 is the world of the future and the unknown. In the future, the only kind of truth that can exist is unprovable and unpredictable. There are two approaches to the future.

- To attempt to impose our current understanding of the present on to the future.
- To be open to doubt and enable ourselves to question our assumptions so that we can perceive different possibilities in the future.

Positivists would be more likely to enjoy the imposition of the current paradigm on to the future, as this would appear to yield a higher return on their current stock of knowledge. The positivists' perception is that this will eliminate most of the uncertainty attached to the future and the unknown. If the future state of the environment and the system they are working with is the same as the present state, they will be proved correct.

Interpretivists would be more comfortable with the second approach to the future, in which uncertainty is dealt with through an openness to reperceiving the world as it evolves, rather than attempting to impose the status quo or maintain the current paradigm. This approach can result in a highly adaptive way of dealing with change in an organisation or the environment. At the extreme, however, the interpretivists' approach may amount to a passive acceptance of whatever is going on, with no attempt to shape or mould it.

Positivists wish to maintain the status quo and will change only if there is hard "proof". (At the extreme, this view would typically be associated with the ISTJ personality profile in Myers-Briggs terminology.) The risk of the positivists is that they will be conserving a smaller and smaller pie for themselves and their like-minded brethren, while the world changes rapidly around them. At its extreme, positivism is similar to religious fundamentalism, where there is only one way to perceive the world and all others are prohibited or filtered out. In other words, it is a closed system.

Interpretivists, however, go with the flow, and generally to adapt to whatever is happening around them. They can sense when things are changing and will be open to trying new ways of seeing and being. (At the extreme, this would be associated with the ENFP personality profile in Myers-Briggs terminology.) The risk of the interpretivists is that they will lose their identity and capability as they literally merge with their surroundings. At its extreme, the interpretivist approach becomes a form of fatalism and collectivism, where individuality disappears in a completely open system.

An evolutionary thinker would transcend both the positivists' and the interpretivists' perspectives, and see that they are simply different ways of dealing with uncertainty and ambiguity. Depending on the context, the evolutionary perspective views both the positivist and interpretivist lenses as ways of dealing with different kinds of situations. For example:

- When dealing with known and comparatively stable systems, some of the positivists' tools – econometrics, fact-based strategic analysis, the configuration school of organisational design, operational research, and so on – are very handy. This is particularly true for the computable, predictable truths of the past.

■ When facing unknown and unstable situations, a dash of interpretivism can be extremely useful, allowing ways of seeing a situation to be reperceived and reframed, and in the process enabling creative new perspectives and new opportunities to emerge. This approach is relevant when dealing with the unprovable, unpredictable truths of the future.

### The new rules of the game: the complexity perspective

The body of evidence and set of theories and models that comprise the new sciences can provide a powerful and unusual way of generating new insights into events and situations. The lens of the new sciences and complexity can enable us to shed the limitations of the modern and the post-modern perspective, and pierce the fog surrounding the apparently random, chaotic or inexplicable nature of most of the complex phenomena in life. At its best, a complexity perspective can generate a richer, more profound, coherent understanding of aspects of life than we ever dreamed possible.

Consider, for example, a flock of birds wheeling high in the sky. You may observe a number of things.

■ A V-shaped flock, in which the strongest birds (the leaders) lead the flock in the direction they choose.
■ Occasionally, a leader delegating the tiring role of piercing the sky first to a favoured subordinate.
■ The rest of the flock following the leaders in a neat V-formation to reduce wind resistance and protect from the dangers of predation.
■ An orderly flock, occasionally doing bizarre things that break this order.

According to the Boids simulation, there appear to be three simple rules generating flocking behaviour, whether a real flock in the sky or one in a computer-generated simulation. In Reynolds's simulation, each boid followed three rules of behaviour.

■ It tried to maintain a minimum distance from other objects in the environment, including other boids.
■ It tried to match velocities with boids in its neighbourhood.
■ It tried to move towards the perceived centre of mass of boids in its neighbourhood.

(As Arthur Battram, a friend of the author, points out: "Notice that there is no rule that says: 'form a flock!'") Applying an understanding of these rules and complexity thinking, one's interpretation of the flock's behaviour would be very different. One would notice:

- the speed with which the positions of the birds change, and the extent to which they are able to change direction suddenly through the emergence of a new collective direction from the spontaneous interaction of each member of the flock each simply obeying their own rules in their local interactions;
- that there are moments when the flock is stable and orderly, with a clear and coherent direction, whereas at other moments the flock is poised on the edge of chaos, so that a small movement in one area can ripple across the entire flock, causing a sudden change in direction.

One can only marvel at how such a complex set of emergent behaviours can come about through such a simple set of rules.

Moving to the human world, it is possible to observe, participate in and understand a vast array of phenomena, in a completely different way, using the lens of complexity. Take jazz musicians, for example.

The key to inspired improvisation is that soloists play a repertoire of simple modules, such as riffs, chords and note patterns, which lie in between the structure of the basic theme of the song. They literally improvise in the gaps between where the core theme should be, with the backing musicians providing a skeletal reminder of the underlying theme. When the real magic happens, making the hairs on the back of your neck stand up in unison, these simple modules combine into an emergent counterpoint, which stands the theme on its head and takes the music into a new dimension.

This phenomenon has been experienced and described by many music aficionados. The twist the lens of complexity provides is that a few basic rules and routines can generate an infinite variety of emergent variations on a theme, spun in the moment like a silvery, gossamer web over the band and audience alike. Yet beneath the surface of this apparent magic (or chaos, as novices appear to react to some improvisational forms) lies the order of the original theme. The players must hold this in their minds but then not play it, so that what happens in the gaps between where the theme should be is the improvisation.

These may be simple (and rather personal) examples of a complexity lens being used to generate a different kind of interaction with and understanding of natural and human phenomena. But complexity is a perspective that can improve everyone's understanding of what is really going on in individuals, teams, organisations, industries and economies.

### Kelly's nine laws of God in organisations
Complexity is a probabilistic science; in other words, it is able to state that under certain conditions, complex adaptive systems are likely to behave in a certain way, given the rules of complexity. These rules were articulated by Kevin Kelly[4] as the "Nine Laws of God" and can be summarised as follows.

#### DISTRIBUTE BEING
Distribute intelligence and resources outwards in any complex adaptive system to the parts, providing redundancy in functionality and resources. Ensure that the parts are, however, designed to be complementary, to ensure their collaboration. The challenge is to ensure effective integration within a complex system of many parts, where that integration is embodied in the genetic code of the parts. Apple Computer grew successfully in this mode during the 1980s through its principle of "Apple genes" in the Apple family of companies.[5]

#### CONTROL FROM THE BOTTOM UP
Let the parts of the complex adaptive system co-ordinate their own control systems rather than imposing them from the top. VISA is a successful network of banks offering the VISA card around the world. The network operates around some basic standards for issuing cards and processing transactions. The members of VISA agree to a code of practice, which ensures that fraud is minimised and that good service to customers is guaranteed. Although there is a VISA head office, the system only works because of the bottom-up control exercised by its members.

#### CULTIVATE INCREASING RETURNS
Increase the leverage of small actions that have large cumulative effects as they amplify their power through feedback processes. This is often done through a win-win action. For example, Netscape distributed its first version of Navigator software free over the Internet, and within months had more than a 90% share of the browser market. It was then able to sell much more server software to companies that wanted a presence on the net.

GROW BY CHUNKING

Chunk multiple simple components or layers into more complex systems using simple rules, much as DNA uses four building blocks to create a large number of proteins and cell types. McDonald's grew in this way during its first three decades, where the core design invented by the McDonald brothers in San Bernardino, California, was replicated first across the United States and then around the world, one chunk at a time. Each new outlet provided new lessons and challenges, which were incorporated into the learning process to improve subsequent outlets.[6]

MAXIMISE THE FRINGES

Encourage diversity, eccentricity and instability at the fringes of a system, thereby increasing resilience through perpetual innovation. 3M's Post-it note story[7] is a classic example of how the skunkworks principle in 3M's laboratories enabled a failed sticky glue formula to be reinvented as the weak adhesive on the back of post-it notes by Art Fry, the lab technician involved. Skunkworks are projects at the fringes of 3M, where inventors and technicians are encouraged to work on their own agendas some 10–15% of the time.

HONOUR YOUR ERRORS

Use errors as key signals for new learning that needs to take place in a system, rather than responding by attempting to shift blame. It is a little-known fact that the complaints department in most organisations is the source of many potential improvements and innovations, if only complaints were treated as opportunities for learning in more organisations. Nordstrom takes this to its extreme when it tells employees that the only company rule is that "there are no rules". Delighting the customer is the chief priority at Nordstrom, and employees are empowered to do just about anything to do this, particularly when a customer complains or there is some sort of internal problem.

PURSUE NO OPTIMA; HAVE MULTIPLE GOALS

In constantly shifting strategic landscapes (otherwise known as fitness landscapes or knowledge landscapes) optima are expensive to pursue as they not only take major investment to achieve, but also rigidify an organisation into an over-specialised position, making change and adaptation difficult. The concept of a portfolio is one way of hedging against uncertainty, whether the portfolio contains markets, products, services, goals, shares or people. It also positions the organisation to pursue opportunities in "adjacent possible" terrains, accessible to it by virtue of the flexibility inherent in having multiple goals.

### SEEK PERSISTENT DISEQUILIBRIUM

Encourage change and learning in an organisation through disequilibrium. This is a recurring theme in much of Tom Peters's work, from *In Search of Excellence* to *Liberation Management*, which revolves around *Thriving on Chaos*, the title of his second book. Disequilibrium enables an organisation to move quickly from one position to another, in much the same way as sprinters are poised at the starting blocks before a race rather than lying flat on their backs or standing to attention (that is, at equilibrium). All living systems operate at the edge of chaos, which is far from equilibrium. Equilibrium is the state of inanimate objects, or dead things. For example, the human body reaches equilibrium upon death, but while it is alive it relies on chains of catalytic reactions, which are prevented from causing chaos within the body by regulatory functions at many levels.[8]

### CHANGE CHANGES ITSELF

The dynamics of change ensure that living systems are continually undergoing change at one or more levels. Because successful species and individuals are regularly initiating, responding to, adapting to and changing as a result of changes in themselves and their environment, the process of life itself can be seen as fluid and highly unstable. Learning organisations[9] recognise the ninth law by institutionalising the change process into the genetic code of their processes and systems. This re-emphasises the point made by Senge that the fifth discipline (systems thinking) is essential to deal with all the complex feedback in living systems, particularly organisations. If change changes itself, then we must be capable of understanding the consequences of change and design our organisations and business ecosystems accordingly.

# Appendix 2
# Leadership

NO JOB IS MORE VITAL TO OUR SOCIETY THAN THAT OF THE LEADER. IT IS
THE LEADER WHO DETERMINES WHETHER OUR INSTITUTIONS SERVE US
WELL OR WHETHER THEY SQUANDER OUR TALENTS AND RESOURCES. IT IS
TIME TO STRIP AWAY THE FOLKLORE ABOUT THE WORK OF LEADERS, AND
TIME TO STUDY IT REALISTICALLY SO THAT WE CAN BEGIN THE DIFFICULT
TASK OF MAKING SIGNIFICANT IMPROVEMENTS IN ITS PERFORMANCE.

After Henry Mintzberg, McGill University, 1973[1]

## Navigating uncertainty

Leaders, entrepreneurs and managers all operate towards the top right-
hand quadrant of the complexity/uncertainty box depicted in Figure A2.1
on the following page. In other words, the more complex and uncertain
the task, the more likely it is to be carried out by some kind of leader,
entrepreneur or manager. Conversely, the simpler and more certain the
task, the more likely it is to be carried out by an operational worker. Of
course, some highly complex tasks are carried out by technical specialists,
and some highly uncertain tasks involving people are carried out by
human resources, organisational change and negotiating specialists. But
the unique characteristic of most general management tasks is their
combination of complexity and uncertainty.

There is an old saying: "you are where you come from". In the third
millennium, it is the way you think about who you are and what you do
that drives who you become. Successful purposive action involves finding
the right context in which what you do aligns with what needs to be
done and, if you are in business, what people are prepared to pay you
for. Our individual or corporate purpose, whether deliberate or emergent,
needs to deploy those things we can do uniquely (our distinctive
capabilities) in situations in which these capabilities are most valuable
(relevant markets). The process by which individuals and organisations
become successful is through developing a sustainable competitive
advantage, as illustrated in Figure A2.2 on page 251.

Purposive action, which harnesses distinctive capabilities and applies
them to the most relevant markets, stems from individual and corporate
intentions, whether we are aware of these intentions or not.

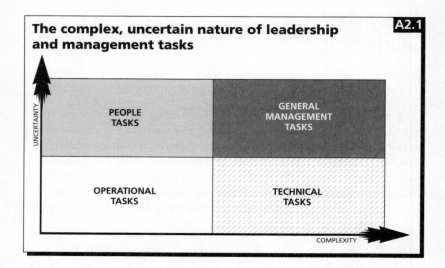

Intentionality, which is the directional aspect of our existence, is a result of our individual uniqueness and our shared heritage. We are all coming from somewhere and going somewhere, even if at times it may seem as though we are standing still. We may be aware of such intentionality, or it may be unconscious. If we are aware of it, then we are able to articulate intentionality as the "I want" or "I should" at the micro-level of our existence, or as the realisation of our inner essence and destiny as an individual or organisation at the macro-level.

Because we are generally not aware of the operation of our subconscious processes, intentionality appears to come from somewhere beyond the place where we perceive its presence or influence. Intentionality is a product of a learning process that has resulted in the recognition of a coherent pattern formed between ourselves and our environment, which defines who we are, why we are here and what we do. Such patterns are stored as mental models; an organisation is the sum total of the interactions between people and their mental models, constructing shared meaning through these models so as to undertake collective action for a shared purpose.

In organisational terms, intentionality is most frequently expressed in terms of a vision, a mission, objectives or a goal. At its most comprehensive, intentionality is capable of creating a picture of a desirable future state for large numbers of people, acting as a motivator and guide for the attainment of that state. At its simplest, intentionality

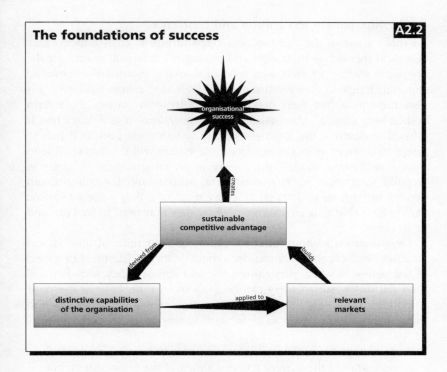

**The foundations of success**                                    A2.2

can be expressed in terms of an individual's purpose, role and objectives in an organisation or society.

In human affairs, the intentionality of human beings is seldom directly realised in its native form. Instead, the coherent outcomes desired by individuals, groups and organisations emerge from the interaction of the collective intentionality of groups of people and organisations in an often surprising fashion with unpredictable side-effects. This is something called the paradox of intentional emergent coherence, which is paradoxical because we gain emergent and surprising collective outcomes in groups, teams and organisations through the interaction of relatively fixed intentions. This was first noticed by a classical economist, Adam Smith, who wrote: "It is not from the benevolence of the butcher, the brewer or the baker that we expect our dinner, but from regard to their own self-interest." Yet out of such simple intentions and interactions emerge entire, complex economies.

### Leadership, pattern recognition and coherence

To make sense of the complex and often turbulent environments they now find themselves in, leaders and managers are having to increase the "requisite variety" of their own ways of thinking about and responding to rapid change in their environment, as well as to ensure such variety is also present within their organisations. "Requisite variety" is a term coined by a pioneer cybernetician, Ross Ashby, known as Ashby's law. It is used to describe the requirement any system must possess if it is to adapt to changes in its environment; the system will need to be able to mirror and even "model" the variety in its environment in order to respond to changes in its environment. Amphibians, for example, can breathe in both air and water; in a very basic way, they possess requisite variety for a changing environment where they may need to feed on land or in water.

Organisations without requisite variety in their internal models and structures will eventually encounter a mode of the environment or a kind of competitor to which they cannot respond appropriately, and they will then fail unless such variety can be built in in time. Four of the most important things leaders or managers can do to enable themselves and their organisation to learn to create such variety are as follows.

◪ Encourage the judicious exploration of new possibility spaces not only around the current strategic thrust of the organisation, but also in places where new forms of demand for what the firm may be or become good at are emerging.

◪ Stimulate the natural ability of the organisation to self-organise around new opportunities, using the minimum of effort and resources for exploration.

◪ Ensure that a rich ability is present in the firm to recognise new patterns of behaviour in both the organisation and its environment.

◪ Manage the co-evolution of the organisation with the other significant players in its business environment.

These four prerequisites for creating appropriate variety-enhancing behaviours and models in an organisation are shown in Figure A2.3. Within these four functions, the role of leaders is to enable their organisation to navigate complexity and uncertainty by:

◪ discerning patterns in events, making sense of them, and taking

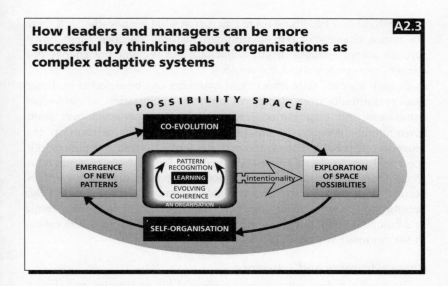

**How leaders and managers can be more successful by thinking about organisations as complex adaptive systems**

A2.3

action that will enhance the chances of survival of themselves and their organisation (pattern recognition); and

☑ creating contexts within which those they lead can make sense of their world and align their own values with those of the organisation, enabling them to make a unique personal contribution to the organisation and its future (evolving coherence).

Pattern recognition is crucial to the evolution of coherence within an organisation, without which learning of any kind cannot occur. The sharpness and clarity of the intentionality depicted by the arrow in Figure A2.3 is a result of a healthy strategic learning process in an organisation that is capable of discerning new patterns in itself and its environment, and of evolving new ways of adding value in the changing world.

As long as there is some degree of alignment between our interpretation of ourselves and of our environment (and hence the interpretations others hold of us), we can continue to operate in a steady-state, single-learning loop. In other words, as long as we see ourselves and the situations we get into as others do, there will be no surprises and we will simply continue to behave as we normally do. Any learning we do in this context will be limited to deepening the grooves of behaviour we already have and becoming more efficient at what we already do. If there are minor changes in our environment we will dampen them down through minor changes in our behaviour, but we will not change our deeper assumptions about the world.

In such a steady state leaders and managers can be expected to derive peak performance from themselves and their organisation, as individual behaviours and organisational routines become perfected over time. Intentionality goes on to autopilot, and we simply perform in the moment out of habit. The competence we derive from such activities feels good and we develop a reinforcing feedback loop, which encourages us to do more of the same. We also notice, however, that such routines become boring if they are unvaried. More ominously, these routines can become stultifying in an organisation, leading to extinction if they result in a failure to adapt, just as surely as the dinosaurs died from suffocation in the primeval swamps.

## Change, learning and coherence

In the good old days many people perceived life as simpler and slower. Transport and information technology had not connected up the world in many more intricate webs, speeding goods, services, people and information across these webs. Thus we had more time to evolve along with our environment and network of friends, colleagues and family. Now, however, this has all changed. In particular, managers are operating on an apparently endless treadmill of doing more for less, faster and cheaper. The globalisation of the world's economy will accelerate this effect further over the next few decades.

Given the nature of this "future shock", which Alvin Toffler first described in the early 1970s, the reaction of most people to rapid modernisation and globalisation is similar: they act to maintain the coherence of their worldview. Common sense, backed by research, demonstrates that our mental and physical health is at risk if we are shocked too often. Our natural defences include denial, anger, bargaining and grieving when something or someone we value is removed from our lives. If these fail, we undergo a nervous breakdown, or suffer serious physical symptoms. Or we can retreat into a form of ethnic, religious or corporate fundamentalism, in which we attempt to re-impose our worldview and will on a hostile world. Or, if we are managers, we can become hooked on wave after wave of management fads, which are based upon over-simplified success recipes, desperately hoping that the next wave will actually explain the complexity and turbulence we perceive around us and give our business the fix it desperately needs.

Even without severe future shock, we find that when we apply our usual intentionality, and there are changes in our environment or ourselves to which we have not yet had the time to evolve, we experience surprises and shocks, which we can deal with in several ways.

- Filter: our pre-existing cognitive filters may simply screen the presence of important changes from our awareness, either because we did not have the pre-existing mental models to "see" the event or trend, or because we deemed it to be unimportant and other stimuli were more overwhelming at the time.
- Deny: we may simply deny these changes have happened, and reject the evidence, if we do not like the nature or implications of the change.
- Hope: we may recognise the changes, but do nothing in the hope that they are only temporary and will go away.
- Learn: we not only recognise the changes around us, but also understand that they imply a need for change in ourselves, which causes us to modify our behaviour to respond to the change.
- Adapt: not only can we change our behaviour, but if the change in our environment is on a large and permanent scale we can structurally alter some aspect of ourselves or our organisation to enhance an existing capability, enabling us to survive in the new environment.
- Transform: we can respond to major, persistent levels of change in and around us by transforming ourselves and our organisation, creating completely new capabilities, which could not have previously been foreseen.

Our survival as an individual or organisation will depend on whether we make the correct judgment as to what we should do to respond to a change, and at what level we respond to it. Once we have, consciously or unconsciously, made the decision to deny, hope, learn, adapt or transform, we are committed to a different course of action, which implies a different intentionality. This intentionality could remain implicit and unarticulated, or it could rise into our awareness and be codified and shared among our colleagues, associates and friends. Yet it does not necessarily mean that it will come to pass.

During this process of personal and organisational change in response to internal and external events, we interact with others in a space of possibility, as shown in Figure A2.3 on page 253. In other words, the outcomes of our interactions are not completely predictable, even though we may have formed some expectations about the range of outcomes that are possible. The more challenging the situation we are in, the greater the range and kind of possible outcomes we should attempt to generate, to create more options for ourselves and our organisations.

When we apply our intentionality within a space of possibilities, we begin to co-evolve with other people and organisations interacting in this space. Every day most of us have many conversations, make many phone calls, go to many meetings and write letters or e-mails; in short, we interact. Each set of interactions with each set of parties we interact with comprises a possibility space, in which we can open up or close down options, or generate new options and possibilities.

Depending upon our psychological make-up, we may choose to co-evolve in different ways. Some of us may be suffering from high anxiety levels and attempt to control our interactions, other people and our environment to limit the range of outcomes to what we are comfortable with (closing down or limiting). Others, who are feeling more confident or self-aware, may be able to allow self-organisation to operate in a situation, thereby creating the conditions in which new patterns of relationship, processes and structure can emerge (opening up and generating). The latter approach is the only way we can adapt or transform ourselves or our organisations; only basic learning is possible within closed situations.

## The role of self-organisation

Stuart Kauffman, a doyen of complexity theorists, illustrates the way complex adaptive systems such as people and organisations evolve, using an example he calls "buttons and threads". Imagine 20 buttons spread out on the table in front of you. Randomly choose two buttons and connect them with a thread. As you continue to do this you will notice that at first you will only pick up buttons that have not been picked up before and that are unconnected to any other buttons. After some time, however, you are more likely to pick at random a pair of buttons and find that one of the pair is already connected to another by one of the threads you wove earlier.

Eventually, the buttons start becoming connected to each other in large clusters. When the ratio of threads to buttons passes 0.5, a giant cluster suddenly forms. After this point the growth of the giant cluster slows again as the ratio of threads to buttons increases beyond the

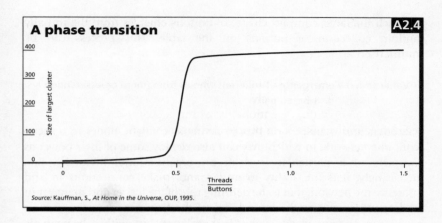

**A phase transition** A2.4

Size of largest cluster

400
300
200
100
0

0        0.5        1.0        1.5

Threads
Buttons

Source: Kauffman, S., *At Home in the Universe*, OUP, 1995.

halfway point. At 0.5, the threads and button system experiences a "phase transition": a sudden change in the size of the largest connected cluster of buttons. In a graph the relationships between the number of threads and buttons mapped on to the size of the largest cluster demonstrates a sigmoid curve, as shown in Figure A2.4.[2]

This kind of phase transition appears to happen in many different kinds of systems: water suddenly emerges from ice between 32 and 34 degrees celsius; life emerges from an autocatalytic web of chemical reactions; the human body emerges from 100,000 human genes, which have evolved into 256 cell types.

Kauffman demonstrated that, using computer simulations, an interactive network of 100,000 units switching each other on and off (as observed among genes) will quickly gravitate to a smaller number of systems, which is roughly the square root of the number of units in the original pool, in this case 316 patterns, close to the 256 cell types found in humans. Stability, Kauffman concluded, emerges from the adaptive interactions of a network of units. These stable patterns do not emerge because of hit-or-miss natural selection; they are the result of the dynamics of interaction, and are not randomly generated.

In a nutshell, a large, coherent pattern (the central cluster) emerges quite quickly from a random distribution of items (the buttons), simply through the iteration of a simple set of activities (connecting one button to another with thread) over time. In other words, a form of order emerges from randomness, with no designer required. So, in this context, what is it that leaders and managers do? They create the conditions in which valuable new "wholes" can emerge, in a similar fashion to the way in which the large, complex cluster of buttons emerges from the initially random collection of buttons on the table. This process can be summarised as:

Value added = emergence of coherent wholes from (more or less) randomly distributed parts

Leaders and managers do this by acting as catalytic nodes in a socio-economic network, in which they can also deploy some of their power as occupiers of a particular level in an organisational hierarchy. But, increasingly, it is the ability to understand, make connections in and influence the network that is the defining role of the leader and manager in the knowledge age, as the boundaries of the firm blur into those of its neighbours, and knowledge evolves in the relationships within the network.

The art of management in the 21st century thus lies in the ability to spot the potential for adding value in the construction and deconstruction of networks. This enables the creation of new knowledge and applying it so as to increase the value of an existing offering to customers, or the creation of brand new offerings that provide superior value to existing ways of doing things. These possibilities emerge from the co-evolution of new technologies and ways of doing things (business designs) and changing customer priorities, resulting in dynamic new patterns of customer decision in interaction with an organisation. The net outcome of this interaction, given that the firm is properly led and managed, should be economic and shareholder value-added.

These things happen because leaders and managers are acting as entrepreneurs in their networks, as well as operating as occupiers of roles within a hierarchy, in which they can exercise specific powers of attention focusing, resource allocation and people selection. Managers set boundaries, identify emerging patterns and work through their networks to make an organisation focus on the activities that will add value for both customers and stakeholders.

When a set of components interacts to produce a higher-order whole where the value of the whole is worth more than the sum of its parts, the value of the whole may become worth a great deal more than the sum of its parts. This is particularly true in knowledge businesses with network economies: the Microsoft/Intel (known as Wintel) business ecosystem is worth trillions of dollars, and produces $1 trillion of output revenue each year. This ecosystem is worth much more than the value of its components, which would probably fetch less than $50 billion-100 billion

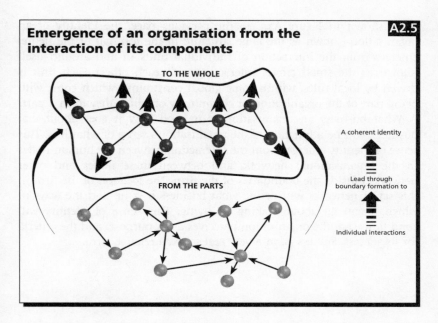

**Emergence of an organisation from the interaction of its components**

A2.5

TO THE WHOLE

FROM THE PARTS

A coherent identity

Lead through
boundary formation to

Individual interactions

on break-up. The intrinsic value of the network of relationships, and the capability that the knowledge embedded in these relationships can bring to clients of the Wintel ecosystem, exceeds the asset value of the components by orders of magnitude.

If proof were needed that the value is added through the emergence of coherent wholes from randomly distributed parts, then the ratio of Microsoft's market value to its net asset value speaks volumes: $270 billion market value to $5 billion net asset value gives a ratio of 54 times more value for the intangible whole of Microsoft than for the sum of its tangible parts.

Murray Gell-Mann observed that:

> A complex adaptive system acquires information about its environment and its own interaction with that environment, identifying regularities in that information, condensing those regularities into a kind of "schema" or model, and acting in the real world on the basis of that schema. In each case, there are various competing schemata, and the results of the action in the real world feed back to influence the competition among those schemata.[3]

As shown in Figure A2.5 on the previous page, the identity of an organisation (shown as the large structure in the top half of the figure) emerges from the interaction of individual units in and around itself (shown as the small circles interacting with each other). Each unit is driven by local rules, within some global constraints, which come with being part of the organisation or community of which they form a part.

What business an organisation is in, and how it goes about that business, will be a function of the organisation's sense of what it is. This sense of identity emerges from the interaction between the human nodes in the organisational network, and between these nodes and other networks outside the boundaries of the firm. The location of the firm in this set of networks will define what business it is in, and the ways in which it can go about making its living. This sense of identity will condition what the organisation perceives as its purpose, and the criteria for its success. Success is, in a very real sense, a relative term.

# Appendix 3
# The wheel of business evolution questionnaire

## Instructions

Please note that this questionnaire is best used in conjunction with Chapter 4 of *Managing Complexity*, which explains the wheel of business evolution in much greater detail.

### 1. To complete the questionnaire
Please use the **right hand column** to indicate the score which you believe most accurately describes the:

- ◪ the **current position** of your organisation or elements of its environment (using a circle)
- ◪ the **desirable or likely future state** of your organisation or elements of its environment within the next three years (using a tick)

Note that there are usually **two dimensions** to any question:

- ◪ the **scale** of the impact/effects of the item in question
- ◪ the **direction** of the impact/effects of the item in question

You are requested to take into account **both the scale and directionality** of the impact/effects of each item, by scoring each item higher or lower as appropriate.

A few lines have been left below each question to make any **comments** you wish to clarify your answer or explain your reasoning.

### 2. To score the questionnaire
The purpose of the wheel of business evolution is to enable you to identify the evolutionary challenges facing your organisation. These challenges will emerge from the gaps between the levels of the current state variables, and the levels of the future state variables. In the score column "N" is NOW and "+3" is IN 3 YEARS.

Once you have added up the scores for the current and future states of each variable at the bottom of each section, work out the average score as instructed. Then take the average score for each of the current and future state variables and plot it on to the wheel diagram on page 275.

Use different colours for the NOW and IN 3 YEARS variables, in order to distinguish easily between them when reviewing your wheel profile. Black (for NOW) and red (for IN 3 YEARS) are ideal contrasts. Then shade in the gaps between the NOW and IN 3 YEARS variables. Use black to shade in areas where the NOW score is further to the outside than the IN 3 YEARS score, and red to shade in areas where the IN 3 YEARS score is further to the outside than the NOW score.

The evolutionary challenges for your organisation lie in the red shaded areas, while the black shaded areas are not priority areas for change, but may be serving as catalysts for change. Also check the alignment of your two scores – if the NOW score is circular in shape your organisation is well aligned.

### 3. To interpret the questionnaire
Compare the shape of your current wheel profile (NOW), with the eight profiles in Chapter 4. Which profile does it most closely resemble? What similarities are there between your current situation and the situation your "lookalike" was in when its wheel profile was created?

What can you do in your organisation to emulate the successes of your lookalike and avoid its mistakes?

*The business environment* comprises a set of political, economic, social and technological actors and forces which are largely outside the control and influence of a business, and which can potentially have both positive and negative impacts on the business.

| A. BUSINESS ENVIRONMENT | Score pad | Score |
|---|---|---|
| | State of variable now and in 3 years | N   +3 |

---

1. How stable is the political and regulatory environment within which your organisation is operating?

   Which are the most unstable elements in the environment?

   Why?

   *Stable*          *Unstable*

   -3 -2 -1 0 1 2 3

   *(circle for now,*
   *tick for 3 years' time)*

---

2. What impact might major swings in the global economy have on your organisation, its businesses and its investments, today and in the future?

   Which regions are/may be most volatile?

   Why?

   *Positive*          *Negative*

   -3 -2 -1 0 1 2 3

   *(circle for now,*
   *tick for 3 years' time)*

---

3. How complex and dynamic are the current and future social trends in the principal marketplaces within which your organisation operates?

   For example, your customers' lifestyles and employee aspirations/demands.

   *Simple*          *Complex*
   *Stable*          *Dynamic*

   -3 -2 -1 0 1 2 3

   *(circle for now,*
   *tick for 3 years' time)*

---

4. What is/will be the net impact of new technology trends (for example, e-commerce) on your organisation's business and organisation?

*Stabilising*      *Destabilising*

-3 -2 -1 0 1 2 3

*(circle for now,*
*tick for 3 years' time)*

Which technologies are having/might have major impacts?

---

**A. TOTAL BUSINESS ENVIRONMENT SCORE**

Add the scores for the "NOW" and "3 years from now" columns on the right

**A. AVERAGE SCORE**

Divide the total scores for the "NOW" and "3 years from now" columns by 4

---

**The business ecosystem** is the community of organisations and stakeholders ("players") operating within your business environment. These players collaborate and compete in an economic web of relationships. This web of relationships co-evolves through time subject to the general forces in the business environment and the specific moves made by the web of players, including your organisation.

**B. BUSINESS ECOSYSTEM**     Score pad     Score

State of variable now and in 3 years    N   +3

5. How many players compete directly with your organisation for your customers and markets?

Less than 5      More than 50

-3 -2 -1 0 1 2 3

*(circle for now,*
*tick for 3 years' time)*

Who are they?

---

6. How diverse are the business designs/models of the key players in your industry?

What unique kinds of design are there?

What makes them unique?

*All the same*      *Very diverse*

-3 -2 -1 0 1 2 3

*(circle for now, tick for 3 years' time)*

---

7. How interdependent are the key businesses/players in your industry and the underlying business ecosystems?

What is the nature of the dependencies?

*Isolated*       *Highly*
*players*     *interdependent*

-3 -2 -1 0 1 2 3

*(circle for now, tick for 3 years' time)*

---

8. How complementary are/might be the product/service offerings you and other players in the industry offer?

What opportunities might there be to redesign the rules of the game?

*No*        *High*
*synergy*    *complementarity*

-3 -2 -1 0 1 2 3

*(circle for now, tick for 3 years' time)*

---

9. How rapidly are the structures, alliances and groupings within your industry and underlying business ecosystem changing?

Will this rate of change slow or increase?

*Stable*     *Rapid change*

-3 -2 -1 0 1 2 3

*(circle for now, tick for 3 years' time)*

---

**B. TOTAL BUSINESS ECOSYSTEM SCORE**

Add the scores for the "NOW" and "3 years from now" columns on the right

---

**B. AVERAGE SCORE**

Divide the total scores for the "NOW" and "3 years from now" columns by 5

*Business designs* describe different possible configurations of a business idea, and how that idea adds value and is embodied through the application of distinctive capabilities to relevant markets to create sustainable competitive advantage. Like species in natural ecosystems, business designs have fitness and sustainability functions which can be improved in a number of ways, through more appropriate strategic moves being made on the strategic landscape, and a broader range of robust and complementary options being available to the firm from which to make strategic moves.

## C. BUSINESS DESIGN

*Score pad*                    *Score*

State of variable now and in 3 years     N     +3

---

10. Does your current business model for your organisation (or the aggregate of the various business models in the group) operate more as a systematic processor, or is it more a versatile innovator?

*Systematic processor*          *Versatile innovator*

-3  -2  -1  0  1  2  3

(circle for now, tick for 3 years' time)

How is it changing?

---

11. How centralised are key strategy and operating decisions in your organisation group? Or are the units highly disaggregated with a large degree of strategic and operational autonomy?

*Centralised*          *Disaggregated*

-3  -2  -1  0  1  2  3

(circle for now, tick for 3 years' time)

---

12. To what extent do you see your organisation operating as a knowledge business leveraging innovation, versus an asset/capital intensive business leveraging a hard infrastructure?

*Asset-based*          *Knowledge-driven*

-3  -2  -1  0  1  2  3

(circle for now, tick for 3 years' time)

And in the future?

---

13. How much do you believe your organisation's key business processes focus outwards into its environment and sense the key issues relevant to your organisation's future?

*Internal/*          *External/*
*past focus*          *future focus*

-3 -2 -1 0 1 2 3

*(circle for now,*
*tick for 3 years' time)*

14. How diverse are the different business designs/models within your organisation or group? How conscious and intentional is this diversity?

*Homogeneous*       *Diverse*

-3 -2 -1 0 1 2 3

*(circle for now,*
*tick for 3 years' time)*

**C. TOTAL BUSINESS DESIGN SCORE**

Add the scores for the "NOW" and "3 years from now" columns on the right

**C. AVERAGE SCORE**

Divide the total scores for the "NOW" and "3 years from now" columns by 5

**Leadership style** is a property possessed both by individuals leading an organisation and by the firm itself in its business ecosystem. In order to make a unique contribution within a business ecosystem and find a special niche for a firm, a specific kind of leadership style is required within the business ecosystem for the role the firm wishes to play. This style also underlies the way in which the campaign a firm needs to orchestrate must be conducted, in order to create and maintain the components of the value web around it for its success.

| D. LEADERSHIP STYLE | Score pad | Score |
|---|---|---|
| | State of variable now and in 3 years | N    +3 |

---

15. Does the way in which your organisation collectively exercises leadership in its industry and the underlying business ecosystems reflect a focus on a clear vision of its unique future contribution?

To what extent is this vision known in your industry?

*Unfocused*      *Focused*
*shared*      *model*

-3 -2 -1 0 1 2 3

*(circle for now,*
*tick for 3 years' time)*

---

16. Does the predominant leadership style within the top echelons of your organisation tend towards a charismatic or an autocratic style?

*Autocratic*      *Charismatic*

-3 -2 -1 0 1 2 3

*(circle for now,*
*tick for 3 years' time)*

---

17. How participative is the top leadership style in your organisation? Are most key decisions taken by a small inner circle without consultation of others, or are many people involved and consulted?

*Monarchic*      *Participative*

-3 -2 -1 0 1 2 3

*(circle for now,*
*tick for 3 years' time)*

---

**D. TOTAL LEADERSHIP STYLE SCORE**

Add the scores for the "NOW" and "3 years from now" columns on the right

**D. AVERAGE SCORE**

Divide the total scores for the "NOW" and "3 years from now" columns by 3

---

*Organisational values* describe the network of expectations about what is desirable behaviour in a firm: "The way things get done around here". This network of expectations is generally dynamic, and evolves together with the network of relationships and business activities of a firm. In this sense, values describe the "how and why" of what happens in an organisation, rather than the "what, where, who and when". Both the motivation for behaviour and the behavioural style form part of the value set in an organisation.

| E. ORGANISATIONAL VALUES | Score pad | Score |
| --- | --- | --- |
| | *State of variable now and in 3 years* | N    +3 |

| | |
| --- | --- |
| 18. Are the values driving behaviour in your organisation driven more by specific survival needs, or by self-actualisation? | *Survival*　　　*Self-actualisation*<br><br>-3 -2 -1 0 1 2 3<br><br>(circle for now,<br>tick for 3 years' time) |
| 19. To what extent is behaviour in your organisation driven by hierarchical considerations versus networks of influence? | *Hierarchy*　　　　*Networks*<br><br>-3 -2 -1 0 1 2 3<br><br>(circle for now,<br>tick for 3 years' time) |
| 20. How conservative would you say your organisation/culture is?<br><br>For example, how rapidly are new practices and ideas taken up? | *Conservative*　　　*Radical*<br><br>-3 -2 -1 0 1 2 3<br><br>(circle for now,<br>tick for 3 years' time) |
| 21. How much of a divergence is there between the formal ("legitimate") system in your organisation, and the informal ("shadow") system? | *High divergence*　*Convergence*<br><br>-3 -2 -1 0 1 2 3<br><br>(circle for now,<br>tick for 3 years' time) |

|  | Score pad | Score |
|---|---|---|
|  |  | N   +3 |

**E. TOTAL ORGANISATIONAL VALUES SCORE**    Add the scores for the "NOW" and "3 years from now" columns on the right

**E. AVERAGE SCORE**    Divide the total scores for the "NOW" and "3 years from now" columns by 4

---

**Management processes** are those clusters of activities required to enable, support and control the business processes in an organisation. This includes core enabling processes such as selecting and managing people, managing operations, managing money, building and maintaining infrastructure, managing reputation/brands and developing and managing information systems. In addition, the strategic management process, stakeholder management, business and organisational development processes need to operate in the appropriate fashion to lead and reinforce change.

### F. MANAGEMENT PROCESSES

|  | Score pad | Score |
|---|---|---|
|  | State of variable now and in 3 years | N   +3 |

22. Is your organisation's management process geared towards tight control, or does it allow initiatives and programmes to emerge and replicate?

Tight control               Emergent

-3  -2  -1  0  1  2  3

(circle for now,
tick for 3 years' time)

---

23. To what extent are the individuals, teams/groups and departments in your organisation encouraged to operate as semi-autonomous, self-organising agents?

Formal                          Self-
organisation              organisation

-3  -2  -1  0  1  2  3

(circle for now,
tick for 3 years' time)

24. How much innovation is encouraged by your management processes? Do they reward entrepreneurs, or are they focused primarily on preventing mistakes?

*Mistake prevention   Innovation*

-3 -2 -1 0 1 2 3

*(circle for now,
tick for 3 years' time)*

25. Would you characterise your organisation's management and decision processes as mainly rational, or mainly intuitive?

*Rational              Intuitive*

-3 -2 -1 0 1 2 3

*(circle for now,
tick for 3 years' time)*

**F. TOTAL MANAGEMENT PROCESS SCORE**

Add the scores for the "NOW" and "3 years from now" columns on the right

**F. AVERAGE SCORE**

Divide the total scores for the "NOW" and "3 years from now" columns by 4

*Knowledge management* provides the cornerstones around which the distinctive capabilities of a firm can be developed. In the heat of real-time online action, such distinctive capabilities form the basis of **corporate intelligence** (individual and collective) in a firm. This means the application of knowledge within a specific known context. **Corporate instinct** emerges as the spontaneous application of acquired and latent intelligence to unknown situations with unspecified contexts.

| **G. KNOWLEDGE MANAGEMENT** | *Score pad* | | *Score* |
| | *State of variable now and in 3 years* | | N   +3 |

26. How is new knowledge generated and applied in your organisation – is it driven top-down, or does it emerge bottom-up?

*Top-down            Bottom-up*

-3 -2 -1 0 1 2 3

*(circle for now,
tick for 3 years' time)*

| | *Score pad* | *Score* |
|---|---|---|
| | *State of variable now and in 3 years* | **N**   **+3** |

---

27. Are training and development in your organisation driven mainly by task and role defined skill needs, or is the focus on more general competencies and personality?

*Task/role*          *General*
*focus*          *competencies*

-3 -2 -1 0 1 2 3

*(circle for now,*
*tick for 3 years' time)*

---

28. How good are people in your organisation at coming up with innovative new ideas and applying them in the business? Are people generally bureaucratic, or entrepreneurial?

*Bureaucratic     Entrepreneurial*

-3 -2 -1 0 1 2 3

*(circle for now,*
*tick for 3 years' time)*

---

29. How centralised and rigid are information systems in your organisation?

*Centralised,          Decentralised,*
*rigid          flexible*

-3 -2 -1 0 1 2 3

*(circle for now,*
*tick for 3 years' time)*

---

30. Do your organisation's management information systems deliver mainly operationally focused information, or is it more strategic?

*Operational          Strategic*

-3 -2 -1 0 1 2 3

*(circle for now,*
*tick for 3 years' time)*

---

**G. TOTAL KNOWLEDGE MANAGEMENT SCORE**

Add the scores for the "NOW" and "3 years from now" columns on the right

**G. AVERAGE SCORE**

Divide the total scores for the "NOW" and "3 years from now" columns by 4

---

*Performance measures* provide feedback to executives on the results of their actions. They form part of the learning loop which enables an organisation to develop its intelligence and succeed. Performance measures vary from high-level, strategic measures such as market share or customer satisfaction, to low-level, operational measures such as cost per unit. It is crucial in an organisation wishing to succeed that there is a balance between strategic, operational, functional and financial performance measures, and that these measures are driven appropriately by balanced customer, internal, stakeholder and learning and innovation measures.

## H. PERFORMANCE MEASUREMENT

Score pad
*State of variable now and in 3 years*

Score
N   +3

31. Do the key management performance measures in your organisation focus on inflexible operational outcomes, or do they tend to be strategic and flexible in their nature?

*Inflexible*        *Strategic*
*operational*          *flexible*

-3 -2 -1 0 1 2 3

*(circle for now,
tick for 3 years' time)*

32. How context-sensitive are the key performance measures in your organisation? That is, are they general across all situations, or do they recognise a diverse array of situations?

*Context sensitivity*
*Low*                    *High*

-3 -2 -1 0 1 2 3

*(circle for now,
tick for 3 years' time)*

33. How far into the future is your organisation thinking and planning? Is the time horizon of managers short, medium or long term?

(Note – this does not mean they are attempting to predict the future, simply that they are considering longer and more complex feedback loops and bigger pictures.)

*Time horizon*
*Short*                    *Long*

-3 -2 -1 0 1 2 3

*(circle for now,
tick for 3 years' time)*

34. To what extent are the performance measures in your organisation internally focused versus focusing on outcomes outside the organisation and external stakeholders?

*Internal*                *External*

-3 -2 -1 0 1 2 3

*(circle for now,
tick for 3 years' time)*

**H. TOTAL PERFORMANCE MEASUREMENT SCORE**

Add the scores for the "NOW" and "3 years from now" columns on the right

**H. AVERAGE SCORE**

Divide the total scores for the "NOW" and "3 years from now" columns by 4

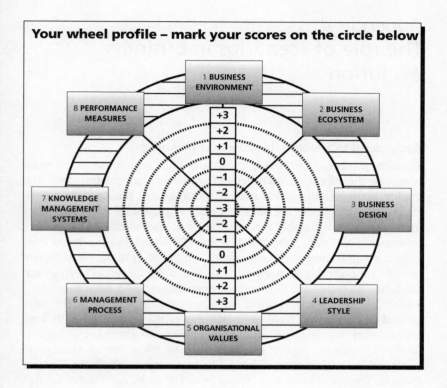

**Your wheel profile – mark your scores on the circle below**

# Appendix 4
# The role of scenarios in business evolution

## Background to scenario thinking and planning

Scenario planning,[1] or strategic thinking with scenarios,[2] is currently sweeping the world of management much like its predecessors total quality management, organisational learning[3] and business process re-engineering[4] did in the late 1980s and early 1990s. It is therefore surprising that apart from the publications of de Geus, and several of his ex-Shell colleagues[5] (including, most notably, Peter Schwarz[6]), not much has been written about scenarios in comparison with the other major management trends. (Although this is changing, with several useful works having been published recently – see Further recommended reading, page 294.)

The author is a management consultant and entrepreneur. The work he and his colleagues have been doing over the past 15 years in large organisations has required them to peer into and construct a range of futures for practical gain. In attempting to make robust strategy in organisations as diverse as Citicorp, Chase Manhattan, Shell, 3M, Hewlett-Packard, Jardine-Matheson, Unilever, the UK National Health Service, Telesure, NYNEX, British Telecom and Dutch Telecom, it has become clear that the future is not only unpredictable, it is also becoming increasingly uncertain for organisations of all descriptions.

Scenario planning comes in various shapes and forms. Most big firms are using it, experimenting with it, or attempting to understand it. Many of the major management consulting firms claim to be doing it for their clients. Yet, as with most fads, the results are patchy. In the author's experience, many firms have experimented with and then discarded scenarios, even while they acknowledge the benefits. Others have embedded scenarios into the fabric of their management and leadership processes and are reaping significant rewards. The focus of this appendix is, from a practical perspective, to understand the following.

- ◩ Why scenarios are necessary and what makes them useful in the field.
- ◩ How the scenario process works, and what we can learn from the

cognitive, complexity and evolutionary sciences about the logic of this process.

◪ The role of scenarios in making transformative strategy, which helps organisations anticipate evolution.

◪ The role scenarios may be playing in organisational evolution, and in the larger context, social evolution, and why this is important for business people to understand.

## A concise history of scenarios

The role of scenarios in evolution may perhaps, one day, come to be viewed as one of the breakthrough moments in the history of our species. Although it is difficult to say when the discipline of scenario thinking began, it is probable that Pleistocene man needed to be able to plan for the unexpected in order to survive. Homo sapiens has had to do some form of primitive scenario planning simply to survive, by having to ask questions such as: what if it snows, and all our crops are destroyed/our prey is unavailable/we all die of cold? We can also see that this particular form of foresight acted as a stimulus for stores of food to be accumulated (what if we have a bad harvest next year?), infrastructure to be built (what if the wolf comes?) and many artefacts of civilisation to emerge.

Many scholars would argue that many other species need to deal with contingencies and behave as if they are asking the question "what if?" even though they demonstrate little or no reflective consciousness. Thus most species that build infrastructures and store food have evolved phenotypes and/or instinctive behaviours, including social systems that protect them from all manner of unpredictable contingencies, from having to deal with the flooding of a termite mound to the need to build nests invisible to or away from predators.

We will restrict ourselves here to human beings and their complex social systems, with particular reference to organisations. It appears that formal scenario planning emerged originally in a military context, and became documented during and after the second world war. Given the increasing sophistication of warfare and the ability of combatants to deceive each other as to their intentions, it became necessary to prepare several sets of possible plans, depending upon the strategy eventually deployed by the other side(s).

Although rehearsal for a number of contingencies has always been a key element of military training and organisation, this in itself is not a form of scenario planning. What is required in scenario planning is not only the concept of multiple possible moves by another player, but also the further concept of multiple possible future worlds.

It is clear that scenario planning has evolved rapidly as a technique since the second world war, but much of the evidence for this is anecdotal. The author has come across several examples of the conscious implementation of scenario planning in major organisations in the 1960s and 1970s; earlier accounts do not appear to be available.[7] The US Air Force (USAF) appears to have been conducting war-game exercises for many years, and certainly since the advent of nuclear weapons has been conducting advanced simulations on some of the world's fastest supercomputers. One of their focuses has been scenarios based on the following question: what if a thermonuclear device is detonated or thermonuclear war is started? As most of the documentary evidence of what the former Soviet Union and the USAF were doing in their respective computerised war games is still classified information, it is only possible to speculate about what happened.

### Scenarios at Royal Dutch Shell

Although Peter Schwartz tells some of the story of how scenario planning at Shell evolved, there are several other accounts that enrich it.

In 1972 Shell was the second largest oil company in revenue terms, but it was regarded as the weakest of the "seven sisters" (as Anthony Sampson called them in his book). Among this group were American oil companies such as Exxon, Standard Oil and Texaco, together with other players such as British Petroleum. Although many Shell people harboured the vision of becoming bigger and more profitable than Exxon (the world's largest oil company during the 1970s and 1980s), this appeared a distant dream in 1972.

Oil companies throughout the world were facing the threat of expropriation by many countries of their fields and equipment. Shell was vulnerable, not having upstream operations and reserves comparable with the other oil majors (although the fact that Shell had few fields in the Arabian Gulf was later to prove something of an asset).

In the late 1960s Herman Kahn at the Stanford Research Institute had begun to refine scenarios as a tool for business planning, based on his involvement with the USAF exercises mentioned above. Companies such as IBM and other giants such as General Motors (GM) would begin to use these techniques over the next few decades, although they kept their efforts largely secret. (It will be shown later that their methods were particularly analytic and gave less credence to the role of insight and intuition, which played such an important role in Shell's successful use of scenarios.)

Pierre Wack, a planner in the newly formed Shell Group Planning Department, together with two colleagues, was looking for events that might affect the price of oil, which had been roughly $2 per barrel for several decades. The team's conclusion in the early 1970s was that members of the Organisation of Petroleum Exporting Countries (OPEC), which hold the bulk of the world's oil reserves, could begin to demand higher prices for their oil, given the shortage of proven reserves elsewhere and the ever-rising demand for oil throughout the world. In particular, the fact the almost all OPEC members were Islamic and resented the western world's support for Israel after the 1967 six-day war might provide them with a motive.

Wack and his colleagues put forward two scenarios to the Shell directors. The first was a default scenario in which the price of oil did not change much. The second was based on their OPEC research and made the Shell directors take notice. Their business would be highly vulnerable if the oil price shot up, and they realised they might have to change their business dramatically. Wack and his colleagues, moreover, were instrumental in getting managers throughout Shell to rehearse for this scenario, so that when OPEC members expropriated oil company assets and raised oil prices in revenge for western support for Israel in the 1973 Yom Kippur war, Shell was ready.

Needless to say, after alerting the company to this event, group planning was given more resources, and scenario planning became the pivot around which Shell's planning process revolved. Over the next two decades, scenarios came to Shell's aid in a number of other situations (in securing low-cost fields in the North Sea and in prognosticating the collapse of the Soviet Union, for example). This, together with the spread of planning as learning by Arie de Geus, who became head of group planning in the early 1980s, was one of the principal ingredients enabling Shell to become the world's largest and most profitable oil company in the space of just over two decades. (In 1995 Shell overtook Exxon in terms of both revenue and profit, with revenue of over $100 billion and profit of over $7 billion).

The question that arises is: why was scenario planning so successful at Shell, when it appears to have less impact in many other corporations? What can this tell us about why scenarios work, and how they work best?

## What makes scenarios work?

Why was it that IBM and GM, which were both using scenario planning, fell from grace as leaders in their respective industries, while Shell went from strength to strength? Although it cannot be said categorically that it was because of the different ways in which they carried out scenario planning, most observers agree that scenarios were an important ingredient in Shell's success. Some of the factors involved, particularly how the different cultures in these organisations may have enhanced or diluted the effects of scenario planning, are examined below.

### Three important differences
Historically, there have been three major differences between Shell and the "Phoenix twins", IBM and GM.

#### MANAGERIAL AND CULTURAL DIVERSITY VERSUS CONFORMITY
Shell is a multicultural organisation which has had to integrate British, Dutch and many other nationalities and cultures into its senior management ranks. It has a consensus culture in which issues have to be argued out, even if there is a residual hierarchy that makes the final decisions. GM and IBM were both, during the two decades under review, run by strong leaders who valued the strong, American-dominated culture they had both developed over several decades. Unusual people such as Pierre Wack and surprising points of view were not particularly welcome in what amounted to highly conformist cultures.

#### INTUITION VERSUS ANALYSIS
IBM and GM were both highly analytic organisations, where having the right answer was the way to get to the top. They were both industry leaders who prided themselves on their ability to predict and control. This mindset had a powerful effect on the way in which they used scenarios: both attempted to select the right strategies given the futures they felt were most probable.

Both failed to realise that what they saw as probable would be likely to reflect their current paradigms, rather than any objective view of where their industries and the world were heading. Unusual scenarios, such as the Japanese invasion of the American motor industry, the decline of mainframes and dominance of personal computers, a radical change in consumer tastes towards smaller cars and computers, or fundamental changes in auto and computer manufacturing techniques as a result of globalisation and technology, did not have the impact on planners and decision-makers they might have, owing to their inability to entertain these possible futures as real.

Such changes in paradigm must come about through intuition and imagination rather than analysis. As Shell understood, the human mind prepares for the future through a process of play and learning, which are highly visual and imaginative. It used the scenario process to help managers re-perceive the world, to yield fundamentally different insights into what might be, rather than as a defensive mechanism to avoid unwanted change. Shell scenario planners helped the organisation learn that they were not using scenarios as just a better method to forecast or predict, but rather as a tool to stimulate creative thought and learning so that better decisions could be made in the present.

COLLABORATIVE LEARNING VERSUS TOP-DOWN DECISION-MAKING
Although many of the early examples of Shell's use of scenarios focus on the committee of managing directors and their decisions, during the late 1980s Shell began to institutionalise planning as learning. The emphasis of group planning was to act as a facilitator of the learning process in the frontline Shell units, rather than as a head-office expert think-tank. As de Geus points out in his classic article on planning as learning: "It may be that the only sustainable competitive advantage an organisation can have is to learn faster than its competitors."

Shell took organisational learning seriously, and although it would be the first to admit that it has still not achieved its goal of being a total learning organisation, it is well on its way. IBM and GM, although they have both recently embraced organisational learning, were slow to recognise the importance of this process in their organisations and, in particular, failed to institutionalise planning as learning, which is much harder to do than it may first appear. Scenarios can only be as effective as the ability of an organisation to use them creatively to generate new insights to make better decisions in the present, rather than to attempt to accurately portray the future.

## The theory underlying scenarios
THE ABILITY TO PERCEIVE AND THINK DIFFERENTLY IS MORE IMPORTANT THAN THE KNOWLEDGE GAINED.

David Bohm[8]

An understanding of the theory underlying scenarios is critical to being able to use them well and, more importantly, is essential if they are to be successfully institutionalised in an organisation.

The first reason is that scenarios are an important tool in the process of individual, team and organisational learning. To learn effectively and quickly, the learners need to be able to reflect on their learning process, thereby learning how to learn. They thus need to know how to use scenarios to learn how to learn in a strategic context. The second reason is the need for precision in the process of applying scenarios in ever more complex business ecosystems.[9] As industry boundaries blur, and our ability radically to reinvent the customer value proposition and the total customer offer depends increasingly on our ability to work across industry and organisational boundaries in often novel alliances and partnerships, we have to use scenarios to address the relevant environments, issues, processes, markets and organisations we are dealing with.

To align increasingly complex stakeholder groups in and around the organisation and the business ecosystems in which it participates, the scenario process has to become more inclusive, and thus more transparent. If people do not truly understand what they are doing and why, it becomes exceptionally easy for them to lose their way in what may amount to the most complex yet powerful management technique.

Strategic thinking with scenarios goes to the root of what individuals and organisations must do to:

◾ adapt successfully to a changing environment;
◾ produce a more desirable future state for themselves.

The human race is uniquely placed in evolution as the only species with a highly developed language capability and the capacity for self-reflection and representation of knowledge in symbolic form.[10] Although we can see examples of pre-adaptation in many animal species, which represent a form of contingency planning, there appears little evidence that any of these species are capable of developing complex conscious images, descriptions and representations of the future. What exists appears to be largely hard-wired, with some capacity for behavioural flexibility in application, but the basic future-producing and future-proofing routines in almost all species are pre-set.

Having said this, we must recognise that much of human and organisational behaviour is also in the nature of conditioned reflex and well-drilled routine. Indeed, we rely on the near-flawless operation of these basic processes for the smooth and effective running of our lives and organisations. From lawyers to airline pilots, accountants to computer operators, doctors to construction workers, the standardisation of skills and routines is essential for their functioning. In business, we standardise outputs, processes and skills; if we did not, mass production as we know it would be impossible. Even mass customisation and flexible manufacturing rely on predictable routines in the software of manufacturing systems. Service businesses too, rely upon routine, from the clerk at the bank to the McDonald's counter assistant.

So at what level can we speak of the need for multiple possible future thinking in an individual or organisation? Innovation, both technical and social, is accelerating rapidly throughout the world. The transfer of know-how and best practice among individuals, organisations and countries is taking place more fluidly than at any time in history. Social institutions are evolving rapidly, moving increasingly towards democracy, although demagoguery is still a potent and unpredictable force.[11] Co-evolution is taking place throughout the world among industries, organisations, technologies and social systems, requiring us to be capable of understanding and responding to more forces, events and uncertainties across a broader front than ever before.[12]

There are also some permanent structural changes taking place in our global trading, financial, and information and communications systems. The wired world open for business 24 hours a day is a reality. Common technological platforms now unite most of the world, enabling information and people to be exchanged, whether over the Internet or via a 747 plane. Organisations that do not respond to these changes and the corresponding trends driving the modern consumer[13] will lose customers, markets and eventually their livelihoods. Shanghai is much closer to main street America or high street UK than it ever was, whether it is producing goods for export or consuming Hollywood's output.

Given this level of change in our environment, the only response is to accelerate our capability to learn and change so as to adapt, which then buys us time to produce a more desirable future state for ourselves. Scenarios are the most powerful technology we have yet encountered to accelerate learning and provoke change, in both individuals and organisations. Learning from and about the future to create more desirable outcomes requires the ability to question some of our most cherished assumptions, in order to generate the profound mindset (or paradigm) changes in those involved.

The work the author and his colleagues do for major corporations[14] in developing and implementing strategy using scenarios is based on five fundamental propositions about the world.

### ORGANISATIONS ARE FUTURE-PRODUCING COMPLEX ADAPTIVE SYSTEMS

Organisations and people are future-producing complex adaptive systems displaying intentionality and behaviour that are a function of their design and situation. To the extent that organisations are designed, and the people in them are capable of designing their own working environments and relationships, they can be understood as mechanisms comprising mechanical and organic components, whose behaviour will follow the logic of their structure. Form (design) must ultimately follow function (purpose or intentionality) in any well-adapted complex system.

### CONSCIOUS AND SUBCONSCIOUS INTENTIONALITY

Individuals, groups, teams and organisations are capable of displaying both subconscious and conscious forms of intentionality. Subconscious (or automatic, conditioned) intentionality is harder to change than the conscious variety, as it is more deeply embedded in the individual or corporate physique and psyche, and we are, by definition, largely unaware of its operation. This is healthy when such intentionality is functional and adaptive, but these deeply ingrained "habits of a lifetime" are often what stall or reverse organisational change and transformation programmes carried out purely at the conscious level. Scenario work cannot ignore such routines and cultures.

### PROLIFERATION OF VARIETY THROUGH INNOVATION

Business systems are the engine of innovation in the global economy, throwing up a huge variety of technical and social inventions, of which some endure and others simply disappear. There are few products, services or processes in business at present that do not require regular, if not almost constant, mutation and adaptation. Variety creation through innovation is usually a multi-stakeholder process, resulting in the co-evolution of industries and players. The Intel business ecosystem would not be much use without the continual innovation of players such as Microsoft, Hewlett-Packard and many others, which create demand for the processing power of Intel's microchips.

### COMPLEX ADAPTIVE AND DELIBERATE SELECTION

Evolution operates on the basic elements of business, such as products, services, technologies, individuals, groups and teams, organisations and business ecosystems, selecting the best-adapted elements and endorsing the most promising combinations. Although this takes place largely in a co-evolutionary sense (that is, evolution selects configurations of the elements rather than simply among the elements themselves), the market or the hierarchy ultimately makes its judgment known as to whether a product, person, process, department, company or industry should survive in its current form. There is room for both competition and co-operation (or co-opetition)[15] in this process, and intelligent players usually work out how to get the system on their side, or they get on side with the system if the former is not possible. The smartest players change the rules of the game to favour their strengths, although this is usually exceptional.[16]

LEARNING ENABLES PRE-ADAPTATION AND FUTURE CREATION

Rather than simply adapting blindly to the forces of evolution, risking annihilation or demotion at the next step, organisations and individuals can take matters into their own hands to some extent. Learning about the complex web of pre-determined elements, driving trends and critical uncertainties in the business and social environment, and the way in which these trends and uncertainties interact with each other to produce different futures, enables an organisation to learn about and prepare for multiple possible futures. In the process it is possible to identify the nature of particular futures for which it seems the organisation's strengths and capabilities are well suited. It is then possible to identify how the organisation might influence the trends and uncertainties around it to bring about such an outcome, and define what combination of change programmes, alliances, innovations and other managerial actions could make this more likely.

To do this effectively with the desired outcomes, strategic thinking using scenarios should be properly integrated into the fabric of the decision processes and mindset of an organisation. Anything less will ensure that an organisation, at best, gets only a one-off "hit" from scenarios with no further enduring benefits. One of the most powerful of these enduring benefits is an increase in organisational intelligence and the speed with which an organisation can respond to or initiate strategic change to its advantage.

# Appendix 5
# Glossary of terms

Vision, mission, objectives, goals, scenarios and so on are some of the most ambiguous and misunderstood words in the managerial vocabulary. Given that they are used interchangeably and often create more confusion than insight, it is hoped that the following is a clear and succinct set of definitions for the way in which these words and other terms are used in the book.

### Aims
The high-level activities to be undertaken to fulfil the mission. In complexity science terms, decomposition of exploitation rules into sets of activities that use business processes to exploit the resources, competencies and infrastructures available to the firm, to deliver the customer value proposition.

### Aspirations
A description of what the organisation intends to become and achieve over the medium to long term. A statement of identity that embodies the set of interactions between the organisation, its stakeholders and its environment, and how this identity is extending itself into the future.

### Beach-head map
A time-based extension of (part of) an ecosystem map, showing the possible unfolding of plays and games by the interlinked actors.

### Business design
Describes the specific way in which an organisation creates, appropriates and protects value in its ecosystem. A business design comprises a set of distinctive competencies applied to relevant markets through a specific configuration of business and management processes. Within each ecosystem are co-evolving fitness landscapes, which are defined by the boundaries between different business designs and the territories within which they compete and collaborate. Business designs have been selected to offer the optimal trade-off between exploitation and exploration congruent with the expectations of stakeholders in the firm and the demands of the business environment.

## Business environment

A set of political, economic, social and technological forces that are largely outside the control and influence of a business, and that can potentially have both a positive and a negative impact on the business.

## Business ecosystem

A community of organisations and stakeholders (the players) operating within a particular business environment and collaborating and competing in an economic web of relationships. These relationships co-evolve through time subject to the forces operating in the business environment and the specific moves made within the web of players.

## Customer value proposition

Organisations deliver a particular customer value proposition to a definable market in order to exist. The delivery of the customer value proposition relies on a business design, which uses key business processes to harness the distinctive competencies and resources of the firm to deliver superior value to relevant markets. Customer value propositions and business designs compete and collaborate for customers, resources, infrastructures and skills on strategic landscapes.

## Direction

What an organisation is as a business enterprise, and what it should be trying to achieve. The purpose and scope of an organisation, together with its principles, success formulae and long-term aspirational goals. It encompasses what are known separately as mission, vision, strategic intent and aspirations. In complexity science terms, the rules (both written and unwritten) by which an organisation exploits and explores the landscape and business ecosystem. Exploitation rules are what an organisation must do to be economically viable and politically legitimate with its stakeholders. Exploration rules are the search rules that define how it will search the strategic landscape and business ecosystem(s), and what it is looking for (scanning).

## Ecosystem map

A strategic landscape taken at a moment in time covering space (the environment) and the actors, together with their interrelationships. The map can be largely pictorial and indicates the scale of the value creation that takes place, together with the types of successful value propositions.

## Future ecosystem environments

A name for a set of scenarios that relate specifically to ecosystems. The set shows how a snapshot current ecosystem map could evolve over time. All standard scenario characteristics apply to this specialised type of storyline.

## Mission

The business an organisation is in and its motivation for being here. In complexity science terms, exploitation rules and their expression in the values of the organisation (written and unwritten rules or "memes"), which together form what is commonly termed culture.

## Scenarios

Tools for ordering an organisation's perceptions about the future environment in which its decisions might be played out. Although the descriptions of scenarios are pictures of future configurations of the business ecosystem, their usage is for taking decisions today.

## Strategy

Traditionally, strategy is the chosen means by which an organisation coherently anticipates and adapts itself to its environment so as to realise its vision and win against competitors. It is a frame of mind – a thinking and learning process concerned with long-term adaptation and the survival and well-being of the organisation. Within complexity science, the definition broadens to encompass the process by which an organisation generates, develops and maintains a robust business design capable of both exploiting its current distinctive capabilities (its fitness function) on or near its current fitness peak, and exploring its strategic landscape and business ecosystem for entrepreneurial opportunities beyond the life cycle of its current business design (its sustainability function) away from its current fitness peak.

## Strategic intent

A high-level statement of the means by which an organisation will achieve its vision. In complexity science, decomposition of exploration rules into the next level of detail, the linkages to the exploitation rules and the transition rules that define how it will migrate from its current business design and ecosystem to a future business design and ecosystem.

## Value

An attribute of a company. It comprises both its ability to generate future cash in amounts which, when discounted at the cost of capital, give a positive net present value over time, and its ability to create and realise options for future wealth generation.

## Value migration

What happens to an industry and organisation when the business model used successfully in the creation of value no longer works. This happens either because the model is based on false assumptions of what customers now value, or because the distinctive resources and competencies used to create customer value have lost their competitive advantage in a particular market.

## Value proposition

The specific part of a business design (or business model) that shows how the company will (continue to) utilise resources and competencies to provide (future) value to customers, while retaining and building its own value.

## Value web

An extension of the value chain; the mutually dependent set of supplier/customer interactions that can successfully co-exist within an ecosystem. (Hence the value web describes the critical components of an ecosystem.)

## Vision

A short, succinct statement of what the organisation intends to become and to achieve at some point in the future, often stated in competitive terms. In complexity science terms, exploration rules and their expression in the prospective memory of an organisation, which define the path-dependent variables and states required to deliver the strategic intent.

# Notes and references

## Chapter 1 Introduction

1 Kelly, K., *Out of Control: The New Biology of Machines*, Addison-Wesley, 1994.
2 Watts Wacker is the author (with Jim Taylor and Howard Means) of *The 500-year Delta: what happens after what comes next* (HarperBusiness, 1997). A futurist is someone who is concerned with or studies the future.
3 *The Economist*, June 5th 1999.
4 Metcalf's law states that the value of a network rises as a square of the number of nodes in the network.
5 Davis, S. and Meyer, C., *Blur: The Speed of Change in the Connected Economy*, Capstone Publishing, 1998.
6 Toffler, A., *Future Shock*, Bantam, 1971.
7 See de Geus, A., *The Living Company*, Nicholas Brealey, 1997, p. 7.
8 See, for example, Slywotzky, A., *Value Migration*, Harvard Business School Press, 1996.
9 Garratt, R., *Creating a Learning Organisation*, Director Books, 1991.
10 For example, Anglo-American, Asea Brown Boveri, AT&T, BA, BancOne, BMW, Body Shop, BT, Canon, Citicorp, Coca-Cola, Corning, Direct Line, Disney Productions, Eastman-Kodak, Federal Express, Ford, GE, General Motors, Glaxo-Wellcome, Hewlett-Packard, IBM, IKEA, Intel, ISS, Kao, Komatsu, 3M, McDonalds, Microsoft, Nestlé, Nintendo, PepsiCo, Philips, Rank-Hovis, Samsung, Semco, Shell, Toyota, Unilever, Virgin, VISA and Xerox.
11 Toffler, A., op. cit.; *The Third Wave*, Bantam, 1981; *Powershift*, Bantam, 1991.
12 Naisbitt, J., *Megatrends 2000*, Sidgewick and Jackson, 1990; *Megatrends Asia*, Nicholas Brealey, 1995.
13 Mandel and Kondratieff have documented those technology long waves occurring since 1792. See Davidson, M., *The Transformation of Management*, Butterworth-Heinemann, 1996.
14 Such as ABB, Apple, AT&T, BA, BancOne, Body Shop, Corning, Disney Productions, Dreamworks, GE, Goretex, IKEA, Imagination, Intel, ISS, Kao, Komatsu, 3M, Microsoft, Pepsico, Philips, Rank-Hovis, Toyota, the US Army, Virgin and VISA, among others.

## Chapter 2 Achieving success in a complex world

1 Kelly, K., *New Rules for the New Economy*, Viking, 1998.
2 A cognitive filter restricts the quantity and type of information that need to be processed by a person, according to the rules operating in the filter. For example, most people focus only on what is relevant to them on the news or in a supermarket, otherwise they would be overwhelmed with the amount of information they would have to process to make even simple decisions.
3 Miller, 1956, from Howard, P.J., *The Owner's Manual for the Brain*, Leonian, 1994.
4 See Lissack, M. and Roos, J., *The Next Common Sense*, Nicholas Brealey, 1999, p. 14.
5 Grinyer, P.H., Mayes, D.G. and McKiernan, P., *Sharpbenders*, Blackwell Publishers, 1988.
6 Peters, T. and Waterman, R., *In Search of Excellence*, Harper & Row, 1982.
7 Goldsmith, W. and Clutterbuck, D., *The Winning Streak*, Random House, 1984.
8 Peters, T., *Thriving on Chaos*, Pan Books, 1989.
9 Hansen, G.S. and Wernerfelt, B., "Determinants of Firm Performance", *Strategic Management Journal*, Vol. 10, 1989, pp. 399–411.
10 Kotler, P., *Leading Change*, Harvard Business School Press, 1996.
11 Samuelson, P., *Economics*, McGraw-Hill Inc, 1976.
12 Mintzberg, H., *Strategy Safari*, Prentice Hall, 1999.
13 Buzzell, R., *The PIMS Principles*, Free Press, 1987.
14 De Geus, A., "Planning as Learning", *Harvard Business Review*, March-April, 1988. "Planning as Learning" is the *Harvard Business Review*'s most reprinted article of all time.

## Chapter 3 Complexity management in action

1 The ability to lift by air, land or sea a sufficient number of troops and equipment to deal with any military or peacekeeping challenge anywhere in the world, within 48–72 hours.
2 Courtesy of Valdis Krebs and his modelling software.

## Chapter 4 The wheel of business evolution

1 Emery, F.E. and Trist, E.I., "The Causal Texture of Organisational Environments", in *Systems Thinking: Selected Readings*, Emery, F.E. (ed.), Penguin, 1980.

2   Moore, J.F., "Predators and Prey: The Ecology of Competition",
    *Harvard Business Review*, May-June 1993.
3   Slywotzky, A., *The Profit Zone*, Times Business, 1997.

Chapter 5 **FutureStep: a new strategic management process**
1   Gell-Mann, M., "Plectics", in Brockman, J. (ed), *The Third Culture*,
    Simon and Schuster 1996.
2   As illustrated in books such as Moore, G.A., *Crossing the Chasm*,
    HarperBusiness, 1999, and *Inside the Tornado*, HarperBusiness, 1995.

Chapter 6 **The future of the e-conomy**
1   Gates, Bill, *Business @ the Speed of Thought*, Warner Books, 1999.
2   Lissack and Roos, op. cit.
3   Sherman, H. and Schultz, R., *Open Boundaries*, Perseus Books, 1999.
4   Gates, op. cit.
5   Kelly, S. and Allison, M., *The Complexity Advantage*, McGraw-Hill,
    1999.
6   Petzinger, T., *The New Pioneers*, Simon & Schuster, 1999.
7   Chicoine-Piper, G.B. and N., with Hodgson, A.M., "Requisite
    Cognitive Skills for Decisions about Systems". Paper presented to the
    1994 International System Dynamics Conference, Stirling, UK.
8   Building on Gardner's theory of multiple, distinct intelligences
    (Gardner, H., *Frames of Mind: The Theory of Multiple Intelligences*,
    Basic Books, New York, 1983), the author distinguishes between 12
    discrete intelligences: factual, analytical, physical, musical, spatial,
    logical, linguistic, practical, mathematical, intrapersonal,
    interpersonal and kinaesthetic. Each of these intelligences can exist
    without the others, both physically and functionally, although they
    are mutually supportive in most instances.
9   De Bono, E., *Lateral Thinking for Management*. McGraw-Hill, 1971.
10  Hodgson, T., *Thinking with Hexagons*, Idon Publications, 1988.
11  Checkland, P. and Scholes, J., *Soft Systems Methodology in Action*,
    John Wiley and Sons, 1990.
12  Using systems dynamics modelling software called i-Think, on an
    IBM PC under Windows.
13  Ingvar, D.H., "Memory of the Future: an Essay on Temporal
    Organisation of Conscious Awareness", *Human Neurobiology*, No. 4,
    1985, pp. 127–136.
14  Russo, J.E. and Schoemaker, P.J.H., *Decision Traps*, Simon & Schuster,
    1990.

15  De Bono, E., *Six Thinking Hats*, Penguin, 1990.
13  Wood, R.L. and Taylor, G., *Tactical Re-engineering for Rapid Results*, Strategic Directions Publishers, Zurich, 1994.
14  Petzinger, op. cit.

## Appendix 1 **A brief primer on the new sciences, complexity and organisations**

1  Definition courtesy of Alex Trisoglio in his paper "Managing Complexity", given at the LSE Strategy Seminar, January 25th 1995.
2  Kauffman, S., *At Home in the Universe*, Oxford University Press, 1995.
3  Dennett, D., in Brockman, J. (ed.), *The Third Culture*, Simon & Schuster, 1996.
4  Kelly (1994), op. cit.
5  See Sculley, J., *Odyssey: Pepsi to Apple*, Fontana, 1987.
6  See Love, J.F., *McDonalds – Behind the Arches*, Bantam Books, 1995.
7  First told in Peters and Waterman, op. cit.
8  Medina, J.J., *The Clock of Ages*, Cambridge University Press, 1996.
9  Senge, P., *The Fifth Discipline*, Doubleday, 1990.

## Appendix 2 **Leadership**

1  The author has changed the word "manager" to "leader".
2  Kauffman, op. cit., p. 57.
3  Gell-Mann, M., "Plectics", in Brockman, J. (ed), *The Third Culture*, Simon and Schuster 1996.

## Appendix 4 **The role of scenarios in business evolution**

1  De Geus (1988), op. cit., pp. 70–74.
2  Hodgson, A., paper on "Strategic Thinking with Scenarios", Idon Ltd, 1993.
3  Senge, op. cit.
4  Wood, R. and Taylor, G., "Tactical Re-engineering for Rapid Results", *Strategic Directions*, 1994.
5  Schwartz, P., *The Art of the Long View – Planning for the Future in an Uncertain World*, Doubleday Currency, 1996.
6  Van der Heijden, K., *Scenarios – The Art of Strategic Conversation*, John Wiley and Sons, London, 1996.
7  For an abridged version of these events see Schwartz, op. cit., pp. 7–11.
8  Bohm, D., quoted in Jaworski, J., *Synchronicity*, Berrett-Koehler, 1996.
9  Moore, J.F., *The Death of Competition*, 1996.

10 Dennett, D.C., *Kinds of Minds – Toward an Understanding of Consciousness*, Basic Books Science Master series, 1996.
11 Toffler, op. cit.
12 Naisbitt, op. cit.
13 Popcorn, F., *Clicking*, 1996. Popcorn identifies 16 consumer trends that appear likely to transform a wide variety of industries.
14 In Ernst and Young's management consultancy practise. Their approach is derived from complexity theory and the concept of the emergence of order in complex adaptive systems from the bottom up.
15 Brandenburger, A.J. and Nalebuff, B., *Co-opetition*, Doubleday, 1996.
16 Hamel, G. and Prahalad C.K., *Competing for the Future*, Harvard Business School Press, 1994.

# Further recommended reading

In addition to the books and articles listed in the bibliography, here is a short list of useful further reading.

## Books

Anderson, P.W., Arrow, K.J. and Pines, D. (eds), *The Economy as an Evolving Complex System*, Addison-Wesley, 1988

Arthur, W.B., *Increasing Returns and Path Dependence in the Economy*, University of Michigan Press, 1994

Buchholz, T.G., *New Ideas from Dead Economists: An Introduction to Modern Economic Thought*, Penguin Books, 1990

Cairncross, F., *The Death of Distance: How the Communications Revolution Will Change Our Lives*, Harvard Business School Press, 1997

Castells, M., *The Rise of the Network Society* (Volume 1 of *The Information Age*), Blackwell Publishers, 1996

Coyle, D., *The Weightless World: Strategies for Managing the Digital Economy*, Capstone Publishing, 1997

Davis, S. and Meyer, C., *Blur: The Speed of Change in the Connected Economy*, Addison-Wesley, 1998

Dorn, J.A. (ed.), *The Future of Money in the Information Age*, Cato Institute, 1997

Downes, L. and Mui, C., *Unleashing the Killer App: Digital Strategies for Market Dominance*, Harvard Business School Press, 1998

Drucker, P., *Post-Capitalistic Society*, HarperCollins, 1993

Dyson, E., *Release 2.0: A Design for Living in the Digital Age*, Broadway Books, 1997

Frank, R.J. and Cook, P.J., *The Winner-Take-All Society*, Penguin Books, 1995

Gardener, H., *Frames of Mind: The Theory of Multiple Intelligences*, Basic Books, 1983

Hagel, J. III and Armstrong, A.G., *Net Gain: Expanding Markets Through Virtual Communities*, Harvard Business School Press, 1997

Holland, J.H., *Hidden Order: How Adaptation Builds Complexity*, Perseus Books, 1996

Holland, J.H., *From Chaos to Order*, Perseus Books, 1999

Kalakota, R. and Whinston, A.B., *Electronic Commerce: A Manager's Guide*, Addison-Wesley, 1997

Krugman, P., *The Self-organizing Economy*, Blackwell Publishers, 1996

Lewin, R., *Complexity*, Phoenix, 1995

Lipnack, J. and Stamps, J., *The Age of the Network: Organizing Principles for the 21st Century*, Oliver Wright Publications, 1994

Lynch, D. and Lundquist, L., *Digital Money: The New Era of Internet Commerce*, John Wiley & Sons, 1996

Martin, C., *The Digital Estate: Strategies for Competing, Surviving, and Thriving in an Internetworked World*, McGraw-Hill, 1996

Martin, J., *Cybercorp: The New Business Revolution*, Amacon, 1996

McKnight, L.W. and Bailey, J.P. (eds), *Internet Economics*, MIT Press, 1997

Moore, J.F., *The Death of Competition: Leadership and Strategy in the Age of Business Ecosystems*, HarperCollins, 1996

Penrose, R., *Shadows of the Mind*, Oxford, 1994

Peppers, D. and Rogers, M., *Enterprise One to One: Tools for Competing in the Interactive Age*, Doubleday, 1997

Pilzer, P.Z., *Unlimited Wealth: The Theory and Practice of Economic Alchemy*, Crown Publishers, 1990

Quinn, J.B., Baruch, J.J. and Zien, K.A., *Innovation Explosion*, The Free Press, 1997

Rothschild, M., *Bionomics: Economy as Ecosystem*, Henry Holt and Company, 1990

Saxenian, A., *Regional Advantage: Culture and Competition in Silicon Valley and Route 128*, Harvard University Press, 1994

Schrage, M., *Shared Minds: New Technologies of Collaboration*, Random House, 1990

Schwartz, E.I., *Webonomics*, Broadway Books, 1997

Shapiro, C. and Varian, H.R., *Information Rules: A Strategic Guide to the Network Economy*, Harvard Business School Press, 1998

Tapscott, D., *The Digital Economy: Promise and Peril in the Age of Networked Intelligence*, McGraw-Hill, 1996

Toffler, A., *The Third Wave*, Bantam, 1980

Whinston, A.B., Stahl, D.O. and Choi, S., *The Economics of Electronic Commerce*, Macmillan Technical Publishing, 1997

Wood, R. and Taylor, G., "Tactical Re-engineering for Rapid Results", *Strategic Directions*, 1994

Wood, R. and Coulson-Thomas, C., *Developing the Top Team*, Institute of Management, 1996

Wriston, W.B., *The Twilight of Sovereignty*, Charles Scribner's Sons, 1992

## Journals

*Emergence: A Journal of Complexity Issues in Organizations and Management,* Laurence Enbbaum & Sons, http://emergence.org
*Complexity,* John Wiley & Sons

## Websites

George Gilder's Telecosm Index:
www.seas.upenn.edu/%7Egaj1/ggindex.html
The Economics of Networks:
http://raven.stern.nyu.edu/networks/site.html
The Information Economy: www.sims.berkeley.edu/resources/infoecon/
http://necsi.org
http://www.santafe.edu
http://www.aom.pace.edu

# Index of companies

Numbers in *italics* indicate
Figures.

## A

ABB 54, 114, 205
ABC *81*
ACT Group 138
Adobe *81*
Aldi 135
Amazon.com 8, 12, 13, *81*, 205,
   206, 207, 220, 225
AMD 83
American Airlines 118
Ameritech *81*
Amoco 70
Anadigics 68
Analytical Graphics 68, 82–3
AOL 13, 52–3, *81*, 170, 206, 207
AOL Compuserve *81*
Apple Computer *81*, 83, 97, 104,
   213, 236, 246
Asda 135
AT&T 21, 65, *81*, 170, 206
@Home *81*
Atally 172
Autobytel 8
Autonomy 226
Avedis Zildjian 205

## B

BAAN 218, 221
BackWeb *81*
Barclays 65, 68
Barclays Global Investors 76
Bay Networks *81*
BBC *170*
BBN *172*
Bell Atlantic (NYNEX) 68, *170*,
   279
BellSouth *81*
Bertelsmann 53, *170*
Bethlehem Steel 11
BIB *170*
BIOS Group 68, 77
BIS Banking Systems 137–8
BizProLink 223
BMW 107
bn.com (Barnes & Noble) 86
Body Shop 104, 114
Boeing 68
BP 68, 68, 69, 70, 281
BP-Amoco 207
British Telecom (BT) 65, 67, 68,
   85–6, *142*, *170*, 279
Broadvision 221
BSkyB *170*
Bull 83
BUPA 91
Burger King 106
Burroughs 83

## C

C5 *170*
Cable & Wireless *170*
Canon 129
Capital One 225, 68
Carlton *170*
CBS 12
Cementos Mexicanos (Cemex)
   68, 87–8
Charles Schwab 205
Chase Manhattan 279
Chemdex 33, 223
Chrysler 105, 107, 114
Cisco *81*, *172*, 205, 207
Citibank 3
Citicorp 65, 75, 76, 204, 279
Citicorp Organisation 68
Citicorp Trading 68
Citigroup 207
City Soft 205
Civil Aviation Authority (CAA)
   134–5, 163
Coca-Cola 104
Commerce One 221
Compaq 12, *81*, 83, 104, 109
Control Data 83
Corel *81*
Cray 83
CWC *170*
Cyber 83
CyberCard *81*
CyberCash *172*
CyLink *172*

## D

Daimler-Benz 86
Datakey *172*
Deere & Co 65, 89
Dell 8, 109
Digital *81*
Digital Equipment Corporation
   (DEC) 11, 12, 83, *111*
Direct Line 104
Disney *170*, 188
Drugstore.com 8
Du Point 205
Dutch Telecom *142*, 279

## E

E-Tech 212–16
e-Trade 225
eBay 8, 33, 224, 225
EDS 109, *111*
Egg 133
Ernst & Young 9, 68
eToys.com 8, 224
Excite *81*, 223
Exxon 281, 282

## F

Fedex 87
Firefly 68, 86
Ford 104, 105, 107
Forrester.com 222
Freeserve 223
Frontier *172*
FT.com 222
Fujitsu 83

## G

Gateway 205
GEIS *81*
General Electric 47, 68, 82, 203,
   205
General Motors (GM) 21, 52, 65,
   68, 83, 88, 105, 107, 108, 173,
   281–4
Genetic Arts 66, 68
Granada *170*
Great Harvest Bakeries 205

## H

Hanson plc 114
Hasbro *170*
Hewlett-Packard (HP) 62, 65, 68,
   70–75, 80, *81*, 82, 109, 114, 115,
   117, *142*, 145, 146, 156, 157, 163,
   *172*, 188, 193, 205, 207, 227, 279,
   287
Honeywell 83
Horse.com 8

## I

IBM 11, 75, *81*, 83, 104, 106, 107,
   *111*, 137, 163, 205, 213, 221, 281–4
iChat *81*
ICI 91, 163
ICI Fibres 131–3
ICL 83
ICSA *172*
IdeaLab 209
IETF *172*
Individual *81*
Intel 12, 80, *81*, 82, 83, 109, *111*,
   227, 258, 287
Intelligenesis 68, 85
Interface 68
Intergraph *81*
Internet Mail Consortium *172*
Intuit *81*
Investor.com 8
ISPs *170*
ITV *170*
iVillage 223

## J

Jardine Matheson *142*, 147
Jardine Office Services (JOS) 147,
   279

# General index